Protection of Natural Persons with Regard to Automated Individual Decision-Making in the GDPR

European Monographs Series Set

VOLUME 113

Editor

Prof. Andrea Biondi is Professor of European Law and Director of the Centre of European Law at King's College London

Introduction & Contents/Subjects

As the process of European integration assumes an increasingly complex character, the EU legal system continues to undergo sweeping changes. The European Monographs series offers a voice to thoughtful, knowledgeable, cutting edge legal commentary on the now unlimited field of European law. Its emphasis on focal and topical issues makes the series an invaluable tool for scholars, practitioners, and policymakers specializing or simply interested in EU law.

Objective

The aim is to publish innovative work appealing to academics and practitioners alike. The result is an original and ongoing library of detailed analyses, theories, commentaries, practical guides, and proposals, each of which furthers the cause of meaningful European integration. Cumulatively, the series may be regarded as a 'work in progress' engaged in building a sharply defined representation of law in Europe.

Readership

Academics and practitioners dealing with EU law.

The titles published in this series are listed at the end of this volume.

Protection of Natural Persons with Regard to Automated Individual Decision-Making in the GDPR

Aleksandra Drożdż

 Wolters Kluwer

Published by:
Kluwer Law International B.V.
PO Box 316
2400 AH Alphen aan den Rijn
The Netherlands
E-mail: international-sales@wolterskluwer.com
Website: lrus.wolterskluwer.com

Sold and distributed in North, Central and South America by:
Wolters Kluwer Legal & Regulatory U.S.
7201 McKinney Circle
Frederick, MD 21704
United States of America
Email: customer.service@wolterskluwer.com

Sold and distributed in all other countries by:
Air Business Subscriptions
Rockwood House
Haywards Heath
West Sussex
RH16 3DH
United Kingdom
Email: international-customerservice@wolterskluwer.com

Printed on acid-free paper.

ISBN 978-94-035-2045-2

e-Book: ISBN 978-94-035-2051-3
web-PDF: ISBN 978-94-035-2053-7

Printed and bound by CPI Group (UK) Ltd, Croydon, CR0 4YY

For Maks

Doctoral dissertation prepared in the Department of International Law and International Relations under the supervision of dr hab. Joanna Połatyńska, prof UŁ

Łódź 2019

About the Author

Dr Aleksandra Drożdż is an advocate, member of the Warsaw Bar Association. Aleksandra specialises in new technologies law, in particular, in personal data protection law, intellectual property law and consumer law. She also advises on merger & acquisition transactions.

Aleksandra graduated from the Faculty of Law and Administration of the Warsaw University and the American Law Centre organised by the Warsaw University, Poland under the auspices of the University of Florida. She is an alumna of numerous prestigious courses in the field of intellectual property law, *inter alia*, at the Harvard University.

Aleksandra founded one of the most successful student associations at the Warsaw University – Law & Art. She is a winner of the award for the best thesis in the field of intellectual property awarded by the Polish Patent Office and the Confederation Lewiatan in 2016. She is a laureate of the '30 under 30' programme led by the American Chamber of Commerce in 2018.

Table of Contents

Preface

The evolution and expansion of the internet, as well as the advancement of other information and communication technologies, have resulted in the processing of various types of personal data on an unprecedented scale. This data is extensively used to optimise processes in an increasing number of sectors, both private and public. New business models, particularly online, tend to offer services seemingly for free, leaving monetisation to come from the personal data collected at a large scale along the way, what is referred to as surveillance capitalism.[1] Obviously, the more transparent and predictable individuals are, the better for those who have insights into this knowledge. Thus, personal data is considered a valuable resource; it is even referred to as the oil of the twenty-first century.[2]

Nowadays, important decisions, previously left to humans, are delegated to algorithms, which may advise, if not decide, how personal data should be interpreted and what actions should be taken as a result. Algorithm-driven computer programs are deemed key instruments for market success in a digitalised economy.[3] Consequently, business models driven by personal data or at least supported by the processing of such data have become the rule and not the exception.[4] The automation of individual decision-making processes becomes an everyday reality in banking and finance, insurance, employment, healthcare, taxation, as well as broadly understood marketing and advertising. This is because it allows improving efficiency and accuracy of decisions considerably, especially when it is necessary to analyse large amounts of data

---

1. S. Zuboff, *Big Other: Surveillance Capitalism and the Prospects of an Information Civilization*, 30 (1) Journal of Information Technology (2015), pp. 75-89.
2. *The world's most valuable resource is no longer oil, but data*, Economist, 6 May 2017, available at: https://www.economist.com/leaders/2017/05/06/the-worlds-most-valuable-resource-is-no-lo nger-oil-but-data, accessed 1 May 2019.
3. P.G. Picht, B. Freund, *Competition (Law) in the Era of Algorithms*, 10 (3) Max Planck Institute for Innovation and Competition Research Paper No. 18-10 (2018), p. 2.
4. K. Wiedemann, *Automated Processing of Personal Data for the Evaluation of Personality Traits: Legal and Ethical Issues*, 10 (1) Max Planck Institute for Innovation and Competition Research Paper No. 18-04 (2018), p. 3.

in a limited time, while also reducing their cost.[5] In short, increasingly, algorithms regulate our lives.

Nonetheless, in recent years, society's deferential attitude toward algorithmic objectivity has weakened. The shift from more subjective and less structured human decision-making processes to automated ones has provoked a large and diverse critical literature concerned with the risks of such a black box society.[6] Scholars have identified a range of problems that completely lack of or limited human involvement in the decision-making process can introduce or exacerbate. For instance, it is common knowledge that most databases contain inaccurate or incomplete data, which may be blindingly applied to individuals in the process of automated individual decision-making. The use of profiling in automated individual decision-making unavoidably involves a margin of error and it may lead to inaccurate predictions about individuals. In addition, algorithms are designed by humans, so they are unavoidably value-laden and may contain latent bias. This, in turn, may lead to discrimination. Even self-learning algorithms are likely to recreate or even intensify discrimination present in the past decision-making because they are trained on historical data. Above all, automated individual decision-making is oftentimes non-transparent, making the capacity of individuals to examine and understand such processes and their results largely subdued. Meanwhile, for individuals, crucial opportunities are on the line, including the ability to get credit, insurance, a job or even receive medical treatment. Those risks can significantly affect the rights and freedoms of natural persons, which means that appropriate safeguards must be provided.

To the extent that automated individual decision-making is based on personal data, in the European Union (hereinafter 'EU') it is subject to the General Data Protection Regulation (hereinafter 'GDPR').[7] However, it is still unclear whether and how the numerous challenges can be addressed within the existing framework of data protection law, or even if it is even the best candidate to tackle them. At first glance, it seems to defer control to the data subjects with regard to automated individual decision-making, as it contains dedicated provisions in this regard. Nevertheless, the analysis carried out in this doctoral dissertation demonstrates that such protection is, in fact, curtailed. Thus, supplementarily, general provisions of the regulation relevant to such processing are examined as well. It is shown that they play a major role with regard to automated individual decision-making.

---

5. Article 29 Data Protection Working Party, *Guidelines on Automated individual decision-making and Profiling for the purposes of Regulation 2016/679*, as last revised and adopted on 6 February 2018, p. 5.
6. F. Pasquale, *The Black Box Society: The Secret Algorithms That Control Money and Information*, Harvard University Press 2015; J. Bambauer, T. Zarsky, *The Algorithm Game*, Arizona Legal Studies Discussion Paper No. 18-09, March 2018, p. 2. *See*, in particular, B. Mittelstadt, P. Allo, M. Taddeo, S. Wachter, L. Floridi, *The Ethics of Algorithms: Mapping the Debate*, 3 (2) Big Data & Society (2016), pp. 1-21; J.A. Kroll, et al., *Accountable Algorithms*, 165 (3) University of Pennsylvania Law Review (2017), pp. 633-705.
7. Regulation (EU) 2016/679 of the European Parliament and of the Council of 27 April 2016 on the protection of natural persons with regard to the processing of personal data and on the free movement of such data, and repealing Directive 95/46/EC (General Data Protection Regulation) (Text with EEA relevance), Official Journal of the European Union L 119, 4 May 2016, pp. 1-88.

The purpose of this doctoral dissertation is to describe and analyse the GDPR framework aimed at protecting natural persons with regard to automated individual decision-making. Its objective is to examine whether this legislative act affords sufficient protection of natural persons with regard to such processing. In addition to that, the focus of the thesis is to identify the loopholes that hinder or prevent the above. Above all, this doctoral dissertation is aimed at identifying *de lege lata* rules and *de lege ferenda* postulates that could provide individuals with effective protection in relation to automated individual decision-making. Therefore, this thesis contributes to the existing discussion concerning algorithmic accountability.

To achieve the above objectives, various sources and research methods are required. To describe the relevant legal framework, the research applies classical doctrinal legal methods, including the formal-dogmatic, logical-linguistic and judicial interpretation. They are applied to identify, analyse and synthesise the content of the law. To interpret the rules of the GDPR, this thesis refers, principally, to the preamble to the regulation; its *travaux préparatoires*; case law of the Court of Justice of the EU and national courts that concerns the previous Data Protection Directive (hereinafter 'DPD');[8] guidelines and opinions of the Article 29 Working Party and its successor from 25 May 2018, the European Data Protection Board; various reports and recommendations along with numerous academic writings.

In view of its goal, the doctoral dissertation is structured as follows. Chapter 1 describes the legal framework of the GDPR, *videlicet* its background, terminology, as well as its material and territorial scope of application. In addition to that, it outlines the key concerns with regard to automated individual decision-making, which serve as a background to the legal analysis in this doctoral dissertation. The second chapter analyses specific provisions of the GDPR aimed at the protection of natural persons with regard to automated individual decision-making. In the third chapter, the thesis further elaborates on the special rights of the data subject with regard to automated individual decision-making provided for in the GDPR. It also examines the key limitations of algorithmic transparency, whereas the fourth and fifth chapters take a broader perspective. Namely, in the fourth chapter, to complement specific provisions of the GDPR aimed at protection of natural persons with regard to automated individual decision-making, the general provisions of the GDPR relevant to this type of processing are taken under the loop. Whereas in the fifth chapter, the general rights of the data subject provided for in the GDPR relevant to automated individual decision-making are discussed. Finally, the doctoral dissertation presents the conclusions.

The scope of this doctoral dissertation is confined to the protection of natural persons with regard to automated individual decision-making in the GDPR. This delineation means that it focuses on the specific and general provisions of this legislative act relevant to this type of processing. It does not consider the procedural aspects of the GDPR, in particular relating to its enforcement. Neither does it contain a comprehensive analysis of the Member State law implementing the GDPR, which plays

---

8. Directive 95/46/EC of the European Parliament and of the Council of 24 October 1995 on the protection of individuals with regard to the processing of personal data and on the free movement of such data, Official Journal of the European Union L 281, 23 November 1995, pp. 31-50.

a secondary role in the regulation, in particular with regard to the scope of the thesis. Hence, it is only touched upon where necessary. Last but not least, the thesis does not analyse the issue in question from a fundamental rights perspective.[9] Although the GDPR is underpinned by the respect for the fundamental rights, it constitutes a separate legal regime with largely different goals.[10] Thus the fundamental rights perspective is only signalled briefly with regard to the key problems connected with automated individual decision-making.

The subject matter of this doctoral dissertation has not been comprehensively analysed in domestic or foreign literature. This is primarily due to the fact that the GDPR is a relatively recent legislative act and automated individual decision-making has so far rarely been the subject of legal analysis. Nonetheless, the topic of the thesis falls within the ambit of the current trend of scholarly research at the confluence of law and new technologies. It is considered that these are some of the most controversial issues in the realm of personal data protection and at the same time, one of those whose role in the information society will grow.[11]

The doctoral dissertation takes into consideration the status of normative legal acts and judicature as of 1 October 2019.

---

9. In particular, with regard to the right to protection of personal data, the right to privacy, the right to an effective remedy, the right to a fair trial, the right to equality and non-discrimination or the rights of the child.
10. GDPR, Recital 2, 4.
11. L. Floridi, *Soft Ethics and the Governance of the Digital*, 31 Philosophy & Technology (2018), pp. 1-8; M. Czerniawski, *Commentary on Article 22 of the GDPR*, [in:] *RODO. Ogólne rozporządzenie o ochronie danych. Komentarz*, E. Bielak-Jomaa Edyta, D. Lubasz (eds), Warsaw 2018, LEX.

CHAPTER 1

Introduction

---

§1.01   LEGAL BACKGROUND OF THE GDPR

As clearly enshrined in the normative framework, which underlies the European Union (hereinafter 'EU'), the protection of natural persons in relation to the processing of personal data is a fundamental right.[1] Currently, the key legislative act in this regard is the General Data Protection Regulation (hereinafter 'GDPR'), which applies from 25 May 2018. It replaced the Data Protection Directive (hereinafter 'DPD'), which could no longer meet the challenges of rapid technological and business developments and required revision.

Namely, since the adoption of the DPD in 1995, the scale of data sharing and collecting has increased dramatically. Nowadays, technology allows both private companies and public authorities to make use of personal data on an unprecedented scale in order to pursue their activities. Natural persons increasingly share their personal information publicly and globally.[2] The risks to personal data of the data subjects, therefore, multiply. Moreover, the DPD, being a directive, not a regulation, was subject to twenty-eight different interpretations and enforcement regimes, leading to differences that fomented confusion and inconsistency among industry leaders and

---

1. Consolidated Version of the Treaty on the Functioning of the European Union, Official Journal of the European Union C 326, 26 October 2012, pp. 47-390 hereinafter 'TFEU'), Article 16 (1); Charter of Fundamental Rights of the European Union, Official Journal of the European Union C 202, 7 June 2016, pp. 389-405 (hereinafter 'Charter of Fundamental Rights of the European Union'), Article 8 (1).
2. Commission Staff Working Paper, Impact Assessment accompanying the document Regulation of the European Parliament and of the Council on the protection of individuals with regard to the processing of personal data and on the free movement of such data (General Data Protection Regulation) and Directive of the European Parliament and of the Council on the protection of individuals with regard to the processing of personal data by competent authorities for the purposes of prevention, investigation, detection or prosecution of criminal offences or the execution of criminal penalties, and the free movement of such data, Brussels, 25 January 2012, SEC (2012) 72 final, pp. 7-8. *See also* GDPR, Recitals 5-6.

data protection authorities. Along with the minimal fines available under the directive, the aforesaid fragmentation exacerbated enforcement problems for data protection authorities.[3]

As indicated in the preamble to the GDPR, it was considered that those developments require a strong and more coherent data protection framework, backed by strong enforcement, given the importance of creating the trust that will allow the digital economy to develop across the internal market. It was acknowledged that natural persons should have control of their own personal data. In addition to that, legislators intended to enhance legal and practical certainty for natural persons, economic operators and public authorities.[4] In summary, the two main policy objectives of the GDPR are: (i) to enhance the internal market dimension of data protection, by reducing fragmentation, strengthening consistency and simplifying the regulatory environment, thus eliminating unnecessary costs and reducing administrative burden; (ii) to increase the effectiveness of the fundamental right to data protection and put individuals in control of their data.[5] Conveniently, the Treaty of Lisbon has created a new legal basis for a modernised and comprehensive approach to data protection and the free movement of personal data.[6]

The GDPR is rightly described as a 'Copernican Revolution' in data protection law, 'seeking to shift its focus away from paper-based, bureaucratic requirements and toward compliance in practice, harmonization of the law, and individual empowerment'.[7] Below is an overview of the main advances introduced by the EU data protection reform from a bird's eye view.

First, as opposed to the DPD, the GDPR is a regulation, not a directive. While 'a directive shall be binding, as to the result to be achieved, upon each Member State to

---

3. B. Casey, A. Farhangi, R. Vogl, *Rethinking Explainable Machines: The GDPR's 'Right to Explanation' Debate and the Rise of Algorithmic Audits in Enterprise*, 34 (1) Berkeley Technology Law Journal (2019), p. 165. *See also* GDPR, Recital 9.
4. GDPR, Recital 7.
5. Commission Staff Working Paper, Executive Summary of the Impact Assessment accompanying the document Regulation of the European Parliament and of the Council on the protection of individuals with regard to the processing of personal data and on the free movement of such data (General Data Protection Regulation) and Directive of the European Parliament and of the Council on the protection of individuals with regard to the processing of personal data by competent authorities for the purposes of prevention, investigation, detection or prosecution of criminal offences or the execution of criminal penalties, and the free movement of such data, Brussels, 25 January 2012, SEC (2012) 73 final, p. 4. *See also* Communication from the Commission to the European Parliament, the Council, the European Economic and Social Committee and the Committee of the Regions, *Safeguarding Privacy in a Connected World: A European Data Protection Framework for the 21st Century*, Brussels, 25 January 2012, COM(2012) 9 final, which comprehensively explains the overall strategy of the EU data protection reform. *See also* Proposal for a Regulation the European Parliament and of the Council on the protection of individuals with regard to the processing of personal data and on the free movement of such data (General Data Protection Regulation) of 25 January 2012, COM(2012) 11 final, in particular, pp. 1-7.
6. Treaty of Lisbon amending the Treaty on European Union and the Treaty establishing the European Community, signed in Lisbon, 13 December 2007, Official Journal of the European Union C 306, 17 December 2007, pp. 1-271. *See* TFEU, Article 16 (2).
7. C. Kuner, *The European Commission's Proposed Data Protection Regulation: A Copernican Revolution in European Data Protection Law*, Bloomberg BNA Privacy and Security Law Report, 6 February 2012, pp. 1, 14.

which it is addressed, but shall leave to the national authorities the choice of form and methods', a regulation 'shall be binding in its entirety and directly applicable in all Member States'.[8] Therefore, the choice of regulation as a legal instrument for the EU data protection reform ensures consistent and homogenous application of the rules for the protection of the fundamental rights and freedoms of natural persons with regard to the processing of personal data throughout the EU.[9]

Second, the reform includes significant changes with regard to jurisdiction. As already explained above, the territorial scope of the GDPR is de facto global.[10] It does not just apply to the processing of personal data in the context of the activities of an establishment of a controller or a processor in the EU. It also applies to the processing of personal data of data subjects which are in the EU by a controller or processor not established in the EU, where the processing activities are related to (i) the offering of goods or services to the data subjects in the EU; (ii) the monitoring of their behaviour as far as it takes place within the EU. In addition to that, for the purposes of determining jurisdiction, it is irrelevant whether personal data is processed within the EU or not.

Third, the GDPR greatly strengthens the effective protection of the rights of data subjects. It does so by setting them out in detail along with the obligations of those which process and determine the processing of personal data and equivalent powers for monitoring and ensuring compliance with the rules for the protection of personal data and equivalent sanctions for infringements in the Member States.[11] *Inter alia*, it continues the legacy of the DPD with regard to restrictions on solely automated individual decision-making. Of course, since the adoption of the DPD over two decades ago, the practical importance of such restrictions has significantly increased with augmented use of solely automated individual decision-making.[12]

Fourth, the reform introduces many new legal mechanisms for promoting strong enforcement which were previously lacking.[13] Crucially, the GDPR introduces hefty administrative fines up to EUR 20,000,000, or in the case of an undertaking, up to 4% of the total worldwide annual turnover of the preceding financial year, whichever is higher.[14] As rightly observed by C. Kuner, one of the purposes of the reform is to elevate the significance of data protection to the level of primary corporate compliance areas such as competition, anti-bribery, and anti-money laundering laws.[15]

As reflected in the preamble to the GDPR, the main changes described above are meant to promote the trust that will allow the digital economy to develop across the

---

8. TFEU, Article 288.
9. GDPR, Recitals 7, 10, 170.
10. GDPR, Article 3. *See* detailed remarks in §1.04.
11. GDPR, Recital 11.
12. M. Brkan, *Do Algorithms Rule the World? Algorithmic Decision-Making in the Framework of the GDPR and Beyond*, Terminator or the Jetsons? The Economics and Policy Implications of Artificial Intelligence, Technology Policy Institute (Conference held 22 February 2018 in Washington, D.C., United States of America), p. 5, L. Edwards, M. Veale, *Enslaving the Algorithm: From a 'Right to an Explanation' to a 'Right to Better Decisions'?*, 16 (3) IEEE Security & Privacy (2018), pp. 47, 50-51.
13. *See*, in particular, Chapters VI-VIII of the GDPR. *See also* GDPR, Recitals 7, 11.
14. GDPR, Article 83 (5).
15. C. Kuner, *The European Commission's Proposed Data Protection Regulation: A Copernican Revolution in European Data Protection Law*, p. 12.

internal market, thereby encouraging economic growth and the competitiveness of the EU industries.[16]

§1.02   TERMINOLOGY

[A]   Personal Data

Personal data is one of the key notions of data protection law determining the material scope of the GDPR. Only when personal data is processed, the rules relating to the protection of natural persons set out in the regulation apply.[17] As provided for in Article 4 (1) of the GDPR, personal data 'means any information relating to an identified or identifiable natural person ("data subject"); an identifiable natural person is one who can be identified, directly or indirectly, in particular by reference to an identifier such as a name, an identification number, location data, an online identifier or to one or more factors specific to the physical, physiological, genetic, mental, economic, cultural or social identity of that natural person'. There are four main building blocks of this definition, *videlicet* 'any information', 'relating to', 'an identified or identifiable' and 'natural person'. Although they are interrelated, for the purpose of clarity, they are explained separately below.[18]

First, the term 'any information' signals the intent of the legislator to design a broad concept of personal data. It covers both objective and subjective information about a natural person, including opinions and assessments without regard to their truthfulness or accurateness.[19] As a matter of fact, the GDPR already envisages the possibility that personal data is inaccurate and grants the data subject the right of access to that information and the right to rectify or erase it.[20]

Second, information can be considered 'relating to' a natural person when it is about that natural person.[21] In numerous instances, it is straightforward to establish such a connection. However, in some situations, information seems to concern only

---

16. GDPR, Recitals 2, 7. For additional legal background on the GDPR, *see* C. Kuner, *The European Commission's Proposed Data Protection Regulation: A Copernican Revolution in European Data Protection Law*, pp. 1-15; G. Hornung, *A General Data Protection Regulation for Europe? Light and Shade in the Commission's Draft of 25 January 2012*, 9 (1) SCRIPTed (2012), pp. 64-81; B. Casey, A. Farhangi, R. Vogl, *Rethinking Explainable Machines*, pp. 163-167; B. Goodman, S. Flaxman, *European Union Regulations on Algorithmic Decision Making and 'a Right to an Explanation'*, presented at 33rd International Conference on Machine Learning, Workshop on Human Interpretability in Machine Learning, New York, United States of America, 19-24 June 2016, published in 38 (3) AI Magazine (2017), pp. 51-53; European Data Protection Supervisor, *Opinion 3/2015 (with addendum). Europe's big opportunity. Recommendations on the EU's options for data protection reform*, 27 July 2015 (updated with addendum, 9 October 2015), (2015/C 301/01), pp. 1-13.
17. GDPR, Article 2 (1): 'This Regulation applies to the processing of personal data wholly or partly by automated means and to the processing other than by automated means of personal data which form part of a filing system or are intended to form part of a filing system'.
18. This approach is proposed by the Article 29 Data Protection Working Party, *Opinion 4/2007 on the concept of personal data*, adopted on 20 June 2007, p. 6.
19. *Ibid.*
20. GDPR, Articles 15 and 16.
21. Article 29 Data Protection Working Party, *Opinion 4/2007 on the concept of personal data*, p. 9.

material things and not natural persons. Nevertheless, objects are usually owned or used by natural persons, so it may be concluded that such information indirectly relates to them.[22] Therefore, one may assume that in the age of datafication, any information 'relates to' a person within the meaning of the definition.[23]

Third, 'identified' refers to a natural person who is known, or distinguished in a group whereas 'identifiable' is a person who is not identified yet, but such identification is possible. In order to determine whether a natural person is identifiable, one has to perform a test of a reasonable likelihood of identification, *videlicet* consider all of the means reasonably likely to be used, either by the controller or anybody else, at a given time considering the costs, the time and the state of technology.[24] To identify a natural person 'directly' most commonly includes a name and a surname, while to do it 'indirectly' involves a combination of other unique identifiers that allow the natural person in question to be singled out. This is a tailored, context-specific analysis which has to be performed *a casu ad casum*, as the same piece of information may be considered personal data or not depending on the circumstances.[25] It is worthy of note that, both Article 4 (1) of the GDPR and its preamble acknowledge that natural persons may be associated with online identifiers such as IP addresses, cookies or Radiofrequency identification (RFID) tags, which may be used to identify them.[26]

Fourth, information has to relate to 'a natural person', that is, to a human being.[27] Hence the right to the protection of personal data is not restricted to nationals or

---

22. S. Eskens, *Profiling the European Citizen in the Internet of Things: How Will the General Data Protection Regulation Apply to This Form of Personal Data Processing, and How Should It?*, written on 29 February 2016, available at SSRN, pp. 18-21; Article 29 Data Protection Working Party, *Opinion 4/2007 on the concept of personal data*, p. 9.
23. N. Purtova, *The Law of Everything: Broad Concept of Personal Data and Future of EU Data Protection Law*, 10 (1) Law, Innovation and Technology (2018), p. 42.
24. GDPR, Recital 26: '[...] To determine whether a natural person is identifiable, account should be taken of all the means reasonably likely to be used, such as singling out, either by the controller or by another person to identify the natural person directly or indirectly. To ascertain whether means are reasonably likely to be used to identify the natural person, account should be taken of all objective factors, such as the costs of and the amount of time required for identification, taking into consideration the available technology at the time of the processing and technological developments. [...]'.
25. P. Schwartz, D. Solove, *Reconciling Personal Information in the United States and European Union*, 102 (4) California Law Review (2014), pp. 877-916; B.J. Koops, *The Trouble with European Data Protection Law*, 4 (4) International Data Privacy Law (2014), p. 250.
26. GDPR, Recital 30: 'Natural persons may be associated with online identifiers provided by their devices, applications, tools and protocols, such as internet protocol addresses, cookie identifiers or other identifiers such as radio frequency identification tags. This may leave traces which, in particular when combined with unique identifiers and other information received by the servers, may be used to create profiles of the natural persons and identify them'. *See also* Judgment of the Court (Second Chamber) of 19 October 2016, Patrick Breyer v Bundesrepublik Deutschland, Case C-582/14, ECLI:EU:C:2016:779, paragraph 31, issued on the basis of the DPD (the predecessor of the GDPR), where the court adopted a broad approach to identifiability and ruled that a dynamic IP address constitutes personal data. *See also* Article 29 Data Protection Working Party, *Opinion 4/2007 on the concept of personal data*, pp. 16-17.
27. United Nations General Assembly, Universal Declaration of Human Rights, 10 December 1948, 217 A (III), Article 6: 'Everyone has the right to recognition everywhere as a person before the law'.

residents in a certain country.[28] The concept of the personality of human beings understood as the capacity to be the subject of legal relations from the birth of the individual and ending with his death is laid down in the Member States law, usually in the civil law. *Ergo,* the regulation does not apply to the personal data of deceased persons.[29]

All of the main building blocks described above allow that notion of personal data is understood broadly, flexibly and it remains adaptable to rapidly evolving technological context. Lately, it is even argued that personal data has the potential to become an all-encompassing notion.[30] However, it is not unlimited, and the data protection authorities and judicature play an essential role in finding an appropriate balance in its application, keeping in mind the objectives of the data protection legislation.[31]

[1]   *Anonymous Information*

Conversely, anonymous information is the opposite of personal data and refers to information which does not relate to an identified or identifiable natural person or to personal data rendered anonymous in such a manner that the data subject is not or no longer identifiable.[32] Consequently, processing anonymous information does not trigger the application of the GDPR.

This is exploited by numerous private entities aiming to escape the data protection regime. They wrongly claim that their activity involves the processing only of supposedly anonymised information just because they do not process the data subject's name and surname, when, in fact, the remaining personal data at their

---

28. GDPR, Recital 14: 'The protection afforded by this Regulation should apply to natural persons, whatever their nationality or place of residence, in relation to the processing of their personal data'. *See also* Recital 2 of the GDPR.
29. GDPR, Recital 27: 'This Regulation does not apply to the personal data of deceased persons. Member States may provide for rules regarding the processing of personal data of deceased persons'. *See also* L. Edwards, M. Veale, *Slave to the Algorithm? Why a 'Right to an Explanation' Is Probably Not the Remedy You Are Looking For,* 16 Duke Law & Technology Review (2017), p. 74, who explain that data protection is a paradigm based on human rights which means it does not contemplate remedies for groups or for non-living persons such as corporations, or the deceased.
30. N. Purtova, *The Law of Everything: Broad Concept of Personal Data and Future of EU Data Protection Law,* p. 45.
31. For further remarks about the concept of personal data *see* Article 29 Data Protection Working Party, *Opinion 4/2007 on the concept of personal data,* which remains significant for data protection compliance under the GDPR, since, as Advocate General Kokott has observed, 'the latter will not affect the concept of personal data', Opinion of Advocate General Kokott delivered on 20 July 2017 in Case C-434/16 Peter Nowak v Data Protection Commissioner, paragraph 3.
32. GDPR, Recital 26: '[...] The principles of data protection should therefore not apply to anonymous information, namely information which does not relate to an identified or identifiable natural person or to personal data rendered anonymous in such a manner that the data subject is not or no longer identifiable. This Regulation does not therefore concern the processing of such anonymous information, including for statistical or research purposes'. For extensive remarks about anonymous information, *see* Article 29 Data Protection Working Party, *Opinion 05/2014 on Anonymisation Techniques,* adopted on 10 April 2014.

disposal allows to single out a specific user anyway.[33] For the above reason, such activity remains within the material scope of the GDPR.

Further, considering the development of technology and a large amount of data available for analysis, it is argued that it is straightforward to re-identify individuals even on the basis of anonymous information, which undeniably undermines the whole idea of it.[34] Thus, both the controller and the processor should mitigate the risk of re-identification to the point it is highly negligible if they wish to avoid the data protection regime.

[2] Pseudonymisation

In the view of the foregoing, during the legislative process leading up to the adoption of the GDPR, a compromise concept of pseudonymisation was introduced.[35] As defined in Article 4 (5) of the GDPR, it means 'the processing of personal data in such a manner that the personal data can no longer be attributed to a specific data subject without the use of additional information, provided that such additional information is kept separately and is subject to technical and organisational measures to ensure that the personal data are not attributed to an identified or identifiable natural person'.

In short, personal data which has undergone pseudonymisation may still be attributed to a natural person by the use of additional information, which is kept separately. Thus, importantly, it is still considered to be personal data, so it remains under the data protection regime to the full extent.[36] Nevertheless, as it is distinctly reflected in the preamble to the GDPR and its relevant provisions, application of pseudonymisation to personal data can reduce the risks to the data subjects concerned.[37] Therefore, the controllers and processors are incentivised to use this

---

33. L. Edwards, *Data Protection: Enter the General Data Protection Regulation*, [in:] *Law, Policy and the Internet*, L. Edwards (ed.), Hart 2018, p. 84.

34. P. Ohm, *Broken Promises of Privacy: Responding to the Surprising Failure of Anonymization*, 57 UCLA Law Review (2010), pp. 1701-1777; L. Sweeney, *Simple Demographics Often Identify People Uniquely*, Carnegie Mellon University, Data Privacy Working Paper 3, Pittsburgh 2000; P. Schwartz, D. Solove, *The PII Problem: Privacy and a New Concept of Personally Identifiable Information*, (86) New York University Law Review (2011), pp. 1814-1894; F. Di Porto, *In Praise of an Empowerment Disclosure Regulatory Approach to Algorithms*, 49 (5) International Review of Intellectual Property and Competition Law (2018), pp. 507-511.

35. Position of the European Parliament adopted at first reading on 12 March 2014 with a view to the adoption of Regulation (EU) No .../2014 of the European Parliament and of the Council on the protection of individuals with regard to the processing of personal data and on the free movement of such data (General Data Protection Regulation) (Text with EEA relevance), P7_TC1-COD(2012)0011; Position (EU) of the Council at first reading with a view to the adoption of a Regulation of the European Parliament and of the Council on the protection of natural persons with regard to the processing of personal data and on the free movement of such data, and repealing Directive 95/46/EC (General Data Protection Regulation), Adopted by the Council on 8 April 2016, Official Journal of the European Union C 159/1, 3 May 2016, pp. 1-82.

36. GDPR, Recital 26: '[...] Personal data which have undergone pseudonymisation, which could be attributed to a natural person by the use of additional information should be considered to be information on an identifiable natural person. [...]'.

37. GDPR, Recitals 28, 29, 78, Articles 6 (4) (e), 25 (1), 32 (1) (a).

measure, as it is deemed one of the appropriate safeguards to be taken to ensure that the requirements of the GDPR are met.

[B]   Special Categories of Personal Data

There is a subset of personal data, which is, by its nature, particularly sensitive. Article 9 (1) of the GDPR includes an exhaustive list of such special categories of personal data, i.e., data revealing racial or ethnic origin, political opinions, religious or philosophical beliefs, or trade union membership, and the processing of genetic data, biometric data for the purpose of uniquely identifying a natural person, data concerning health or data concerning a natural person's sex life or sexual orientation. Considering that their processing could create significant risks to a person's fundamental rights and freedoms, special categories of personal data merit higher protection.[38] Specifically, there is a general prohibition on processing such personal data, although it is not absolute and there are exemptions from it.[39] Such a higher level of protection concerns, *inter alia*, use of special categories of personal data in solely automated individual decision-making.[40]

Taking into account that profiling can create special categories of personal data by inference from 'ordinary' personal data, it is crucial to realise the above-mentioned restrictions apply to the special categories of data, which are inferred from other data as well.[41] For example, the controller can now use thousands of 'non-traditional' third party data sources, such as consumer buying history, to predict a life insurance applicant's health status with an accuracy comparable to a medical exam.[42] In this case, even though concerning health is inferred from 'ordinary data' it constitutes a special category of personal data within the meaning of Article 9 (1) of the GDPR and, therefore, it is subject to a higher level of protection in accordance with the GDPR.[43]

In another study, researchers combined Facebook 'likes' with limited survey information which allowed them to predict a male user's sexual orientation accurately 88% of the time; a user's ethnic origin 95% of the time; and whether a user was Christian or Muslim 82% of the time.[44] It is worth noting that Facebook had assigned an ad preference involving sensitive personal data to 73% of the EU users, primarily *via* inferred rather than explicitly shared data.[45] Such inferred special categories of

---

38. GDPR, Recital 51: 'Personal data which are, by their nature, particularly sensitive in relation to fundamental rights and freedoms merit specific protection as the context of their processing could create significant risks to the fundamental rights and freedoms [...]'.

39. GDPR, Article 9 (1) and (2).

40. *See* Chapter 2, §2.07.

41. Creating new data by inference from other data is explained in depth below in §1.02[F].

42. A. Rieke, D. Robinson, H. Yu; *Civil Rights, Big Data, and Our Algorithmic Future: A September 2014 Report on Social Justice and Technology by Robinson + Yu*, September 2014, p. 6.

43. *See*, in particular: GDPR, Articles 9, 22 (4), 35 (3) (b), 37 (1) (c).

44. M. Kosinski, D. Stilwell, T. Graepel, *Private Traits and Attributes Are Predictable from Digital Records of Human Behavior*, 110 (15) Proceedings of the National Academy of Sciences of the United States of America (2013), pp. 5802-5805.

45. J. González Cabañas, Á. Cuevas, R. Cuevas, *Facebook Use of Sensitive Data for Advertising in Europe*, submitted on 14 February 2018, available at arXiv, pp. 1-15.

personal data used in automated individual decision-making are afforded greater protection under the GDPR.

Of course, besides the above-mentioned restrictions, the general principles and other rules of the GDPR apply to special categories of personal data as well.[46]

[C]   Controller

Article 4 (7) of the GDPR defines the controller as 'the natural or legal person, public authority, agency or other body which, alone or jointly with others, determines the purposes and means of the processing of personal data; where the purposes and means of such processing are determined by Union or Member State law, the controller or the specific criteria for its nomination may be provided for by Union or Member State law'.

In brief, the controller has the decision-making power concerning the purposes and means of the processing of personal data, regardless of whether it is derived from a legal designation or factual circumstances. When assessing whether a person or body is a controller, it ought to be considered whether it determines the reasons justifying the processing and whether it has control over the processing methods, the choice of personal data to be processed and who is allowed to access it.[47] As reflected in the above definition, in some cases, there may be multiple controllers or joint controllers.[48]

[D]   Processor

The processor, in accordance with Article 4 (8) of the GDPR, is 'a natural or legal person, public authority, agency or other body which processes personal data on behalf of the controller'. Pursuant to the GDPR, the controller may only use the processor providing sufficient guarantees to implement appropriate measures in such manner that processing will meet the regulation requirements and ensure the protection of the rights of the data subject.[49] In addition to that, processing activities by the processor on behalf of the controller must be governed by a contract or other legal act under EU or Member State law that sets out the subject matter and duration of the processing, the nature and purpose of the processing, the type of personal data and categories of data subjects and the obligations and rights of the controller.[50] In essence, the instructions given by the controller establish the limits of what the processor is allowed to do with personal data.[51]

---

46. In particular, the conditions for lawful processing of personal data set out in Article 6 (1) of the GDPR.
47. Council of Europe, Explanatory Report to the Protocol amending the Convention for the Protection of Individuals with regard to Automatic Processing of Personal Data, Council of Europe Treaty Series No. 223, Strasbourg, 10.10.2018, paragraph 22, pp. 4-5.
48. GDPR, Article 26. For further remarks on the controller, *see* Article 29 Working Party, *Opinion 1/2010 on the concepts of 'controller' and 'processor'*, adopted on 16 February 2010.
49. GDPR, Article 28 (1).
50. GDPR, Article 28 (3).
51. GDPR, Article 28 (3) (a). For further remarks on the processor, *see* Article 29 Working Party, *Opinion 1/2010 on the concepts of 'controller' and 'processor'*.

[E]   Processing

As provided for in Article 4 (2) of the GDPR processing 'means any operation or set of operations which is performed on personal data or on sets of personal data, whether or not by automated means, such as collection, recording, organisation, structuring, storage, adaptation or alteration, retrieval, consultation, use, disclosure by transmission, dissemination or otherwise making available, alignment or combination, restriction, erasure or destruction'.

To simplify, the term 'processing' is defined extremely widely, and it refers to any handling of personal data wholly or partly by automated means or manually, as the above list is non-exhaustive. This open wording results from the legislators' intention to prevent any risk of circumvention and to ensure that the protection of natural persons is technologically neutral and does not depend on the techniques used.[52]

[F]   Profiling

As will be explained below, profiling technologies are deemed invaluable as they enable the controller to derive additional information about a particular person from already available personal data concerning it. By way of explanation, one of the best-known applications of profiling is credit scoring, that is estimating the likelihood that if a person is granted credit, it will repay it. Financial institutions have used it for many years, as it achieves significantly greater decision-making accuracy than human decision makers.[53]

In the light of increasing usage of such technologies both in the private and public sector and their far-reaching implications for the data subjects, during the legislative process, it was considered necessary to introduce a legal definition of profiling in the GDPR,[54] which was missing in the DPD. As provided for in Article 4 (4) of the GDPR, profiling means 'any form of automated processing of personal data consisting of the use of personal data to evaluate certain personal aspects relating to a natural person, in particular, to analyse or predict aspects concerning that natural person's performance at work, economic situation, health, personal preferences, interests, reliability, behaviour, location or movements'. This definition supplemented by Recital 30 of the GDPR,

---

52. GDPR, Recital 15: 'In order to prevent creating a serious risk of circumvention, the protection of natural persons should be technologically neutral and should not depend on the techniques used. [...]'.

53. J. Kingston, *Using Artificial Intelligence to Support Compliance with the General Data Protection Regulation*, 25 (4) Artificial Intelligence and Law (2017), p. 439.

54. Article 29 Data Protection Working Party, *Advice paper on essential elements of a definition and a provision on profiling within the EU General Data Protection Regulation,* adopted on 13 May 2013, p. 2; Article 4 (3a), Position of the European Parliament adopted at first reading on 12 March 2014 with a view to the adoption of Regulation (EU) No .../2014 of the European Parliament and of the Council on the protection of individuals with regard to the processing of personal data and on the free movement of such data (General Data Protection Regulation); Article 4 (4), Position (EU) of the Council at first reading with a view to the adoption of a Regulation of the European Parliament and of the Council on the protection of natural persons with regard to the processing of personal data and on the free movement of such data, and repealing Directive 95/46/EC (General Data Protection Regulation).

which rightly notes that numerous traces left by the data subjects *via* online identifiers such as IP addresses, cookies or RFID tags facilitate the creation of individual profiles of the natural persons.[55]

According to the influential guidelines of the Article 29 Data Protection Working Party, endorsed by the European Data Protection Board,[56] the above-mentioned definition was inspired by, although is not identical to, the definition provided in the Recommendation CM/Rec (2010)13, which was the first text to lay down internationally agreed minimum privacy standards in the context of profiling.[57] Although the said recommendation is not legally binding, it constitutes an influential standard of reference to be implemented both by the public and private sector, through national legislation and self-regulation. It was adopted by the Council of Europe,[58] and it complements the Convention for the Protection of Individuals with regard to Automatic Processing of Personal Data.[59]

Simply put, profiling within the meaning of Article 4 (4) of the GDPR is an automated form of processing, which is carried out on personal data and its objective is to evaluate personal aspects about the data subject. The term evaluating suggests that profiling involves some assessment or judgement about a person. It allows the controller to deduce consumer preferences through each data subject's digital footprint. Profiling entails constructing a profile of an individual in order to separate it from the mass of individuals and to infer additional information about it. Hence, it is aimed at the differentiation of individuals.[60]

---

55. GDPR, Recital 30: 'Natural persons may be associated with online identifiers provided by their devices, applications, tools and protocols, such as internet protocol addresses, cookie identifiers or other identifiers such as radio frequency identification tags. This may leave traces which, in particular when combined with unique identifiers and other information received by the servers, may be used to create profiles of the natural persons and identify them'.
56. Article 29 Data Protection Working Party, *Guidelines on Automated individual decision-making and Profiling*, p. 7. With the entry into force of the GDPR, on 25 May 2018, the European Data Protection Board succeeded the Article 29 Working Party as an independent body responsible for ensuring the consistent application of the GDPR. To acknowledge the continuity of the work provided by the predecessor pertaining to the GDPR, the European Data Protection Board endorsed over a dozen guidelines and other documents on various aspects of the GDPR adopted by the Article 29 Working Party in Endorsement 1/2018 issued on 25 May 2018. It is key to note the European Data Protection Board is composed of representatives of the national data protection authorities, and the European Data Protection Supervisor. Although the guidelines issued by the European Data Protection Board do not have the direct force of law, they are strongly indicative of how it will be eventually interpreted.
57. Council of Europe, Recommendation CM/Rec(2010)13 of the Committee of Ministers to Member States on the protection of individuals with regard to automatic processing of personal data in the context of profiling of 23 November 2010, point 1 (e) p. 9. Therein, 'Profiling' means an automatic data processing technique that consists of applying a 'profile' to an individual, particularly in order to take decisions concerning her or him or for analysing or predicting her or his personal preferences, behaviours and attitudes. In contrast to the definition of profiling included in the GDPR, it excludes processing that does not include inference.
58. The Council of Europe was founded in 1949, in the aftermath of the Second World War, currently covering virtually the entire continent of Europe. It seeks to develop common democratic and legal principles based on the European Convention on Human Rights and other reference texts on the protection of individuals.
59. Convention for the Protection of Individuals with regard to Automatic Processing of Personal Data of 28 January 1981, European Treaty Series No. 108.
60. Council of Europe, Recommendation CM/Rec (2010)13, paragraph 108, p. 41.

A simple classification of individuals based on known characteristics such as their age, sex, and height does not necessarily constitute profiling. This depends on the purpose of the classification. For instance, the controller may wish to classify data subjects according to their age or gender for statistical purposes and to acquire an aggregated overview of them without making any predictions or performing any analysis about particular individuals. In this case, the purpose is not evaluating certain personal aspects relating to a natural person and is, therefore, not profiling.[61]

Further, Article 4 (4) of the GDPR refers to 'any form of automated processing' as opposed to 'solely' automated processing (referred to in Article 22 (1) of the GDPR). Hence although profiling has to involve some form of automated processing, some degree of human involvement does not take the activity out of the above definition.

The GDPR calls particular attention to profiling aimed at analysing or predicting aspects concerning that natural person's performance at work, economic situation, health, personal preferences, interests, reliability, behaviour, location or movements. Apart from unambiguous personal data such as the location of the data subject, the above examples cover complex and vague information such as its reliability. The discussed list encompasses both personal characteristics of the data subject such as personal preferences or health and its deliberate conduct such as behaviour and movements.[62] Given the breadth of these very different categories, the GDPR's *desideratum* for profiling evidently errs on the side of inclusion, to put it mildly.[63] Aside from that, the list of aspects concerning a natural person, that may be analysed or predicted during profiling is only exemplary, and it is non-exhaustive.[64] The regulation follows a modern and pragmatic approach; therefore, evaluation of any personal data is covered by the GDPR's definition, because, in reality, any information can be valuable and decisive, even when it is seemingly unimportant.[65]

As explained in the Recommendation CM/Rec (2010)13, profiling may involve three distinct stages.[66] The first stage consists of a large-scale data collection. During the second stage, this data undergoes automated analysis in order to identify correlations. Additionally, statistical methods are used to determine the probability factors of the spotted correlations. This stage may also be vividly described as 'the process of

61. Article 29 Data Protection Working Party, *Guidelines on Automated individual decision-making and Profiling*, p. 7.
62. This distinction is underlined also by K. Wiedemann, *Automated Processing of Personal Data for the Evaluation of Personality Traits*, p. 5. K. Wiedemann notes also that in some cases, it is difficult or even impossible to draw the line between personal characteristics and conduct and provides an example of the evaluation of a person's 'performance at work', which might take into consideration personal characteristics, such as creativity or empathy, as well as (deliberate) conduct, such as work ethics or courtesy.
63. B. Goodman, S. Flaxman, *European Union Regulations on Algorithmic Decision Making and 'a Right to an Explanation'*, p. 52.
64. D. Lubasz, et al., *Commentary on Article 4 of the GDPR*, [in:] *RODO. Ogólne rozporządzenie o ochronie danych. Komentarz*, E. Bielak-Jomaa, D. Lubasz (eds), Warsaw 2018, LEX.
65. K. Wiedemann, *Automated Processing of Personal Data for the Evaluation of Personality Traits*, p. 6.
66. Council of Europe, Recommendation CM/Rec(2010)13, paragraphs 96-98, p. 39.

knowledge discovery in databases'.[67] In the third stage, those correlations are applied to a particular individual to identify characteristics of its past, present or future behaviour.

Profiling often uses data from various different sources in order to infer something about an individual based on the qualities of other individuals who appear statistically similar.[68] Therefore, it may create new personal data by applying to particular individual characteristics of other individuals with whom it can be identified through the data collected on it. This means that the new personal data has not been collected, but calculated. Such new data is often called derived or inferred data.[69] Consequently, this most common method of profiling involves some margin of error as it based on a process of statistical extrapolation producing partially accurate and partially inaccurate results.[70] Profiling inevitably leads to false positives, i.e., the assignment of a data subject to a certain group it does not belong to, and false negatives, i.e., the exclusion of a data subject from a certain group it is actually a part of.[71] This is because profiling takes data from its original context and turns it into acontextual derivatives which may or may not turn out to be accurate.[72] By way of illustration, profiles do not necessarily represent reality but rather a version of reality derived from the data.[73]

It is noteworthy that during the process of profiling, special categories of personal data may be derived from seemingly non-sensitive information.[74] This blurs the line between 'ordinary' personal data and special categories of personal data discerned in the GDPR.[75] Considering that processing of special categories of personal data poses significant risks to a person's fundamental rights and freedoms, the GDPR establishes an appropriately higher level of protection for processing such data. The controllers which derive such data from 'ordinary' personal data should meet all of the relevant requirements for processing special categories of personal data. Currently, given the increasing power of algorithms, an inevitable conclusion is that not only is 'everything

---

67. M. Hildebrandt, *Who Is Profiling Who? Invisible Visibility*, [in:] *Reinventing Data Protection?*, S. Gutwirth, Y. Poullet, P. de Hert, C. de Terwangne, S. Nouw (eds), Springer 2009, p. 239.
68. Article 29 Data Protection Working Party, *Guidelines on Automated individual decision-making and Profiling*, p. 7.
69. For a comprehensive legal analysis of such personal data, *see* S. Wachter, B. Mittelstadt, *A Right to Reasonable Inferences: Rethinking Data Protection Law in the Age of Big Data and AI*, 2 Columbia Business Law Review (2019), pp. 494-620.
70. Council of Europe, Recommendation CM/Rec(2010)13, paragraphs 50 and 53, pp. 28-29.
71. K. Wiedemann, *Automated Processing of Personal Data for the Evaluation of Personality Traits*, pp. 11-12; Council of Europe, Recommendation CM/Rec(2010)13, paragraph 54, p. 29.
72. L. Edwards, *Data Protection and e-Privacy: From Spam and Cookies to Big Data, Machine Learning and Profiling*, [in:] *Law, Policy and the Internet*, p. 143.
73. D. Kamarinou, C. Millard, J. Singh, *Machine Learning with Personal Data*, Queen Mary School of Law Legal Studies Research Paper 247 (2016), p. 6.
74. European Data Protection Supervisor, *Opinion 3/2018 on online manipulation and personal data*, adopted on 19 March 2018, p. 7; L. Edwards, M. Veale, *Slave to the Algorithm?*, pp. 36-38.
75. European Parliament resolution of 14 March 2017 on fundamental rights implications of big data: privacy, data protection, non-discrimination, security and law-enforcement (2016/2225(INI)), P8_TA(2017)0076, paragraph 3.

is personal data' but even, 'everything is special category personal as such data is so easily inferred from 'ordinary' personal data.[76]

Last but not least, it is crucial to realise that profiling is not a purpose in itself, but it is used by the controller to facilitate the attainment of a given goal. For example, it may serve the bank's purpose to manage credit risk, the medical researcher's purpose to prevent genetic diseases and the government's purpose to combat tax evasion or benefit fraud.[77] It allows companies to make efficient use of their resources, for instance, by personalising goods and services or using targeted behavioural advertising tailored to the assumed needs and desires of potential customers.[78] It is used for analysing the respective credit card owner's buying patterns in order to prevent the fraudulent use of a credit card.[79] Overall, profiling allows the controller to make better individual decisions, especially those, which are automated.[80]

[G]   Automated Individual Decision-Making

As indicated above, profiling is often the first step in automated individual decision-making. Once the profiling is conducted, the controller may use its outcome to its advance by making automated individual decisions. Although these activities are interrelated, it is imperative to understand that each of these terms has a different scope.

Contrary to the notion of profiling, automated individual decision-making is not expressly defined in the regulation. In spite of this, it is largely self-explanatory. It is a process of making a decision that involves some form of automated processing. Such a decision may be based on any type of personal data, including the data provided directly by the data subject; observed about it, acquired from a third party or obtained as a result of profiling.[81] Naturally, it is possible to make an automated individual decision without profiling, and, vice versa, conduct profiling without making an automated individual decision.

The process of individual decision-making can assume manifold forms, with various levels of automation.[82] In an extreme scenario, there is no human involvement

---

76. *See* N. Purtova, *The Law of Everything: Broad Concept of Personal Data and Future of EU Data Protection Law*, pp. 40-81, where the author rightly argues that given the broad understanding of the notion of personal data, GDPR risks becoming 'the law of everything'. *See also* L. Edwards, *Data Protection: Enter the General Data Protection Regulation*, [in:] *Law, Policy and the Internet*, p. 90, where the author applies the same logic to special categories of personal data.

77. Council of Europe, Recommendation CM/Rec(2010)13, paragraph 48, p. 27 and paragraph 75, p. 34.

78. N.J. King, J. Forder, *Data Analytics and Consumer Profiling: Finding Appropriate Privacy Principles for Discovered Data*, 32 (5) Computer Law & Security Review (2016), pp. 696-697.

79. O. Tene, J. Polonetsky, *Big Data for All: Privacy and User Control in the Age of Analytics*, 11 (5) Northwestern Journal of Technology and Intellectual Property (2013), pp. 249-250.

80. For a comprehensive analysis of legal aspects of profiling, *see* A. Mednis, *Prawo ochrony danych osobowych wobec profilowania osób fizycznych*, Wrocław 2019.

81. Article 29 Data Protection Working Party, *Guidelines on Automated individual decision-making and Profiling*, p. 8.

82. K. Wiedemann, *Automated Processing of Personal Data for the Evaluation of Personality Traits*, pp. 17-18.

in this process or even the execution of the resulting decision. Oppositely, the results of profiling may constitute only one factor among several others, which form the basis of the subsequent decision subject entirely to human authority. In between these two scenarios, different levels of automation can be imagined. The less realistic it is for a human decision-maker to deviate from the results of profiling, the more automation plays a role in the individual decision-making process. In fact, if the human oversight of the individual decision-making process is not meaningful, just a token gesture, a resulting decision may be considered to be based on solely automated processing within the meaning of Article 22 (1) of the GDPR.[83]

Profiling and subsequent automated individual decision-making are used in numerous sectors, both private and public, as it allows to considerably improve the efficiency, consistency and quality of decisions, especially when it is necessary to analyse a large amount of data in a limited time. The most frequently mentioned examples are banking and finance, employment, healthcare, taxation, insurance, as well as broadly understood marketing and advertising.[84] Such systems are primarily designed either to anticipate outcomes that are not yet knowable for sure, such as whether an individual will repay a loan or detect and subjectively classify something unknown but somehow knowable, using inference rather than direct measurement, such as whether a submitted tax return is fraudulent or not.[85]

Automated individual decision-making encompasses a multitude of decision types, ranging from low to high impact. For instance, it may have a bearing on what kind of search results, curated content or ads are displayed to a particular data subject. On the other hand, it may determine whether a data subject receives a credit, insurance, a tax return or a job.

As a side note, progress in automated individual decision-making was initially held back by a lack of large-scale data and algorithmic architectures that could advance them, restraining such systems to relatively simplistic cases. Currently, technologies capable of coping with more input data and highly non-linear correlations have been developed. To a large extent, this has been due to the move away from manually specified rule-based algorithms to machine learning (hereinafter 'ML').[86] In addition to that, computation is considerably cheaper than it used to be.[87]

To reflect the potential risks of such processes, which are increasingly common, the GDPR contains specific provisions, which address solely automated individual decision-making.[88] As provided for in Article 22 (1) of the GDPR, they apply only to processes which are fully automated and which bring about legal effects or other

---

83. G. Malgieri, G. Comandé, *Why a Right to Legibility of Automated Decision-Making Exists in the General Data Protection Regulation*, 7 (4) International Data Privacy Law (2017), p. 243.
84. Article 29 Data Protection Working Party, *Guidelines on Automated individual decision-making and Profiling*, p. 5.
85. L. Edwards, M. Veale, *Slave to the Algorithm?*, p. 24.
86. L. Edwards, M. Veale, *Slave to the Algorithm?*, p. 24. Machine learning (ML), a type of AI, is briefly explained below in §1.02[H][3].
87. *Ibid.*, p. 25.
88. GDPR, Articles 13 (2) (f); 14 (2) g, 15 (1) (h) and 22. Specific provisions on solely automated individual decision-making are described below in Chapter 2, while corresponding rights of the data subjects are described below in Chapter 3.

similarly significant consequences for the data subject.[89] Whereas, with regard to automated individual decisions which fall outside the scope of this definition, numerous general provisions of the regulation apply.[90]

[H]   Other Terms

Multiple advances in technology have made it significantly easier to process personal data, *inter alia*, to conduct profiling and the subsequent automated individual decision-making. Although none of the terms explained below is explicitly mentioned in the GDPR, they are helpful in understanding the rapidly evolving landscape of personal data processing. It has to be noted that this is a non-exhaustive list of terms, as the scope of such as an exercise would be truly prohibitive.

[1]   *Algorithm*

An algorithm is a sequence of instructions or a set of rules designed to complete a task or solve a problem.[91] It is also defined as a mathematical construct with a finite, abstract, effective, compound control structure, imperatively given, accomplishing a given purpose under given provisions.[92] To simplify, an algorithm is any process that can be carried out automatically.[93] As signalled above, profiling usually uses sophisticated algorithms to find correlations within the processed data. They augment or replace analysis and decision-making by humans.

The use of algorithms is, in itself, not an entirely new phenomenon. Albeit, today's possibilities of collecting and processing vast amounts of data without direct human intervention, makes a difference.[94] Algorithms vary from simplistic to complex.[95] Traditionally, they require decision-making rules and weights to be individually defined and programmed 'by hand'. While this remains to be true in many cases, algorithms increasingly rely on their learning capacities owing to artificial intelligence (hereinafter 'AI') and ML.[96]

---

89. GDPR, Article 22 (1): 'The data subject shall have the right not to be subject to a decision based solely on automated processing, including profiling, which produces legal effects concerning him or her or similarly significantly affects him or her'. The scope of this definition is explained in greater detail below in §1.02[G].
90. General provisions relevant to automated individual decision-making are described below in Chapter 4, while corresponding rights of the data subjects are described below in Chapter 5.
91. Information Commissioner's Office, *Automated decision-making and profiling*, Guidelines of 5 June 2018, p. 5; Encyclopaedia Britannica: Definition of Algorithm, 15th edition, 2010.
92. R.K. Hill, *What an Algorithm Is*, 29 (1) Philosophy and Technology (2016), p. 35.
93. J.L. Chabert, [in:] *A History of Algorithms: From the Pebble to the Microchip*, J.L. Chabert (ed.), Springer 1999, p. 2.
94. P.G. Picht, B. Freund, *Competition (Law) in the Era of Algorithms*, p. 3.
95. B. Mittelstadt, P. Allo, M. Taddeo, S. Wachter, L. Floridi, *The Ethics of Algorithms: Mapping the Debate*, p. 3.
96. Information Commissioner's Office, *Automated decision-making and profiling*, Guidelines of 5 June 2018, p. 5. For more information about the current trajectory of algorithm development *see*, in particular: A. Tutt, *An FDA for Algorithms*, 69 (1) Administrative Law Review (2017), pp. 92-105.

[2] Artificial Intelligence

The term Artificial Intelligence (hereinafter 'AI') was coined by John McCarthy in 1956 and, in essence, it refers to machines imitating human intelligence.[97] Currently, AI is understood as systems designed by humans that, given a complex goal, act in the physical or digital world by perceiving their environment, interpreting the collected structured or unstructured data, reasoning on the knowledge derived from this data and deciding the best action(s) to take (according to pre-defined parameters) to achieve the given goal. In other words, 'AI is usually defined as the science of making computers do things that require intelligence when done by humans'.[98] AI systems can also be designed to learn to adapt their behaviour by analysing how the environment is affected by their previous actions'.[99] To simplify even further, AI refers to 'systems that display intelligent behaviour by analysing their environment and taking action – with some degree of autonomy – to achieve specific goals'.[100]

Due to significant growth in computing power, availability of data and progress in algorithms, AI is currently considered one of the most important technologies of the twenty-first century.[101] It is expected to disruptively change almost all areas of human life. As it is capable of analysing vast amounts of data, it may solve complex problems, which are sometimes beyond the scope of human intelligence.[102] It was the major trigger for the 'fourth industrial revolution' characterised by a fusion of technologies that is blurring the lines between the physical, digital and biological spheres, collectively referred to as cyber-physical systems.[103]

It improves products, processes and business models in all economic sectors. Notable contemporary examples of deployment of AI are personal assistants such as

---

97. John McCarthy was the organiser of a summer workshop that took place in 1956, the Dartmouth Summer Research Project on Artificial Intelligence, which is widely regarded as the seminal event for artificial intelligence as a field. For more in-depth information *see* J. Moor, *The Dartmouth College Artificial Intelligence Conference: The Next Fifty years*, 27 (4) AI Magazine (2006), pp. 87-91.

98. J. Copeland, *What Is Artificial Intelligence*, May 2000, available at: http://www.alanturing.net/turing_archive/pages/reference%20articles/what%20is%20ai.html, accessed 1 June 2019.

99. The Europeans Commission's High-Level Expert Group on Artificial Intelligence, *A definition of AI: Main capabilities and scientific disciplines*, Brussels, 18 December 2018, p. 7. This definition expands the previous definition of Artificial Intelligence (AI) as defined in Communication from the Commission to the European Parliament, the European Council, the Council, the European Economic and Social Committee and the Committee of the Regions on Artificial Intelligence for Europe, Brussels, 25 April 2018, COM(2018) 237 final.

100. Communication from the Commission to the European Parliament, the European Council, the Council, the European Economic and Social Committee and the Committee of the Regions, *Coordinated Plan on Artificial Intelligence*, Brussels, 7 December 2018, COM(2018) 795 final, p. 1.

101. *Ibid.*

102. Opinion of the European Economic and Social Committee on '*Artificial intelligence: anticipating its impact on work to ensure a fair transition*', 6 December 2018, (2018/C 440/01), paragraph 2.3.

103. K. Schwab, *The Fourth Industrial Revolution: What It Means, How to Respond*, World Economic Forum, 14 January 2016, available at: https://www.weforum.org/agenda/2016/01/the-fourth-industrial-revolution-what-it-means-and-how-to-respond/, accessed 1 May 2019.

Siri or Alexa, care robots such as Paro, clinical decision support systems, internet search engines, translators like Google Translate, autonomous vehicles, smart thermostats, spam filters, recommendation and filtering systems that compare and group users to provide personalised advertising or content, dynamic price optimisation, biometric facial, voice or dactyloscopic (finger) recognition systems, autonomous robotic vacuum cleaners such as Roomba, to name but a few. In addition to that, it also transforms public services.[104] Remarkably, it may even be used to support compliance with GDPR.[105] It is considered that AI will expand and amplify the scope of job automation.[106] In short, the realm of possible applications of AI is exceedingly vast, and many companies have been heavily investing in it in recent years.[107] Undeniably, it is also the key ingredient in profiling and subsequent automated individual decision-making.

[3]   Machine Learning

ML is a subfield of AI that involves identifying patterns in the available data and then generating algorithms in order to apply the newly found knowledge to the new data, usually for predictive purposes. In other words, ML is defined by the capacity to define or modify decision-making rules autonomously.[108] Unsurprisingly, ML is used extensively in both private and public sector domains, particularly in augmenting individual decision-making processes. The widespread, and low cost, availability of cloud computing, which enables much faster, cheaper, and more scalable processing of large amounts of data, contributes to the progress of ML.[109]

Once trained, ML algorithms can correctly classify new data with accuracies that exceed those of humans.[110] They can perform much more difficult tasks than manually specified rule-based algorithms can, like understanding speech and translating it into different languages, searching for the most relevant answer to a query or manipulating vehicles to drive safely.[111] A well-known example of an application of ML algorithms is an analysis conducted of decisions made by the European Court of Human Rights

---

104. Communication from the Commission to the European Parliament, the European Council, the Council, the European Economic and Social Committee and the Committee of the Regions, *Coordinated Plan on Artificial Intelligence*, Brussels, 7 December 2018, p. 1.
105. J. Kingston, *Using Artificial Intelligence to Support Compliance with the General Data Protection Regulation*, pp. 429-443.
106. D. Acemoglu, P. Restrepo (2018), *Artificial Intelligence, Automation and Work*, NBER Working Paper 24196, January 2018 referenced in Opinion of the European Economic and Social Committee on '*Artificial intelligence: anticipating its impact on work to ensure a fair transition*', 6 December 2018, (2018/C 440/01), paragraph 1.1.
107. F. Rossi, *Artificial Intelligence: Potential Benefits and Ethical Considerations*, European Parliament Briefing, October 2016, PE 571.380, p. 2.
108. B. Mittelstadt, P. Allo, M. Taddeo, S. Wachter, L. Floridi, *The Ethics of Algorithms: Mapping the Debate*, p. 3.
109. D. Kamarinou, C. Millard, J. Singh, *Machine Learning with Personal Data*, p. 4.
110. Communication from the Commission to the European Parliament, the European Council, the Council, the European Economic and Social Committee and the Committee of the Regions, *Coordinated Plan on Artificial Intelligence*, Brussels, 7 December 2018, p. 6.
111. L. Edwards, *Data Protection and e-Privacy: From Spam and Cookies to Big Data, Machine Learning and Profiling*, [in:] *Law, Policy and the Internet*, p. 142.

which attempted to predict the outcome of cases by applying ML techniques to the textual content and the components of cases. The researchers produced a system that was 79% accurate in predicting case outcomes.[112] In short, they are capable of making automated individual decisions rapidly, efficiently and consistently in complex and subtle domains involving even millions of variables.[113]

Contrary to 'ordinary' rule-based algorithms, ML algorithms are able to make automated individual decisions independently of pre-set rules and parameters. In particular, they can find patterns in the available data and develop, by monitoring their own operations, a suitable reaction or strategy with regard to these patterns. Consequently, the automated individual decisions produced by ML algorithms are difficult to predict beforehand or explain afterwards.[114] ML algorithms can remain black boxes, incomprehensible to humans because they are generated with predictive performance rather than interpretability as a priority.[115] This inherent feature of ML can thus severely inhibit the effectiveness of special rights of the data subject with regard to solely automated individual decision-making.[116]

ML enables so-called derived or inferred, predictive data to be created from the available data. However, as already noted above in §1.02[F], these inferences are based on statistical processes and are dependent on the quality and selection of the available data as well as the generated algorithm.[117] Even when the training dataset is accurate, the said inferences contain some margin of error, as they are based on a process of statistical extrapolation producing partially accurate and partially inaccurate results.[118]

Last but not least, predictive analytics involving ML are subject to prevalent criticism for potentially unfair and discriminatory results flowing from the classification of data subjects using the available data in which historical prejudices and assumptions are embedded.[119] By way of explanation, since ML algorithms are trained on historical data, they are intrinsically likely to recreate or even intensify discrimination present in the past decision-making.[120]

---

112. N. Aletras, D. Tsarapatsanis, D. Preoţiuc-Pietro, V. Lampos, *Predicting Judicial Decisions of the European Court of Human Rights: A Natural Language Processing Perspective*, 2 (e93) PeerJ Computer Science (2016), pp. 1-19.

113. L. Edwards, *Data Protection and e-Privacy: From Spam and Cookies to Big Data, Machine Learning and Profiling*, [in:] *Law, Policy and the Internet*, p. 142.

114. As explained by A. Tutt, *An FDA for Algorithms*, pp. 101-102, 'an algorithm's predictability is a measure of how difficult its outputs are to predict, while its explainability is a measure of how difficult its outputs are to explain'.

115. L. Edwards, M. Veale, *Slave to the Algorithm?*, p. 56; P.G. Picht, B. Freund, *Competition (Law) in the Era of Algorithms*, p. 4.

116. *See* at length this argument in L. Edwards, M. Veale, *Slave to the Algorithm?*, pp. 38-43. This issue is also covered below in Chapter 3, §3.10[B].

117. L. Edwards, *Data Protection and e-Privacy: From Spam and Cookies to Big Data, Machine Learning and Profiling*, [in:] *Law, Policy and the Internet*, p. 142.

118. Council of Europe, Recommendation CM/Rec(2010)13, paragraphs 50 and 53, pp. 28-29.

119. E. Bozdag, *Bias in Algorithmic Filtering and Personalization*, 15 (3) Ethics and Information Technology (2013), pp. 209-227; B. Custers, *Data Dilemmas in the Information Society: Introduction and Overview*, [in:] *Discrimination and Privacy in the Information Society*, B. Custers, T. Calders, B. Schermer, T. Zarsky (eds), Springer 2013, p. 4; D. Kamarinou, C. Millard, J. Singh, *Machine Learning with Personal Data*, p. 16.

120. L. Edwards, M. Veale, *Slave to the Algorithm?*, p. 28; M. Veale, R. Binns, *Fairer Machine Learning in the Real World: Mitigating Discrimination Without Collecting Sensitive Data*, 4 (2)

[4]   *Big Data*

Big data refers to huge volumes of diversely sourced data processed either by the private or public sector, which are then extensively analysed using sophisticated algorithms.[121] It relies not only on the increasing capability of technology to support the collection and storage of large amounts of data but also on its ability to analyse, understand and take advantage of the full value of this data.[122]

It is predominantly used to identify general trends and correlations, which may ultimately lead to better and more informed decisions overall. Taking into account that big data has brought controllers the means to understand consumers and predict both their personality traits and their behaviour, it may also be processed in a way that directly affects data subjects.[123] A typical case would be profiling, which often precedes automated individual decision-making, both described above in §1.02[F] and in §1.02[G] respectively. For example, in the field of marketing and advertisement, big data can be used to analyse or predict the personal preferences, behaviour and attitudes of individual customers and subsequently inform 'measures or decisions' that are taken with regard to those customers such as personalised discounts, special offers and targeted advertisements based on the customer's profile.[124]

Although the processed data is not always personal, one of the greatest values of big data for businesses and governments is derived from the monitoring of human behaviour, both collectively and individually and in its predictive potential.[125] It is noteworthy that even if the data is seemingly anonymous or has undergone de-identification, nowadays it is usually easy to match it with other data, in order to re-identify the particular data subject.[126] This means that such data may be considered personal and hence, it remains subject to the provisions of the GDPR.[127]

As a side note, it is worth to know that the above-mentioned process of discovering patterns in large datasets involving methods at the intersection of ML,

---

Big Data and Society (2017), p. 2; B. Goodman, S. Flaxman, *European Union Regulations on Algorithmic Decision Making and 'a Right to an Explanation'*, p. 53; D. Kamarinou, C. Millard, J. Singh, *Machine Learning with Personal Data*, p. 16. This is also acknowledged in Article 29 Data Protection Working Party, *Guidelines on Automated individual decision-making and Profiling*, pp. 5-6. For further remarks as to key concerns regarding automated decision-making *see* §1.05 below.

121. Article 29 Data Protection Working Party, *Opinion 03/2013 on purpose limitation*, adopted on 2 April 2013, pp. 35, 45; European Parliament resolution of 14 March 2017 on fundamental rights implications of big data: privacy, data protection, non-discrimination, security and law-enforcement, lit. A.
122. European Data Protection Supervisor, Opinion 7/2015 *Meeting the challenges of big data*, 19 November 2015, p. 7.
123. K. Wiedemann, *Automated Processing of Personal Data for the Evaluation of Personality Traits*, p. 3; Article 29 Data Protection Working Party, *Opinion 03/2013 on purpose limitation*, p. 45.
124. *Ibid.*
125. European Data Protection Supervisor, Opinion 7/2015 *Meeting the challenges of big data*, 19 November 2015, p. 7.
126. For further information about re-identification of a data subject, *see* P. Ohm, *Broken Promises of Privacy*, pp. 1701-1777; L. Sweeney, *Simple Demographics Often Identify People Uniquely*; P. Schwartz, D. Solove, *The PII Problem*, pp. 1814-1894.
127. GDPR, Articles 2 (1) and 4 (1).

statistics, and database systems is usually called 'data mining' or 'knowledge discovery in databases'.[128] It should be noted that the idea of using massive amounts of data in order to generate new knowledge is not new, and it has been employed for decades.[129] Nevertheless, the widespread use of big data began much later, when data storage and processing costs fell, algorithms improved and vast datasets of personal and non-personal data were created, in particular by online industries.[130]

§1.03 MATERIAL SCOPE OF APPLICATION OF THE GDPR

The protection of natural persons afforded by the regulation applies to the processing of personal data wholly or partly by automated means.[131] The principal concepts determining the material scope of the GDPR *videlicet* notions of personal data and processing are explained above in §1.02[A] and in §1.02[E], respectively. As concluded therein, one and the other are notoriously inclusive. Reiterating, personal data is defined as any information relating to an identified or identifiable natural person, which makes it almost an all-encompassing notion.[132] Whereas processing means any handling of personal data from the point of collection to the point of destruction, whether or not by automated means. Unsurprisingly, given the broad interpretation of both of the above concepts, the material scope of the GDPR is expansive as well.

---

128. U. Fayyad, G. Piatetsky-Shapiro, P. Smyth, *From Data Mining to Knowledge Discovery in Databases*, 17 (3) AI Magazine (1996), pp. 37-54; Encyclopædia Britannica: Definition of Data Mining, 15th edition, 2010.
129. K. Wiedemann, *Automated Processing of Personal Data for the Evaluation of Personality Traits*, p. 12.
130. L. Edwards, *Data Protection and e-Privacy: From Spam and Cookies to Big Data, Machine Learning and Profiling*, [in:] *Law, Policy and the Internet*, p. 141.
131. GDPR, Article 2:

> 1. This Regulation applies to the processing of personal data wholly or partly by automated means and to the processing other than by automated means of personal data which form part of a filing system or are intended to form part of a filing system.
> 2. This Regulation does not apply to the processing of personal data:
>   (a) in the course of an activity which falls outside the scope of Union law;
>   (b) by the Member States when carrying out activities which fall within the scope of Chapter 2 of Title V of the TEU;
>   (c) by a natural person in the course of a purely personal or household activity;
>   (d) by competent authorities for the purposes of the prevention, investigation, detection or prosecution of criminal offences or the execution of criminal penalties, including the safeguarding against and the prevention of threats to public security.
> 3. For the processing of personal data by the Union institutions, bodies, offices and agencies, Regulation (EC) No. 45/2001 applies. Regulation (EC) No. 45/2001 and other Union legal acts applicable to such processing of personal data shall be adapted to the principles and rules of this Regulation in accordance with Article 98.
> 4. This Regulation shall be without prejudice to the application of Directive 2000/31/EC, in particular of the liability rules of intermediary service providers in Articles 12 to 15 of that Directive.

132. N. Purtova, *The Law of Everything: Broad Concept of Personal Data and Future of EU Data Protection Law*, p. 45.

Additionally, the regulation may apply to processing other than by automated means. In contrast to automated processing, which uses technology, manual processing is executed by humans without its use. By its very nature, it is incomparably less efficient and, for this reason, poses fewer risks to the rights and freedoms of natural persons. Subsequently, the manual processing is only subject to the GDPR if personal data is contained or is intended to be contained in a filing system, i.e., a structured set, which is accessible according to specific criteria.[133]

Although the GDPR has a vast material scope, it contains some exclusions. First, it does not apply to the processing of personal data in the course of an activity, which falls outside the scope of EU law, such as activities concerning national security or relating to the common foreign and security policy of the EU.[134]

Second, it does not apply to the processing of personal data by the Member States when carrying out activities falling within the scope of Chapter 2 of Title V of the Treaty on European Union (hereinafter 'TEU'), which contains specific provisions on the common foreign and security policy.[135]

Third, it does not apply to the processing of personal data by a natural person in the course of a purely personal or household activity.[136] According to the preamble to the GDPR, this exception could apply to correspondence and the holding of addresses, or social networking and online activity undertaken within the context of such activities. Albeit the controllers or processors who provide the means for processing personal data for such personal or household activities may not rely on this exclusion from the material scope of the GDPR.

Fourth, it does not apply to the processing of personal data by competent authorities for the purposes of the prevention, investigation, detection or prosecution of criminal offences or the execution of criminal penalties, including the safeguarding against and the prevention of threats to public security, i.e., where the Directive (EU) 2016/680 applies.[137]

---

133. GDPR, Recital 15: '[...] Files or sets of files, as well as their cover pages, which are not structured according to specific criteria should not fall within the scope of this Regulation'.
134. GDPR, Article 2 (2) (a). *See also* Recital 16 of the GDPR: 'This Regulation does not apply to issues of protection of fundamental rights and freedoms or the free flow of personal data related to activities which fall outside the scope of Union law, such as activities concerning national security. This Regulation does not apply to the processing of personal data by the Member States when carrying out activities in relation to the common foreign and security policy of the Union'.
135. GDPR, Article 2 (2) (b), Recital 16.
136. GDPR, Article 2 (2) (c). *See also* Recital 18 of the GDPR: 'This Regulation does not apply to the processing of personal data by a natural person in the course of a purely personal or household activity and thus with no connection to a professional or commercial activity. Personal or household activities could include correspondence and the holding of addresses, or social networking and online activity undertaken within the context of such activities. However, this Regulation applies to controllers or processors which provide the means for processing personal data for such personal or household activities'. *See also* Recital 4 of the GDPR: 'The processing of personal data should be designed to serve mankind. The right to the protection of personal data is not an absolute right; it must be considered in relation to its function in society and be balanced against other fundamental rights, in accordance with the principle of proportionality [...]'.
137. GDPR, Article 2 (2) (d), Recital 19. *See also* Directive (EU) 2016/680 of the European Parliament and of the Council of 27 April 2016 on the protection of natural persons with regard to the

Fifth, for the processing of personal data by the EU institutions, bodies, offices and agencies, Regulation (EU) 2018/1725 applies in parallel with the GDPR.[138] This legal act lays down the specific rules to protect natural persons with regard to the processing of personal data and to ensure the free movement of personal data within the EU in the fields of judicial cooperation in criminal matters and police cooperation, and it is to be interpreted homogeneously and applied coherently with the GDPR.[139]

Lastly, the GDPR is without prejudice to the application of Directive 2000/31/EC, which seeks to contribute to the proper functioning of the internal market by ensuring the free movement of information society services between the Member States, as they should be treated as complementary systems of consumer rights protection.[140]

Overall, none of these exclusions is particularly relevant to the issue of automated individual decision-making, and GDPR remains applicable to most of such cases, both in the private and public sector.

§1.04   TERRITORIAL SCOPE OF APPLICATION OF THE GDPR

The expansive territorial scope of the GDPR is based on two main criteria: the establishment criterion, as per its Article 3 (1),[141] and the targeting criterion as per its Article 3 (2).[142] Where one of these two criteria is met, the relevant provisions of the GDPR apply to the processing of personal data by the controller or the processor

---

processing of personal data by competent authorities for the purposes of the prevention, investigation, detection or prosecution of criminal offences or the execution of criminal penalties, and on the free movement of such data, and repealing Council Framework Decision 2008/977/JHA, Official Journal of the European Union L 119, 4 May 2016, pp. 89-131.

138. GDPR, Article 2 (3). *See also* Regulation (EU) 2018/1725 of the European Parliament and of the Council of 23 October 2018 on the protection of natural persons with regard to the processing of personal data by the Union institutions, bodies, offices and agencies and on the free movement of such data, and repealing Regulation (EC) No. 45/2001 and Decision No. 1247/2002/EC, Official Journal of the European Union L 295, 21 November 2018, pp. 39-98.

139. *See* Recital 17 of the GDPR together with Recitals 5 and 77 of the Regulation (EU) 2018/1725.

140. GDPR, Article 2 (4). *See also* Recital 21 of the GDPR: 'This Regulation is without prejudice to the application of Directive 2000/31/EC of the European Parliament and of the Council, in particular of the liability rules of intermediary service providers in Articles 12 to 15 of that Directive. That Directive seeks to contribute to the proper functioning of the internal market by ensuring the free movement of information society services between Member States'. *See also* Directive 2000/31/EC of the European Parliament and of the Council of 8 June 2000 on certain legal aspects of information society services, in particular electronic commerce, in the Internal Market ('Directive on electronic commerce'), Official Journal of the European Union L 178, 17 July 2000, pp. 1-16. *See,* in particular, Recital 14 of the Directive 2000/31/EC, which notes that the legal framework in the field of personal data is already established and, therefore, it is not necessary to cover this issue in order to ensure the smooth functioning of the internal market, in particular the free movement of personal data between Member States, the implementation and application of this legal act should be made in full compliance with the principles relating to the protection of personal data, in particular as regards unsolicited commercial communication and the liability of intermediaries.

141. GDPR, Article 3 (1): 'This Regulation applies to the processing of personal data in the context of the activities of an establishment of a controller or a processor in the Union, regardless of whether the processing takes place in the Union or not'.

142. GDPR, Article 3 (2): 'This Regulation applies to the processing of personal data of data subjects who are in the Union by a controller or processor not established in the Union, where the processing activities are related to: (a) the offering of goods or services, irrespective of whether

concerned. Additionally, Article 3 (3) of the GDPR confirms its application to the processing where Member State law applies by virtue of public international law.[143] Apart from that, the GDPR also applies in Iceland, Liechtenstein and Norway, which are part of the European Economic Area (hereinafter 'EEA'), but not the Member States.[144]

[A]   The Establishment Criterion

Regarding the first establishment criterion provided for in Article 3 (1) of the GDPR, which states that 'this Regulation applies to the processing of personal data in the context of the activities of an establishment of a controller or a processor in the Union, regardless of whether the processing takes place in the Union or not', it is key to explain the notion of establishment, which is not defined in the GDPR.[145] Recital 22 of the GDPR clarifies that an 'establishment implies the effective and real exercise of activities through stable arrangements. The legal form of such arrangements, whether through a branch or a subsidiary with a legal personality, is not the determining factor in that respect'.

Based on the identical wording of Recital 19 of the DPD, the predecessor of the GDPR, the Court of Justice of the European Union issued several judgments confirming such broad and flexible interpretation of this notion, departing from a formalistic approach where undertakings are established solely in the place where they are registered.[146] In particular, the Court of Justice of the European Union ruled that the meaning of establishment extends to even a minimal real and effective activity exercised through stable arrangements, as it has to be considered in the light of the specific nature of the economic activities and the provision of services concerned.[147]

---

a payment of the data subject is required, to such data subjects in the Union; or (b) the monitoring of their behaviour as far as their behaviour takes place within the Union'.

143. GDPR, Article 3 (3): 'This Regulation applies to the processing of personal data by a controller not established in the Union, but in a place where Member State law applies by virtue of public international law'.

144. Decision of the EEA Joint Committee No. 154/2018 of 6 July 2018 amending Annex XI (Electronic communication, audiovisual services and information society) and Protocol 37 (containing the list provided for in Article 101) to the EEA Agreement [2018/1022], Official Journal of the European Union L 183, 19 July 2018, pp. 23-26.

145. Article 4 (16) of the GDPR defines only the notion of 'main establishment', which is mainly relevant for the purpose of determining the competence of the supervisory authorities concerned according to Article 56 of the GDPR, not 'establishment' as such.

146. See, in particular, Judgment of the Court (Grand Chamber) of 13 May 2014, Google Spain SL and Google Inc. v Agencia Española de Protección de Datos (AEPD) and Mario Costeja González, Case C-131/12, ECLI:EU:C:2014:317; Judgment of the Court (Third Chamber) of 1 October 2015, Weltimmo s. r. o. v Nemzeti Adatvédelmi és Információszabadság Hatóság, Case C-230/14, ECLI:EU:C:2015:639; Judgment of the Court (Third Chamber) of 28 July 2016, Verein für Konsumenteninformation v Amazon EU Sàrl, Case C-191/15, ECLI:EU:C:2016:612; Judgment of the Court (Grand Chamber) of 5 June 2018, Unabhängiges Landeszentrum für Datenschutz Schleswig-Holstein v Wirtschaftsakademie Schleswig-Holstein GmbH, Case C-210/16, ECLI:EU:C:2018:388.

147. Judgment of the Court (Third Chamber) of 1 October 2015, Weltimmo s. r. o. v Nemzeti Adatvédelmi és Információszabadság Hatóság, Case C-230/14, ECLI:EU:C:2015:639, paragraphs 29, 31.

Consequently, the threshold for an establishment is quite low, especially when the activities of a controller or a processor concern the provision of services exclusively online.

Once it is concluded that the controller or the processor is established in the EU, it has to be considered whether the processing in question is carried out in the context of the activities of this establishment, in order to determine whether Article 3 (1) of the GDPR applies. As interpreted by the Court of Justice of the European Union, the meaning of processing of personal data in the context of the activities of an establishment cannot be interpreted restrictively.[148] Thus, an inextricable link between the activities of a local establishment in a Member State and the data processing of the controller or the processor established outside the EU may trigger the applicability of the GDPR, even if that local establishment is not actually taking any role in the data processing itself.[149]

Moreover, it has to be accentuated that Article 3 (1) of the GDPR *in fine* clearly specifies that the regulation applies 'regardless of whether the processing takes place in the Union or not'. In actuality, it is the presence, through an establishment, of the controller or the processor in the EU and the fact that processing takes place in the context of the activities of this establishment that trigger the application of the GDPR to the processing activities. Whereas the place of processing is not relevant in determining whether it falls within the territorial scope of the GDPR.

Similarly, although not explicitly, the wording of Article 3 (1) of the GDPR does not limit the application of the GDPR to the processing of personal data of individuals who are in the EU. Therefore, if other requirements of Article 3 (1) of the GDPR are met, the regulation applies, regardless of the location or the nationality of the data subject whose personal data is being processed.[150]

[B]   The Targeting Criterion

The second targeting criterion sets out the circumstances in which the GDPR applies even to a controller or processor not established in the EU, depending on its processing activities. Specifically, Article 3 (2) of the GDPR, states that 'This Regulation applies to the processing of personal data of data subjects who are in the Union by a controller or

---

148. Judgment of the Court (Grand Chamber) of 13 May 2014, Google Spain SL and Google Inc. v Agencia Española de Protección de Datos (AEPD) and Mario Costeja González, Case C-131/12, ECLI:EU:C:2014:317, paragraph 53.
149. Judgment of the Court (Grand Chamber) of 13 May 2014, Google Spain SL and Google Inc. v Agencia Española de Protección de Datos (AEPD) and Mario Costeja González, Case C-131/12, ECLI:EU:C:2014:317, paragraphs 47, 52. *See also* Article 29 Data Protection Working Party, *Update of Opinion 8/2010 on applicable law in light of the CJEU judgement in Google Spain*, adopted on 16 December 2015, pp. 4-7; European Data Protection Board, *Guidelines 3/2018 on the territorial scope of the GDPR (Article 3) – Version for public consultation*, adopted on 16 November 2018, p. 7.
150. This interpretation is confirmed by the wording of Recital 14 of the GDPR: 'The protection afforded by this Regulation should apply to natural persons, whatever their nationality or place of residence, in relation to the processing of their personal data [...]'. *See also*: European Data Protection Board, *Guidelines 3/2018 on the territorial scope of the GDPR (Article 3)*, p. 9.

processor not established in the Union, where the processing activities are related to: (a) the offering of goods or services, irrespective of whether a payment of the data subject is required, to such data subjects in the Union; or (b) the monitoring of their behaviour as far as their behaviour takes place within the Union'. As clearly reflected in the wording of this provision, the targeting criterion requires that data subject is located on the territory of the EU, but it does not need to be a citizen, resident or hold any other type of legal status.[151] Additionally, there are two alternative requirements which have to be satisfied to apply the said criterion, *videlicet* the processing of personal data must relate to the offering of goods or services, or to the monitoring of data subjects' behaviour in the EU.

The first of the above-mentioned activities occurs when the offer of goods or services is directed at the data subject in the EU, specifically, whether the behaviour of the controller or the processor indicates his intention to do so. This is further clarified in Recital 23 of the GDPR, which states that 'mere accessibility of the controller's, processor's or an intermediary's website in the Union, of an email address or of other contact details, or the use of a language generally used in the third country where the controller is established, is insufficient to ascertain such intention', nonetheless 'factors such as the use of a language or a currency generally used in one or more Member States with the possibility of ordering goods and services in that other language, or the mentioning of customers or users who are in the Union, may make it apparent that the controller envisages offering goods or services to data subjects in the Union'.[152] An activity may constitute an offering of goods or services within the meaning of Article 3 (2) (a) of the GDPR, regardless of whether a payment is made in exchange.[153]

The second of the above-mentioned activities, which triggers the 'targeting criterion' is the monitoring of the data subject's behaviour as far as it takes place within the EU. Besides, the monitored behaviour must relate to a data subject, which is in the EU. As advised in the Recital 24 of the GDPR, 'in order to determine whether a processing activity can be considered to monitor the behaviour of data subjects, it should be ascertained whether natural persons are tracked on the internet including potential subsequent use of personal data processing techniques which consist of profiling a natural person, particularly in order to take decisions concerning her or him

---

151. This interpretation is confirmed by the wording of Recital 14 of the GDPR: 'The protection afforded by this Regulation should apply to natural persons, whatever their nationality or place of residence, in relation to the processing of their personal data [...]'.

152. As noted by the European Data Protection Board, *Guidelines 3/2018 on the territorial scope of the GDPR (Article 3)*, pp. 15-16. *See also* specific factors listed in Judgment of the Court (Grand Chamber) of 7 December 2010, Peter Pammer v Reederei Karl Schlüter GmbH & Co KG (C-585/08), and Hotel Alpenhof GesmbH v Oliver Heller (C-144/09) Joined cases C-585/08 and C-144/09), ECLI:EU:C:2010:740, to consider whether goods or services are offered to the data subject in the EU. Despite the fact that this case law is based on Article 15 (1) (c) of Council Regulation (EC) No. 44/2001 of 22 December 2000 on jurisdiction and the recognition and enforcement of judgments in civil and commercial matters, Official Journal of the European Union L 012, 16 January 2001, pp. 1-23, an interpretation of the notion of 'directing an activity' contained therein is considered helpful in explaining the 'offering of goods or services'.

153. GDPR, Article 3 (2) (a) *in fine*.

or for analysing or predicting her or his personal preferences, behaviours and attitudes'. Whereas the European Data Protection Board rightfully comments that the above recital should be understood broadly and also apply to the tracking of a data subject through other types of network (than the internet) or technology involving personal data processing, such as wearables and different smart devices.[154]

The key consideration to determine whether processing involves monitoring of the data subject, is the controller's data processing objective, especially any automated individual decision-making. Although in some cases it will not be easy to determine whether an activity amounts to monitoring of a data subject, it is likely that, for instance, behavioural advertisement, geo-localisation activities (in particular, for marketing purposes), online tracking (e.g., through the use of cookies), personalised diet and health analytics services online, Closed-circuit television (CCTV) will all trigger the application of Article 3 (2) of the GDPR.[155]

[C]   Processing in a Place Where Member State Law Applies by Virtue of Public International Law

Finally, there is Article 3 (3) of the GDPR, which, as indicated above, provides that 'this Regulation applies to the processing of personal data by a controller not established in the Union, but in a place where Member State law applies by virtue of public international law'. This provision is expanded upon in Recital 25 of the GDPR, which cites diplomatic missions and consular posts as examples of such places.[156]

§1.05   KEY CONCERNS REGARDING AUTOMATED INDIVIDUAL DECISION-MAKING

Automated individual decision-making may bring significant benefits for the controllers, the data subjects and society, including by improving the efficiency, rapidity, accuracy and consistency of decisions.[157] Notwithstanding the above, such processing inherently entails a number of significant risks for individuals' rights and freedoms. It can have various unintended and unexpected effects. Automated individual decisions may profoundly affect individuals' lives in terms of, for instance, discrimination,

---

154. European Data Protection Board, *Guidelines 3/2018 on the territorial scope of the GDPR (Article 3)*, pp. 17-18.
155. European Data Protection Board, *Guidelines 3/2018 on the territorial scope of the GDPR (Article 3)*, p. 18.
156. The definitions and status of diplomatic missions and consular posts are laid down, respectively, in the Vienna Convention on Diplomatic Relations of 18 April 1961, United Nations, Treaty Series, vol. 500, pp. 95 et seq. and the Vienna Convention on Consular Relations of 24 April 1963, United Nations, Treaty Series, vol. 596, pp. 261 et seq.
157. *See also* 40th International Conference of Data Protection and Privacy Commissioners, *Declaration on ethics and data protection in artificial intelligence adopted at 40th International Conference of Data Protection and Privacy Commissioners*, adopted on 23 October 2018 in Brussels, p. 2.

deindividualisation, information asymmetries, and social segregation.[158] Public assessment of these concerns is difficult because the algorithms used in such processes are complex, opaque and, above all else, proprietary. Below is a high profile, non-exhaustive overview of the key concerns regarding automated individual decision-making, which serves as a background to the legal analysis in this doctoral dissertation.

[A]   Inaccurate Personal Data

Automated individual decision-making involves a risk that inaccurate personal data is blindingly applied to an individual.[159] If profiling is used, both the personal data relating to a data subject in respect of whom an automated individual decision is made and the large scale dataset, which is used for 'the process of knowledge discovery in databases' need to be as accurate as possible. Any conclusions which constitute the basis for an automated individual decision can only be as reliable as the personal data they are based on. Thus, if the personal data is inaccurate, or irrelevant, or taken out of context, the risk of rendering a wrong decision is inevitable. This risk is realistic.

For instance, a 2012 study of the United States' Federal Trade Commission on credit report accuracy found that 26% of the participants found at least one error, which was potentially material on at least one of the three credit reports that had been issued on them. In addition to that, in 21% of all cases, at least one of the Credit Reporting Agencies adjusted their scores after going through the dispute process that is provided in the Fair Credit Reporting Act.[160] In 13% of all cases, this had an actual impact on the credit score, and for 5.2% of the consumers, the resulting increase in score was such that their credit risk tier decreased and thus the consumer may be more likely to be offered a lower auto loan interest rate.[161]

[B]   Inconclusive Personal Data

There is also a risk that automated individual decision-making is based on inconclusive personal data. By way of explanation, profiling, which often precedes automated individual decision-making, may use personal data from various different sources in order to infer something about an individual based on qualities of other individuals

---

158. B. Schermer, *The Limits of Privacy in Automated Profiling and Data Mining*, 27 Computer Law and Security Review (2011), pp. 45-52; Article 29 Data Protection Working Party, *Guidelines on Automated individual decision-making and Profiling*, p. 5.
159. Council of Europe, Recommendation CM/Rec(2010)13, paragraphs 55-58, pp. 30-31.
160. An Act to amend the Federal Deposit Insurance Act to require insured banks to maintain certain records, to require that certain transactions in United States currency be reported to the Department of the Treasury, and for other purposes enacted 26 October 1970 (The Fair Credit Reporting Act), title VI of Public Law 91-508, 84 Statutes at Large 1114, 15 U.S. Code §§ 1681 et seq.
161. J. Leibowitz, et al., *Report to Congress under Section 319 of the Fair and Accurate Credit Transactions Act of 2003*, Washington 2012, referenced in K. Wiedemann, *Automated Processing of Personal Data for the Evaluation of Personality Traits*, pp. 11-12.

who are statistically similar.[162] This means that the new personal data has not been collected, but calculated, using inferential statistics or ML algorithms. In other words, such algorithms reason from externally supplied instances to produce general hypotheses, which are used to make predictions about future instances.[163] Hence, inevitably, profiling produces uncertain knowledge and involves some margin of error, as it based on a process of statistical extrapolation producing partially accurate and partially inaccurate results.[164] It may lead either to false positives, i.e., the assignment of a data subject to a certain group it does not belong to or to false negatives, i.e., the exclusion of a data subject from a certain group it is actually a part of.[165] As a consequence, an automated individual decision may be based on unreliable personal data. In other words, the controller may over-rely on correlations and make an automated individual decision about the data subject based on imprecise projections. Besides, it is considered that inferring new or unknown information about the data subject from other data is often highly privacy invasive.[166]

Moreover, correlation does not imply causation and no conclusions should be drawn just on its basis. Correlation is rather insufficient to motivate actions, such as making a decision.[167] Nevertheless, correlations based on a sufficient amount of data are currently increasingly seen as credible enough to bring such action.[168] Accordingly, a lot of automated individual decision-making relies on correlations found within vast datasets without establishing causality of the information. Besides that, algorithms do not perform well with regard to common sense reasoning, and thus, there are legitimate concerns about the intentional and unintentional negative consequences of their use.[169]

Last but not least, attributing to given individual qualities of other individuals who appear statistically similar stands in contradiction with individuals answerability for their own actions.[170] As a result of profiling, an individual is comprehended based on connections with others rather than its actual behaviour.

---

162. Article 29 Data Protection Working Party, *Guidelines on Automated individual decision-making and Profiling*, p. 7. *See also* remarks in §1.02[H][3] above.
163. S.B. Kotsiantis, *Supervised Machine Learning: A Review of Classification Techniques*, 31 (3) Informatica (2007), pp. 249-268.
164. Council of Europe, Recommendation CM/Rec(2010)13, paragraphs 50 and 53, pp. 28-29.
165. K. Wiedemann, *Automated Processing of Personal Data for the Evaluation of Personality Traits*, pp. 11-12; Council of Europe, Recommendation CM/Rec(2010)13, paragraph 54, p. 29.
166. Privacy International, *Data Is Power: Profiling and Automated Decision-Making in GDPR*, p. 7.
167. B. Mittelstadt, P. Allo, M. Taddeo, S. Wachter, L. Floridi, *The Ethics of Algorithms: Mapping the Debate*, p. 4; E. Bayamlıoglu, *Contesting Automated Decisions: A View of Transparency Implications*, 4 (4) European Data Protection Law Review (2018), p. 437. Correlation proves causation fallacy is also known as *cum hoc ergo propter hoc* and *post hoc ergo propter hoc* (Latin for 'with this, therefore because of this' and 'after this, therefore because of this' respectively).
168. M. Hildebrandt, B.J. Koops, *The Challenges of Ambient Law and Legal Protection in the Profiling Era*, 73 (3) Modern Law Review (2010), pp. 428-460.
169. F. Doshi-Velez, M. Kortz, *Accountability of AI under the Law: The Role of Explanation*, Berkman Klein Center Working Group on Explanation and the Law, Berkman Klein Center for Internet & Society Working Paper (2017), p. 1.
170. Council of Europe, Recommendation CM/Rec(2010)13, paragraph 53, pp. 28-29.

[C]   Discriminatory Algorithms

Automation of individual decision-making is often justified by an alleged lack of bias in algorithms.[171] With regard to algorithms, there is so-called neutrality fallacy, as it is believed they will provide a more even and objective treatment of individuals.[172] In reality, they are not ideal neutral decision makers.

Algorithms are designed by humans, and they reflect their values, whether it is intentional or not.[173] As a result, they are unavoidably value-laden and may contain latent bias of numerous members of engineering teams, who develop them over time.

Although algorithms are designed for discerning the data points and differentiate between peers, discrimination, even if predictively valid, is unethical and socially unacceptable, not to mention unlawful.[174] In general, discrimination is understood as the unfair treatment of an individual because it belongs to a particular group.[175] EU's efforts to tackle discrimination are clearly reflected in the normative framework which underlies the EU, i.e., TEU, TFEU, the Charter of Fundamental Rights of the European Union and the European Convention on Human Rights.[176] Accordingly, in the secondary law, there are numerous provisions including varying lists of characteristics about an individual that may not, directly or indirectly, play a role in the decision-making process.[177]

It is widely acknowledged that in the words of the United Nations Human Rights Council: 'automatic processing of personal data for individual profiling may lead to

---

171. L. Edwards, M. Veale, *Slave to the Algorithm?*, p. 27.
172. C. Sandvig, *Seeing the Sort: The Aesthetic and Industrial Defence of 'the Algorithm'*, 11 (1) Journal of the New Media Caucus (2015), pp. 35-51; C. Powell, *Race and Rights in the Digital Age*, 112 American Journal of International Law Unbound (2018), pp. 339-343.
173. B. Mittelstadt, P. Allo, M. Taddeo, S. Wachter, L. Floridi, *The Ethics of Algorithms: Mapping the Debate*, p. 7; L. Edwards, M. Veale, *Enslaving the Algorithm*, pp. 50-51.
174. M. Veale, R. Binns, *Fairer Machine Learning in the Real World*, p. 2; I. Ntokos, *Reality Mining: Privacy and Data Protection Dilemmas in the World of Perpetual Behavioral Monitoring*, written on 13 August 2018, available at SSRN, pp. 36-39.
175. Recital 71 of the GDPR lists the following characteristics as grounds for discrimination: racial or ethnic origin, political opinion, religion or beliefs, trade union membership, genetic or health status or sexual orientation.
176. Consolidated version of the Treaty on European Union, Official Journal of the European Union C 326, 26 October 2012, pp. 13-390 (hereinafter 'TEU'), Articles 2 and 3; TFEU, Articles 8, 10, 18-25; Charter of Fundamental Rights of the European Union, Article 21; Council of Europe, European Convention for the Protection of Human Rights and Fundamental Freedoms, as amended by Protocols Nos 11 and 14, 4 November 1950, ETS 5 (hereinafter 'European Convention on Human Rights'), Article 14.
177. *See*, in particular, the following directives, which are implemented into Member State law: Council Directive 2000/43/EC of 29 June 2000 implementing the principle of equal treatment between persons irrespective of racial or ethnic origin, Official Journal of the European Union L 180, 19 July 2000, pp. 22-26; Council Directive 2000/78/EC of 27 November 2000 establishing a general framework for equal treatment in employment and occupation, Official Journal of the European Union L 303, 2 December 2000, pp. 16-22; Directive 2006/54/EC of the European Parliament and of the Council of 5 July 2006 on the implementation of the principle of equal opportunities and equal treatment of men and women in matters of employment and occupation (recast), Official Journal of the European Union L 204, 26 July 2006, pp. 23-36.

discrimination'.[178] The use of predictive analytics, especially involving ML algorithms, may lead to discriminatory results flowing from the classification of data subjects using the available data in which historical prejudices and assumptions are embedded.[179] Because ML algorithms are trained on historical data, they are intrinsically likely to recreate or even intensify discrimination present in the past decision-making.[180] In other words, they may 'learn' to discriminate.

By way of illustration, when Amazon was building its automated recruiting system, the algorithms were trained to vet applicants by observing patterns in resumes submitted to the company over a ten-year period. Most came from men, a reflection of male dominance across the tech industry. In effect, Amazon's system taught itself that male candidates were preferable. Although Amazon edited the system to make it neutral, there was no guarantee that the algorithms would not devise other ways of sorting candidates that could prove discriminatory, so the project was discontinued.[181]

A 2015 study by Carnegie Mellon University researchers, for instance, found that Google's online advertising system showed an ad for high-income jobs to men much more often than it showed the ad to women.[182] The study suggests that such discrimination could either be the result of advertisers placing inappropriate bids, or an unexpected outcome of unpredictable large-scale ML. Intentional or not – such discrimination is an inherent risk of targeted advertising and impossible for individuals to detect.

As another example, it is key to realise that race can be easily perceived online, based on the products that an individual buys, the websites it visits, and the digital dossiers sold by data brokers.[183] For instance, until recently, Facebook used AI to categorise its users by 'ethnic affinities,' based on posts liked or otherwise engaged with on Facebook.[184] Housing advertisers used the company's 'ethnic affiliations' to exclude particular groups as part of niche advertising strategies.

It is commonly perceived that simply omitting personal data regarding legally protected characteristics in an automated individual decision-making process removes the possibility for discrimination.[185] In fact, this does not successfully prevent

---

178. United Nations General Assembly, Human Rights Council, Resolution: *The right to privacy in the digital age*, adopted on 22 March 2017, A/HRC/34/L.7/Rev.1.

179. *See* reference 119.

180. *See* reference 120.

181. J. Dastin, *Amazon Scraps Secret AI Recruiting Tool That Showed Bias Against Women*, Reuters, 10 October 2018, available at: https://www.reuters.com/article/us-amazon-com-jobs-automation-insight/amazon-scraps-secret-ai-recruiting-tool-that-showed-bias-against-women-idUSKCN1MK08G, accessed 1 May 2019.

182. A. Datta, M.C. Tschantz, *Automated Experiments on Ad Privacy Settings a Tale of Opacity, Choice, and Discrimination*, 1 Proceedings on Privacy Enhancing Technologies (2015), pp. 92-112.

183. C. Powell, *Race and Rights in the Digital Age*, pp. 342-343.

184. J. Angwin, T. Jr. Parris, *Facebook Lets Advertisers Exclude Users by Race*, Propublica, 28 October 2016, available at: https://www.propublica.org/article/facebook-lets-advertisers-exclude-users-by-race, accessed 1 July 2019.

185. *See*, for example, G. Noto La Diega, *Against the Dehumanisation of Decision-Making: Algorithmic Decisions at the Crossroads of Intellectual Property, Data Protection, and Freedom of Information*, 9 (1) Journal of Intellectual Property, Information Technology and Electronic Commerce Law (2018), p. 9.

discrimination from happening. Even supposing, it is possible to design algorithms that do not take into account legally protected characteristics as input variables for decision-making, correlative proxies for those characteristics are not easy to foresee or detect. This may leave room for indirect discrimination. Processing other, seemingly neutral data such as postal code or occupation data may overlap with profiles related to those characteristics, whether it is unwitting or not.[186] Especially in large datasets, correlations can become increasingly complex and problematic to detect, which makes the task exhaustively identifying and excluding data features correlated with legally protected characteristics a priori unfeasible.[187] Thus, existing antidiscrimination laws may be potentially circumvented.[188]

Oddly enough, some authors claim that, in order to avoid discrimination, it is necessary to use personal data regarding legally protected characteristics in the process of building automated individual decision-making models.[189] However, this approach seems to be incompatible with the basic data protection principles set out in Article 5 of the GDPR, specifically: lawfulness, fairness and transparency principle, purpose limitation principle and, finally, data minimisation principle, as well as a general prohibition on processing special categories of personal data provided for in Article 9 of the GDPR, not to mention the antidiscrimination laws.[190]

Moreover, with regard to some groups, which are historically undersampled, or exhibit more complicated, nuanced patterns compared to others, ML algorithms may produce faulty results, simply because the available dataset is too small and non-representative.[191] In spite of that, most data mining methods assume that the available dataset is correct and represents the population well, which leads to incorrect assessments about the data subjects, which are inadequately represented in a given dataset.[192] There is also the so-called uncertainty bias.[193] It occurs when one group is underrepresented in the sample, so there is more uncertainty associated with predictions about this group, and the algorithm is risk averse. Then, the algorithm favours

---

186. B. Mittelstadt, P. Allo, M. Taddeo, S. Wachter, L. Floridi, *The Ethics of Algorithms: Mapping the Debate*, p. 8; L. Edwards, M. Veale, *Slave to the Algorithm?*, p. 28; B. Goodman, S. Flaxman, *European Union Regulations on Algorithmic Decision Making and 'a Right to an Explanation'*, p. 53; I. Žliobaitė, B. Custers, *Using Sensitive Personal Data May Be Necessary for Avoiding Discrimination in Data-Driven Decision Models*, 24 Artificial Intelligence and Law (2016), pp. 185, 189.
187. B. Goodman, S. Flaxman, *European Union Regulations on Algorithmic Decision Making and 'a Right to an Explanation'*, p. 54.
188. K. Wiedemann, *Automated Processing of Personal Data for the Evaluation of Personality Traits*, p. 14.
189. I. Žliobaitė, B. Custers, *Using Sensitive Personal Data May Be Necessary*, pp. 183-201.
190. GDPR, Article 5 (1) (a), (b), (c) and Article 9 (1), respectively.
191. M. Veale, R. Binns, *Fairer Machine Learning in the Real World*, p. 2.
192. T. Calders, I. Zliobaite, *Why Unbiased Computational Processes Can Lead to Discriminative Decision Procedures*, [in:] *Discrimination and Privacy in the Information Society*, B. Custers, T. Calders, B. Schermer, T. Zarsky (eds), Springer 2013, pp. 43-57.
193. B. Goodman, S. Flaxman, *European Union Regulations on Algorithmic Decision Making and 'a Right to an Explanation'*, p. 54; B. Goodman, *Economic Models of (Algorithmic) Discrimination*, 29th Conference on Neural Information Processing Systems, 5-10 December 2016, Barcelona, Spain, pp. 4-6.

groups that are better represented in the training data, as there is less uncertainty in these predictions.

There are also cases when automated individual decision-making is simply unfair, even when it does not consider the above-mentioned legally protected characteristics. In particular, ML algorithms are problematic because they make use of all the associations that exist in the training dataset, whether or not they are explicit and whether or not they are well-justified.[194] As an example, despite the fact that it may be predictively important, judging an individual's suitability for a job based on its web browser abuses a short-lived, arbitrary correlation and restricts individuals' autonomy.[195] Automated individual decision-making can also lock an individual into a specific category and restrict them to their suggested preferences (even when they are inaccurate), which can undermine its freedom to choose, for example, certain products or services.[196]

Finally, discriminatory algorithms may scale exponentially and self-perpetuate in a vicious cycle without adequate control measures.[197] With the use of automation, any injustice is likely to take place on a larger scale.[198] This contributes to social segregation, self-fulfilling prophecies and stigmatisation of certain groups, undermining their autonomy and participation in society.[199] Automated individual decision-making contributes to, or even creates, the situations it claims merely to predict.[200] For instance, designating an individual as a likely credit risk wholly on the basis of profiling, which may be accurate or not, raises the actual cost of future financing for this individual. This, in turn, increases the likelihood of its eventual insolvency. Overall, discriminatory effects on natural persons resulting from automated individual decision-making may not be easily prevented. Thus, there is a high risk that algorithms, instead of being the ideal neutral decision makers, may even fortify any existing injustice.

---

194. J. Kingston, *Using Artificial Intelligence to Support Compliance with the General Data Protection Regulation*, p. 432.
195. *How might your choice of browser affect your job prospects?*, Economist, 11 April 2013, available at: https://www.economist.com/the-economist-explains/2013/04/10/how-might-your-choice-of-browser-affect-your-job-prospects, accessed 1 May 2019. *See also*: L. Edwards, M. Veale, *Slave to the Algorithm?*, p. 30.
196. Article 29 Data Protection Working Party, *Guidelines on Automated individual decision-making and Profiling*, pp. 5-6.
197. R. Williams, *Rethinking Deference for Algorithmic Decision-Making*, written on 31 August 2018, available at SSRN, pp. 9-10.
198. G. Noto La Diega, *Against the Dehumanisation of Decision-Making*, p. 8.
199. A. Mantelero, *Personal Data for Decisional Purposes in the Age of Analytics: From an Individual to a Collective Dimension of Data Protection*, 32 (2) Computer Law & Security Review (2016), p. 241; B. Mittelstadt, P. Allo, M. Taddeo, S. Wachter, L. Floridi, *The Ethics of Algorithms: Mapping the Debate*, p. 9.
200. D.K. Citron, F. Pasquale, *The Scored Society: Due Process for Automated Predictions*, 89 (1) Washington Law Review (2014), pp. 1-33.

[D]   Lack of Transparency

Another concern with regard to automated individual decision-making revolves around transparency, which is paramount to addressing all of the concerns described above. As identified by the European Data Protection Supervisor, the issue is not profiling per se, but rather the 'lack of meaningful information about the algorithmic logic which develops these profiles and has an effect on the data subject'.[201] Transparency remains intimately linked to the ideal of effective control of automated individual decision-making.[202] In relying on automation, there is a risk of important decisions being made by the controllers unaccountably. Transparency is essential to mount a challenge against an automated individual decision of private or public entity.

When personal data is processed to produce evidence for a conclusion, it is reasonable to expect that the connection between this personal data and the conclusion is accessible and open for scrutiny.[203] Additionally, when the connection is not obvious, this expectation may be fulfilled by a further explanation. Nevertheless, taking into account how algorithms operate, this expectation is not easily satisfied.

Notably, profiling, which generates new data about a data subject based on personal data of other individuals who appear similar on the basis of a probability calculation is a priori intrinsically far less transparent than other personal data processing.[204] The data subject cannot suspect the existence of correlations that may result in certain characteristics of other individuals being attributed to it. Individuals might even not know of the existence of profiling or automated individual decision-making or understand what is involved. Hence, when profiling is used in the process of automated individual decision-making, transparency is especially important.

Interestingly, the more accurate an algorithm is, the less transparent it is.[205] Typically, systems with more variables perform better than simpler systems, but there is a trade-off between performance and explicability. For instance, linear decision-making models, which sequentially check each data point in the list until a match is found or the whole list has been searched, are useful only in simple cases, but they remain easy to interpret.[206] Whereas accurate decision-making models are increasingly complex, especially when they use ML algorithms, which turn them into black

---

201. European Data Protection Supervisor, *Opinion 3/2015 (with addendum). Europe's big opportunity. Recommendations on the EU's options for data protection reform*, paragraph 3.1, p. 8. The European Data Protection Supervisor is the EU's independent data protection authority. Its general mission is to monitor and ensure the protection of personal data and privacy when EU institutions and bodies process the personal information of individuals.
202. L. Edwards, M. Veale, *Slave to the Algorithm?*, p. 41.
203. B. Mittelstadt, P. Allo, M. Taddeo, S. Wachter, L. Floridi, *The Ethics of Algorithms: Mapping the Debate*, p. 4.
204. Council of Europe, Recommendation CM/Rec(2010)13, paragraphs 50-53, p. 28.
205. G. Noto La Diega, *Against the Dehumanisation of Decision-Making*, p. 9; L. Edwards, M. Veale, *Slave to the Algorithm?*, p. 59; B. Casey, A. Farhangi, R. Vogl, *Rethinking Explainable Machines*, p. 181.
206. B. Goodman, S. Flaxman, *European Union Regulations on Algorithmic Decision Making and 'a Right to an Explanation'*, p. 55.

boxes.[207] There is an inherent difficulty in the interpretation of how each of the numerous data points used by an ML algorithm contributes to the conclusion it makes. It is driven both by high-dimensionality of data and complexity of an ML algorithm.[208] Besides being intrinsically non-transparent, ML algorithms are dynamic in their ability to evolve according to different data patterns, which further makes them unpredictable.[209] In other words, their decision-making logic is changeable, and it is difficult to predict. Use of AI, which operates with a certain degree of autonomy, makes the rationale of decision-making intrinsically opaque. Such algorithms are difficult to control, monitor and correct.[210] The machine cannot be controlled in real-time due to its processing speed and the multitude of operational variables.[211] AI and ML algorithms aside, even 'ordinary' algorithms with hand-written decision-making rules may be highly complex and practically inscrutable for an average data subject.[212]

On the other hand, it is also acknowledged that using more intelligible automated individual decision-making systems may lead to performance losses which could be far costlier than the social utility of providing individualised explanations of the decisions.[213]

Beside these technical black boxes, there are also legal ones. Unsurprisingly, automated individual decision-making is mostly implemented by private profit-maximising entities operating under the least possible transparency obligations.[214] What is more, to some extent, transparency conflicts with certain rights of controllers, in particular, trade secrets or intellectual property.[215] Proprietary algorithms are kept secret for the sake of competitive advantage.[216] There is an unequal power struggle between data subject's interests in transparency and controller's commercial viability.[217] Obviously, there is an imbalance in knowledge and power favouring the controllers. Transparency is seen as one of the bastions of *inter alia* accountability and restraint on the arbitrary or self-interested exercise of power.[218]

On the other hand, some scholars challenge the dominant position in the legal literature that transparency is a *panacea* for all these problems.[219] They argue that disclosure of source code is often neither necessary nor sufficient to demonstrate the

---

207. L. Edwards, M. Veale, *Slave to the Algorithm?*, p. 56; P.G. Picht, B. Freund, *Competition (Law) in the Era of Algorithms*, p. 4.
208. B. Mittelstadt, P. Allo, M. Taddeo, S. Wachter, L. Floridi, *The Ethics of Algorithms: Mapping the Debate*, p. 6.
209. M. Perel, N. Elkin-Koren, *Black Box Tinkering: Beyond Disclosure in Algorithmic Enforcement*, 69 Florida Law Review (2017), p. 181.
210. A. Tutt, *An FDA for Algorithms*, p. 103.
211. A. Matthias, *The Responsibility Gap: Ascribing Responsibility for the Actions of Learning Automata*, 6 (3) Ethics and Information Technology (2004), pp. 182-183.
212. R. Kitchin, *Thinking Critically about and Researching Algorithms*, 20 (1) Information, Communication & Society (2017), pp. 20-21.
213. B. Casey, A. Farhangi, R. Vogl, *Rethinking Explainable Machines*, p. 181.
214. M. Perel, N. Elkin-Koren, *Black Box Tinkering*, p. 181.
215. *See* remarks in Chapter 3, §3.10[A].
216. R. Kitchin, *Thinking Critically about and Researching Algorithms*, p. 20.
217. L.A. Granka, *The Politics of Search: A Decade Retrospective*, 26 (5) The Information Society (2010), p. 369.
218. L. Edwards, M. Veale, *Slave to the Algorithm?*, p. 19.
219. J.A. Kroll, et al., *Accountable Algorithms*, p. 633.

fairness of a decision-making process. The fact that information is accessible does not mean it is comprehensible, especially for an average data subject, which is not tech-savvy. Furthermore, transparency may be undesirable because it enables the data subject to game algorithms.[220] Once the individual decision-making rules are learned or inferred, they may be exploited. Individuals may use various tactics to manipulate algorithms for their self-serving reasons.

As described above, although there are many concerns with regard to automated individual decision-making, the capacity of individuals to examine and understand this process and results is further subdued by lack of transparency. It has obvious repercussions on the accountability issue, which is key to offset the inherent concerns with regard to automated individual decision-making.

---

220. J. Bambauer, T. Zarsky, *The Algorithm Game*, pp. 1-47; E. Bayamlıoglu, *Contesting Automated Decisions*, p. 437. *Conferatur* L. Edwards, M. Veale, *Slave to the Algorithm?*, pp. 63-64, who downplay this particular concern.

CHAPTER 2

Specific Provisions on Solely Automated Individual Decision-Making

§2.01 INTRODUCTORY REMARKS

The key provision of the GDPR concerning solely automated individual decision-making, Article 22, is highly delimited. Although the data subject has the right not to be subject to such processing, the said right applies only to decision-making processes which are solely automated and produce legal effects or other similarly significant consequences for the data subject.[221] Conversely, automated individual decisions, which fall outside the scope of the definition provided for in Article 22 (1) of the GDPR are not subject to specific provisions on solely automated individual decision-making included in the GDPR.[222] Aside from that, Article 22 (2) of the GDPR sets out three considerable exemptions allowing the controller to undertake the processing described in Article 22 (1) of the GDPR, even if it meets the criteria provided for therein.

Accordingly, this chapter first elaborates on the legal nature of this right; second, it contains an in-depth analysis of the concept of an individual decision based solely on automated processing; third, it explores the possible scope and meaning of legal or similarly significant effects; fourth, it outlines the scope of the exemptions under which such processing is allowed; fifth it interprets separate rules pertaining to solely automated individual decisions based on special categories of personal data; sixth it remarks on such decisions concerning children. Finally, it contains interim conclusions.

---

221. GDPR, Article 22 (1): 'The data subject shall have the right not to be subject to a decision based solely on automated processing, including profiling, which produces legal effects concerning him or her or similarly significantly affects him or her'.
222. GDPR, Articles 13 (2) (f), 14 (2) (g), 15 (1) (h), 22.

§2.02   LEGAL NATURE OF THE RIGHT NOT TO BE SUBJECT TO SOLELY AUTOMATED INDIVIDUAL DECISION-MAKING

Before delving deeper into detailed requirements laid down in Article 22 (1) of the GDPR, it is key to interpret the legal nature of this right. Article 22 (1) of the GDPR states that 'the data subject shall have the right not to be subject to a decision based solely on automated processing, including profiling, which produces legal effects concerning him or her or similarly significantly affects him or her'. Because of its wording, 'right not to', this provision may be understood in two different ways. Namely, it may be read either as a right to opt out that the data subject has to actively exercise or as a general prohibition that does not require any action. Each of these interpretations offers different protection to the interests of the data subject and the controller.

If the right stipulated in Article 22 (1) of the GDPR is interpreted in the former way, solely automated individual decision-making could be lawfully conducted by the controller, as long as the data subject does not exercise its right to opt out. In this scenario, the right may not be invoked by the data subject, if one of the exemptions provided for in Article 22 (2) of the GDPR applies. Conversely, if it is interpreted in the latter way, the controller is not allowed to administer such processing, unless one of the exceptions stipulated in Article 22 (2) of the GDPR applies. In this scenario, the data subject does not need to act to prevent solely automated individual decision-making.

These interpretations are differentiated by whether the data subject's action is required to restrict solely automated individual decision-making. To opt out, the data subject needs to be aware of the existence of solely automated individual decision-making and willing to intercede, both of which require deliberate effort on its part.[223] Alternatively, the data subject is simply protected by default. In conclusion, interpreting Article 22 (1) of the GDPR as a prohibition favours the interests of the data subject, while interpreting it as a right to opt out inclines towards the interests of the controller.

Interestingly, the same issue has already existed in the DPD, which contained a similar provision.[224] Then, the said ambiguity resulted in a split in the implementation of Article 15 of the DPD by the Member States, which considered both options, that is a general prohibition and a right to opt out, as viable.[225]

---

223. S. Wachter, B. Mittelstadt, L. Floridi, *Why a Right to Explanation of Automated Decision-Making Does Not Exist in the General Data Protection Regulation*, 7 (2) International Data Privacy Law (2017), p. 94.
224. DPD, Article 15 (1): 'Member States shall grant the right to every person not to be subject to a decision which produces legal effects concerning him or significantly affects him and which is based solely on automated processing of data intended to evaluate certain personal aspects relating to him, such as his performance at work, creditworthiness, reliability, conduct, etc.'.
225. In particular, Article 15 of the DPD was implemented as a right to opt out in the United Kingdom and the Kingdom of Sweden. *Vide* Article 12 of the United Kingdom Data Protection Act 1998 (c 29): 'An individual is entitled at any time, by notice in writing to any data controller, to require the data controller to ensure that no decision taken by or on behalf of the data controller which significantly affects that individual is based solely on the processing by automatic means of personal data in respect of which that individual is the data subject for the purpose of evaluating matters relating to him such as, for example, his performance at work, his creditworthiness, his reliability or his conduct' and section 29 of the Swedish Personal Data Act

Teleological interpretation of this provision implies that constructing Article 22 (1) of the GDPR as a right that has to be actively exercised by the data subject runs contrary to the purpose of this provision, that is the protection of the data subject with regard to solely automated individual decision-making.[226] Certainly, the protection is weaker if it is dependent on the action taken by the data subject. Systematic interpretation of this provision also presupposes that only solely automated individual decisions exempted under Article 22 (2) of the GDPR are permitted.[227]

Article 22 is included in a chapter of the GDPR entitled 'Rights of the data subject'. Nonetheless, it does not in itself mean that it is a right to opt out it. This chapter does not only contain rights which require the action of the data subject, but also rights which are passive.[228] In addition to that, the circumstance that Article 22 of the GDPR is found in a section of the GDPR named 'Right to object and automated individual decision-making' supports the interpretation that it is not a right to opt out like the right to object. This is also affirmed by the lack of analogous information duty in Article 22 of the GDPR as the one set out with regard to the right to object.[229] Last but not least, the title of Article 22 of the GDPR is not worded as a 'right', in contrast to the titles of the provisions establishing the rights which have to be invoked by the data subject.[230]

On the other hand, Article 22 (4) of the GDPR states that solely automated individual decisions 'shall not' be based on special categories of personal data. Hence, it could be argued that the legislators would have worded Article 22 (1) of the GDPR clearly, just as Article 22 (4) of the GDPR, if they intended to establish a general prohibition on solely automated individual decision-making.

---

issued on 29 April 1998 (1998:204): 'If a decision that has legal effects for a natural person or otherwise has manifest effects for the natural person, is based solely on automated processing of such personal data as is intended to assess the qualities of the person, the person who is affected by the decision shall have an opportunity to have the decision reconsidered by a person upon request. Anybody who has been the subject of such a decision as is referred to in the first paragraph is entitled to on application obtain information from the controller of personal data about what has controlled the automated processing that resulted in the decision. As regards applications and provision of information, the applicable parts of the rules under Section 26 apply'. Notably, some Member States adopted even a hybrid approach, creating a prohibition for some types of decision and a right to object to other types, for example section 14 of the Italian Data Protection Code, Legislative Decree No. 196 of 30 June 2003, prohibited judicial or administrative decisions involving assessment of a person's conduct that were based solely on the automated processing of personal data aimed at defining the person's profile or personality, whereas similar decisions made by private sector actors were simply subject to a qualified right to object by the data subject.

226. M. Brkan, *Do Algorithms Rule the World? Algorithmic Decision-Making in the Framework of the GDPR and Beyond*, p. 7.
227. I. Mendoza, L.A. Bygrave, *The Right Not to Be Subject to Automated Decisions Based on Profiling*, University of Oslo Faculty of Law Legal Studies Research Paper Series No. 20/2017, p. 9.
228. *See*, in particular, Articles 13 and 14 of the GDPR establishing obligations which the controller has to fulfil without any action of the data subject.
229. GDPR, Article 21 (4): 'At the latest at the time of the first communication with the data subject, the right referred to in paragraphs 1 and 2 shall be explicitly brought to the attention of the data subject and shall be presented clearly and separately from any other information'.
230. GDPR, Articles 15, 16, 17, 18, 20, 21.

Nonetheless, the Article 29 Working Party guidelines firmly state that Article 22 (1) of the GDPR establishes a general prohibition on solely automated individual decision-making, not a mere right to opt out which has to be actively invoked by the data subject.[231] This prohibition applies whether or not the data subject takes action regarding such processing of its personal data. The Article 29 Working Party accentuates that the above interpretation reinforces the idea of the data subject having control over its personal data, which is in line with the fundamental principles of the GDPR. Given the position of this body, such reading of this provision is strongly indicative of how it will be eventually interpreted. If this is the case, it is unfortunate that the legislator worded Article 22 (1) of the GDPR as a right, not a general prohibition as it reduces legal certainty as to correct interpretation of this provision both for the data subjects and the controllers.

At the same time, it has to be noted that the scope of the right set out in Article 22 (1) of the GDPR, even if it is interpreted as a general prohibition solely on automated individual decision-making, is limited, as explained further in this chapter.[232]

§2.03   INDIVIDUAL DECISION

First of all, Article 22 of the GDPR requires the existence of a 'decision', though the regulation does not provide any guidance as to what might constitute one, beyond a brief statement in the preamble that it 'may include a measure'.[233]

Under the DPD, which also contained this term,[234] it was argued that it requires a broad interpretation so as to cover any act or result which either changes or has the potential to change the social, psychological, economic or legal status of the individual – including similar concepts and terms such as: plans, suggestions, proposals, advice, or mapping of options.[235] It is submitted that the above interpretation remains valid under the GDPR. In the recent literature, it was added that a decision may be in a way binding on an individual (such as a decision on credit application, granting a visa,

---

231. Article 29 Data Protection Working Party, *Guidelines on Automated individual decision-making and Profiling*, pp. 19-20.
232. For further remarks concerning legal nature of the right not to be subject to solely automated individual decision-making, *see* G. Malgieri, G. Comandé, *Why a Right to Legibility of Automated Decision-Making Exists*, p. 247; M.E. Kaminski, *The Right to Explanation, Explained*, 34 (1) Berkeley Technology Law Journal (2019), p. 197; I. Mendoza, L.A. Bygrave, *The Right Not to Be Subject to Automated Decisions Based on Profiling*, pp. 9-10; S. Wachter, B. Mittelstadt, L. Floridi, *Why a Right to Explanation of Automated Decision-Making Does Not Exist*, pp. 94-95; G. Noto La Diega, *Against the Dehumanisation of Decision-Making*, p. 17; Privacy International, *Data Is Power: Profiling and Automated Decision-Making in GDPR*, p. 14.
233. GDPR, Recital 71: 'The data subject should have the right not to be subject to a decision, which may include a measure […]'.
234. DPD, Article 15 (1): 'Member States shall grant the right to every person not to be subject to a decision which produces legal effects concerning him or significantly affects him and which is based solely on automated processing of data intended to evaluate certain personal aspects relating to him, such as his performance at work, creditworthiness, reliability, conduct, etc.'.
235. L.A. Bygrave, *Minding the Machine: Article 15 of the EC Data Protection Directive and Automated Profiling*, 17 (1) Computer Law & Security Review (2001), p. 22.

choosing taxpayer for audit) or non-binding (such as profiling, e.g., sending targeted online advertisements to an air traveller on the basis of her profile).[236]

Interestingly, it may be asserted that the output of an algorithmic system is merely something, which is then used to make a decision, either by another system or by a human. When queried, such an output contains a classification or an estimation, generally with uncertainty estimates. On their own, the algorithmic system is incapable of synthesising the estimation and relevant uncertainties into a decision for action.[237] Therefore, while it is not possible to treat the bare outcome of data analysis as the decision itself, it is also evident that data subjects should not be compelled to wait until a process fully matures and creates all its intended effects.[238] A decision should be formalised to the extent that it can be distinguished from other stages that prepare, support, complement, or head off decision-making. If a decision meets the requirements of Article 22 (1) of the GDPR, it is subject to its regime, even if it is an interim action in a broader process potentially involving multiple decisions.[239]

Unsurprisingly, taking into account subject matter of the GDPR set out in its Article 1 (1) of the GDPR, which covers the protection of natural persons and henceforth regulates only the protection of individuals and not groups, Article 22 of the GDPR does not apply to collective decisions.[240] An example in this sense is provided by the neighbourhood's general credit score adopted by credit companies, which allows providing opportunities for people living in a given neighbourhood in a way that bears no relationship to their individual conditions, but is based on the aggregate score of the area.[241]

In general, collective decisions are not necessarily linked to the personal data of particular individuals, as they can be easily based on anonymised data which would render the GDPR inapplicable.[242] Nevertheless, anonymisation is not complete as long

---

236. M. Brkan, *Do Algorithms Rule the World? Algorithmic Decision-Making in the Framework of the GDPR and Beyond*, p. 8.
237. H.E. Douglas, *Science, Policy, and the Value-Free Ideal*, University of Pittsburgh Press 2009; L. Edwards, M. Veale, *Slave to the Algorithm?*, p. 46.
238. E. Bayamlıoglu, *Transparency of Automated Decisions in the GDPR: An Attempt for Systemization*, Privacy Law Scholars Conference (PLSC) 2018, p. 6.
239. *Ibid.*
240. GDPR, Article 1 (1): 'This Regulation lays down rules relating to the protection of natural persons with regard to the processing of personal data and rules relating to the free movement of personal data'. For the detailed remarks about material scope of the GDPR, *see* Chapter 1, §1.03. *See also* L. Edwards, M. Veale, *Enslaving the Algorithm*, p. 48. *See also* L. Edwards, M. Veale, *Slave to the Algorithm?*, pp. 22, 74, who explain that data protection is a paradigm based on human rights which means it does not contemplate remedies for groups or for non-living persons such as corporations, or the deceased. For further analysis of the collective dimension of data protection *see* A. Mantelero, *Personal Data for Decisional Purposes in the Age of Analytics*, pp. 238-255; B. Mittelstadt, *From Individual to Group Privacy in Big Data Analytics*, 30 (4) Philosophy & Technology (December 2017), pp. 475-494.
241. P. Dixon, R. Gellman, *The Scoring of America: How Secret Consumer Scores Threaten Your Privacy and Your Future*, World Privacy Forum, 2 April 2014, pp. 21, 44.
242. GDPR, Recital 26: '[...] The principles of data protection should therefore not apply to anonymous information, namely information which does not relate to an identified or identifiable natural person or to personal data rendered anonymous in such a manner that the data subject is not or no longer identifiable. [...]'.

as the data subject remains identifiable.[243] With the increasing importance and use of big data, re-identification of an individual part of a certain group is easier than ever.[244] Additionally, if such collective decisions give rise to a solely automated individual decision within the meaning of Article 22 (1) of the GDPR, even if it is based on personal data of persons other than the data subject, for example, where the latter's creditworthiness is determined not by its own specific financial situation but those of other persons in its neighbourhood, such a decision is subject to a regime of Article 22 of the GDPR.

Undeniably, exclusion of collective automated individual decisions from the scope of application of Article 22 of the GDPR creates an immense imbalance in how individual and collective automated decisions are treated. It opens the door for the controllers to circumvent the data subject's right not to be subject to solely automated individual decision-making by adopting collective automated decisions, whenever possible.

Finally yet importantly, although Article 22 of the GDPR includes an explicit reference to profiling, which often precedes solely automated individual decision-making, it does not exclude from its scope automated individual decision-making which does not include it.[245] As correctly noted by the Article 29 Working Party, 'automated decisions can be made with or without profiling; profiling can take place without making automated decisions'.[246] An example of a solely automated individual decision-making that is not based on profiling is imposing speeding fines purely on the basis of evidence from speed cameras.[247] Such activity is subject to restrictions on solely automated individual decision-making despite not being based on profiling.

§2.04   SOLELY AUTOMATED

Second, Article 22 (1) of the GDPR refers to individual decisions 'based solely' on automated processing regardless of whether it includes profiling or not.[248] Prima facie, this means that there is no human involvement in the decision-making process at all. However, this is not a valid interpretation of this provision.

To start with, it does not mean that even feeding the system with personal data has to be an entirely automated procedure. Undeniably, processing may still be

---

243. For further remarks on identifiability, *see* W.G. Urgessa, *The Protective Capacity of the Criterion of 'Identifiability' under EU Data Protection Law*, 2 (4) European Data Protection Law Review (2016), pp. 521-531.
244. For further remarks on re-identification, *see* P. Ohm, *Broken Promises of Privacy*, pp. 1701-1777; L. Sweeney, *Simple Demographics Often Identify People Uniquely*; P. Schwartz, D. Solove, *The PII Problem*, pp. 1814-1894.
245. G. Noto La Diega, *Against the Dehumanisation of Decision-Making*, pp. 17-18.
246. Article 29 Data Protection Working Party, *Guidelines on Automated individual decision-making and Profiling*, p. 8.
247. Example provided by the Article 29 Data Protection Working Party, *Guidelines on Automated individual decision-making and Profiling*, p. 8.
248. Solely automated individual decision-making within the meaning of Article 22 (1) of the GDPR can but need not involve profiling.

considered solely automated if a human inputs the personal data to be processed and then the decision-making is carried out by a machine.[249]

Furthermore, according to the influential guidelines of the Article 29 Data Protection Working Party, in order for an individual decision not to be solely automated, human oversight of an automated decision-making process has to be meaningful, rather than a mere rubber stamp.[250] Thus, as proposed by L.A. Bygrave, it is necessary to operate with a relative notion of 'solely'.[251] According to this stand, individual automated decisions, which are not actively assessed humans, even if they are formally attributed to them, would be considered to be solely automated within the meaning of Article 22 (1) of the GDPR. For instance, if a human does not actively exercise any real influence on the outcome of a given automated decision-making process, the individual decision is solely automated. Notwithstanding the above, it is worth noting that in many cases, meaningful human involvement is simply unfeasible, if only for the reason of the sheer quantity of personal data being processed. In the legal doctrine, it is even argued that as long as algorithms outperform humans, any human involvement in the decision-making process is effectively nominal.[252]

It may also be argued that depending on the context and the nature of the analysis, every independent conclusion in a process may be treated as a separate decision.[253] In that regard, even an interim stage of the process would if solely automated, be subject to Article 22 of the GDPR despite the involvement of a human in the final decision.

Conversely, in order for an individual decision not to be based solely on automated individual decision-making, human involvement has to be technically possible and executed by someone who is able to assess the individual decision and has the authority and competence to change it.[254] In the legal doctrine, it is generally agreed that the controller cannot avoid the provisions of Article 22 of the GDPR by fabricating human involvement.[255] Otherwise, this provision would be nearly purposeless. Thus, if someone routinely applies automatically generated profiles to individuals without

---

249. M. Brkan, *Do Algorithms Rule the World? Algorithmic Decision-Making in the Framework of the GDPR and Beyond*, p. 3; Information Commissioner's Office, *Automated decision-making and profiling*, Guidelines of 5 June 2018, p. 8.
250. Article 29 Data Protection Working Party, *Guidelines on Automated individual decision-making and Profiling*, pp. 20-21. *See also* Information Commissioner's Office, Feedback request – profiling and automated decision-making of 6 April 2017, p. 19.
251. L.A. Bygrave, *Minding the Machine*, paragraph 4.3, p. 20.
252. M. Veale, L. Edwards, *Clarity, Surprises, and Further Questions in the Article 29 Working Party Draft Guidance on Automated Decision-Making and Profiling*, 34 (2) Computer Law & Security Review (2018), pp. 400-401.
253. E. Bayamlıoglu, *Transparency of Automated Decisions in the GDPR*, p. 7.
254. I. Mendoza, L.A. Bygrave, *The Right Not to Be Subject to Automated Decisions based on Profiling*, p. 10.
255. L.A. Bygrave, *Minding the Machine*, paragraph 4.3, p. 20; G. Malgieri, G. Comandé, *Why a Right to Legibility of Automated Decision-Making Exists*, p. 251; A.D. Selbst, J. Powles, *Meaningful Information and the Right to Explanation*, 7 (4) International Data Privacy Law (2017), p. 235; D. Kamarinou, C. Millard, J. Singh, *Machine Learning with Personal Data*, p. 11; E. Bayamlıoglu, *Transparency of Automated Decisions in the GDPR*, pp. 6-7. For the contrary view, *see* S. Wachter, B. Mittelstadt, L. Floridi, *Why a Right to Explanation of Automated Decision-Making Does Not Exist*, p. 92.

having any actual influence on the result, it would still constitute a decision based on solely automated processing.

Although in the legal doctrine it was pointed out that it could be possible to circumvent Article 22 of the GDPR through organisational designs, which are more sophisticated than simple rubber-stamping.[256] Specifically, if a human could choose freely between several possible scenarios generated by an automated system, its decision space would be severely constrained, but the actual decision would not be performed by an automated system. It is questionable whether this loophole is valid, as the human decision-maker would still lack control over the content of the outcome. In other words, it is currently considered that a minimal human involvement without real influence on the outcome of the decision cannot be sufficient to exclude the applicability of Article 22 (1) of the GDPR. In order to escape the data subject's right not to be subject to solely automated individual decision-making set out in Article 22 (1) of the GDPR, automated processing has to be used only as decision support, whereas the final decision must be taken by the human, who bears some responsibility as to the outcome.[257]

Considering that the necessary level of human involvement is not clarified in the GDPR, there is a risk that the provision may also be interpreted narrowly, which would enable the controllers to keep an increasing amount of data-driven practices out of the reach of the data protection regime.[258] As rightly noted by L. A. Bygrave, one could even argue that few, if any, decisions are solely automated, because the algorithms steering such processes are created by human beings.[259] However, such an argument would deprive the provision in question of any practical effect.

Even though this provision shares some language with its predecessor in the DPD, there is very little determinative guidance about how it should be interpreted and applied in practice.[260] Tellingly, under the DPD, which also contained this loophole, it has been widely used by the controllers to circumvent the provisions on automated

---

256. M. Almada, *Human Intervention in Automated Decision-Making: Toward the Construction of Contestable Systems*, written on 23 April 2019, preprint available at SSRN, pp. 1-10, 17th International Conference on Artificial Intelligence and Law (ICAIL), 17-21 June 2019, Montréal, Canada, Forthcoming.
257. M. Brkan, *Do Algorithms Rule the World? Algorithmic Decision-Making in the Framework of the GDPR and Beyond*, p. 10; L. Edwards, M. Veale, *Slave to the Algorithm?*, p. 45; E. Bayamlıoglu, *Transparency of Automated Decisions in the GDPR*, p. 6.
258. S. Wachter, B. Mittelstadt, L. Floridi, *Why a Right to Explanation of Automated Decision-Making Does Not Exist*, p. 92.
259. L.A. Bygrave, *Minding the Machine*, paragraph 4.3, p. 20. This argument was submitted beforehand by D. Korff, *The Effects of the EC Draft Directive on Business*, [in:] *Recent Developments in Data Privacy Law*, J. Dumortier (ed.), Leuven University Press 1992, pp. 43, 50.
260. DPD, Articles 12 (a) and 15. A.D. Selbst, J. Powles, *Meaningful Information and the Right to Explanation*, p. 235.

individual decisions, simply by a nominal involvement of a human in the process.[261] However, currently, as stressed above, the Article 29 Working Party (on behalf of all of the supervisory authorities, i.e., independent public authorities which are established by the Member States pursuant to Article 51 of the GDPR) takes the position that trivial human involvement will not suffice.[262]

As a side note, to resolve this ambiguity, in the legislative process leading up to the adoption of the GDPR, it was proposed by the Article 29 Data Protection Working Party and the European Parliament that this provision should also cover partly or predominantly automated processing methods.[263] However, this amendment was eventually dropped in the trilogue. Notwithstanding the above, it cannot be the intention of the legislator to open the way for the interpretation of the adverb 'solely' as a backdoor to circumvent the data protection regime. Such a formalistic interpretation does not ensure a sufficiently high level of the protection of personal data envisaged by the GDPR.[264]

Last but not least, it is worth pointing out that even if an automated individual decision-making system is regarded as merely advisory, human's involvement can be rendered nominal anyway by so-called automation bias, a psychological phenomenon where humans over-rely on decision support systems.[265] The human belief in the infallibility of mechanistic processes causes it to assume the validity of decisions made by algorithms and to abdicate his own responsibilities. Interestingly, according to the studies, there is a deep-rooted human tendency to assume the validity of automated individual decisions, even when presented with information that directly contradicts

---

261. E. Bayamlıoglu, *Transparency of Automated Decisions in the GDPR*, p. 6; Commission Staff Working Paper, Impact Assessment accompanying the document Regulation of the European Parliament and of the Council on the protection of individuals with regard to the processing of personal data and on the free movement of such data (General Data Protection Regulation), p. 24. For an example of such a restrictive interpretation of an analogous provision under the DPD, considering that any minimum human intervention excludes the applicability of Article 15 of the DPD, *see* Judgment of the German Federal Court, Bundesgerichtshof of 28 January 2014, Case VI ZR 156/13 (LG Gießen, AG Gießen).
262. Article 29 Data Protection Working Party, *Guidelines on Automated individual decision-making and Profiling*, p. 21.
263. Article 29 Data Protection Working Party, *Opinion 01/2012 on the data protection reform proposals*, adopted on 23 March 2012, p. 14; Article 20 (5) (Profiling), European Parliament Committee on Civil Liberties, Justice and Home Affairs, Report on the Proposal for a Regulation of the European Parliament and of the Council on the Protection of Individuals with Regard to the Processing of Personal Data and on the Free Movement of Such Data (General Data Protection Regulation) of 21 November 2013, A7-0402/2013; Article 20 (5) (Profiling), Position of the European Parliament adopted at first reading on 12 March 2014 with a view to the adoption of Regulation (EU) No .../2014 of the European Parliament and of the Council on the protection of individuals with regard to the processing of personal data and on the free movement of such data (General Data Protection Regulation).
264. M. Brkan, *Do Algorithms Rule the World? Algorithmic Decision-Making in the Framework of the GDPR and Beyond*, p. 10.
265. J.L. Chabert, *A History of Algorithms: From the Pebble to the Microchip*, Springer 1999; K. Goddard, A. Roudsari, J.C. Wyatt, *Automation Bias: A Systematic Review of Frequency, Effect Mediators, and Mitigators*, 19 (1) Journal of the American Medical Informatics Association (2012), p. 121; F. Doshi-Velez, M. Kortz, *Accountability of AI under the Law: The Role of Explanation*, p. 2.

the decision's apparent validity.[266] The drafters of the DPD, themselves, explicitly acknowledged this phenomenon almost three decades ago.[267]

All in all, an assessment of whether a given decision-making process is solely automated must be made by the controller *a casu ad casum*. For instance, the controller could identify and record the degree of any human involvement in it, in particular, at what stage does it take place, which could be included in the data protection impact assessment (hereinafter 'DPIA'), which is required in the case of automated individual decision-making within the meaning of Article 22 (1) of the GDPR anyway.[268]

§2.05   LEGAL OR SIMILARLY SIGNIFICANT EFFECTS

In order to be applicable, Article 22 (1) of the GDPR requires that an individual decision is not only based on solely automated processing but also produces legal effects concerning the data subject or similarly significantly affects it. It is considered that when an individual decision affects one's legal status in the strict sense or other legitimate interests, the law must provide sufficient safeguards to protect such an individual.[269]

Vice versa, individual decisions, which do not have serious impactful effects, will not be subject to Article 22 (1) of the GDPR.[270] Hence, it is key to delineate the boundaries of the above-mentioned terms.

---

266. K. Goddard, A. Roudsari, J.C. Wyatt, *Automation Bias*, p. 121.
267. This phenomenon is explicitly acknowledged in the Commission of the European Communities, Amended proposal for a Council Directive on the protection of individuals with regard to the processing of personal data and on the free movement of such data, COM(92) 422 final – SYN 287, 15 October 1992, p. 26: 'The danger of the misuse of data processing in decision-making may become a major problem in future: the result produced by the machine, using more and more sophisticated software, and even expert systems, has an apparently objective and incontrovertible character to which a human decision-maker may attach too much weight, thus abdicating his own responsibilities'. *See also* Commission communication on the protection of individuals in relation to the processing of personal data in the Community and information security of 13 September 1990, COM/1990/314/FINAL/2, p. 29, which states: 'This provision is designed to protect the interest of the data subject in participating in the making of decisions which are of importance to him. The use of extensive data profiles of individuals by powerful public and private institutions deprives the individual of the capacity to influence decision-making processes within those institutions, should decisions be taken on the sole basis of his data shadow'. As explained by L.A. Bygrave, *Minding the Machine*, p. 19, the said data shadow can be understood as pre-collected data often found in the databases of third parties, independently of any specific input from the affected data subjects.
268. GDPR, Article 35 (3) (a): A DPIA referred to in paragraph 1 shall in particular be required in the case of a systematic and extensive evaluation of personal aspects relating to natural persons which is based on automated processing, including profiling, and on which decisions are based that produce legal effects concerning the natural person or similarly significantly affect the natural person. For further remarks concerning the DPIA in the context of automated individual decision-making, *see* Chapter 4, §4.04.
269. For further remarks on efficiency and fairness in automated individual decision-making T. Zarsky, *The Trouble with Algorithmic Decisions: An Analytic Road Map to Examine Efficiency and Fairness in Automated and Opaque Decision Making*, 41 (1) Science, Technology, & Human Values (2016), pp. 118-132.
270. Article 29 Data Protection Working Party, *Guidelines on Automated individual decision-making and Profiling*, p. 21.

[A] Legal Effects

Even though the GDPR does not define the notion of an individual decision producing legal effects, it seems relatively straightforward to assume that such a decision affects the data subject's rights based on laws or arising under a contract.[271]

For example, calculation of a tax return on the basis of an income, entitlement to or denial of a particular social benefit granted by law, such as child or housing benefit or refused admission to a country or denial of citizenship are all individual decisions having legal effects relating to the data subject within the meaning of Article 22 (1) of the GDPR, which are based on laws.

Whereas, automated individual decisions directly affecting the data subject's rights arising under a contract are primarily seen in domains such as insurance, education, employment, finance, online sales and advertising.[272] For instance, in the insurance sector, data analytics may be used to evaluate the risks unique to each individual and personalise the premium to be paid accordingly.

[B] Similarly Significant Effects

Even if automated individual decision-making does not have an effect on the data subject's legal rights, it could still fall within the scope of Article 22 of the GDPR, if it produces an effect that is equivalent or similarly significant in its impact. In other words, even where there is no change in the data subject's legal rights, it could still be impacted sufficiently to require the protections under this provision. As acknowledged by the Information Commissioner's Office, 'a significant effect is more difficult to explain but suggests some consequence that is more than trivial and potentially has an unfavourable outcome'.[273] As added by I. Mendoza and L. A. Bygrave, while such consequences probably need not be entirely adverse for the person, the more adverse they are, the greater the chance they are deemed to be significant.[274]

It is noteworthy that the GDPR has introduced the word 'similarly' to the phrase 'significantly affects', which was not present in Article 15 of the DPD. It follows that under the GDPR, the threshold for significance is similar to that of an individual decision producing legal effects. While in the legal doctrine, it is proposed that, in order

---

271. G. Noto La Diega, *Against the Dehumanisation of Decision-Making*, p. 18. *Conferatur* an expansive interpretation of G. Malgieri, G. Comandé, *Why a Right to Legibility of Automated Decision-Making Exists*, p. 252, who argue that 'In other words, any influence (e.g., limitation) on existing rights of data subjects, including civil procedural rights, administrative law rights, etc. is a legal effect. Analogously, we can infer that any influence on human rights or constitutional rights of individuals is a legal effect'.
272. As submitted by E. Bayamlıoglu, *Transparency of Automated Decisions in the GDPR*, p. 13, in the context of targeted online advertising, where the content of communication amounts to an 'offer' for a contract, it may also be seen within the scope of the legal effects within the meaning of Article 22 (1) of the GDPR.
273. Information Commissioner's Office, Feedback request – profiling and automated decision-making of 6 April 2017, p. 19.
274. I. Mendoza, L.A. Bygrave, *The Right Not to Be Subject to Automated Decisions Based on Profiling*, p. 12.

for a decision to fall within the scope of Article 22 of the GDPR, it must not necessarily have a quasi-legal effect in terms of content, it is sufficient that it profoundly affects the individual as much as a decision affecting its rights would.[275] These effects can be both material and immaterial, conceivably affecting the data subject's dignity, integrity or reputation.[276]

Despite these hints, the term in question is still extremely vague. In the guidelines of the Article 29 Data Protection Working Party, it is proposed that such an individual decision would have the potential to: significantly affect the circumstances, behaviour or choices of the individuals concerned; have a prolonged or permanent impact on the data subject; or at its most extreme, lead to the exclusion or discrimination of individuals.[277] This understanding is broad enough to encompass many different scenarios of solely automated individual decision-making. Recital 71 of the GDPR provides two typical examples of such decisions: automatic refusal of an online credit application or e-recruiting practices without any human intervention.[278] While guidelines of the Article 29 Data Protection Working Party add two more: decisions that affect someone's access to health services or access to education, for example, university admissions.[279] Usually, both the context and the purpose of the processing are paramount in deciding whether the consequences of an individual decision are similarly significant. For instance, while a recruitment system automatically rejecting job applications from minors as a legal necessity may reasonably escape the data protection regime; such practice would be regarded to be within the scope of Article 22 of the GDPR, where the automated individual decision based on age is carried out to exclude candidates above certain age without an explicit legal basis.[280]

It is a concern that the requirement of 'significance' may be manoeuvred by the controllers for the purpose of exclusion of certain processing operations from the scope of Article 22 of the GDPR. This concern has been already expressed by the Article 29 Data Protection Working Party, which noted that the provision in question is imprecise and that 'it should be clarified that it also covers the application of, for example, web analysing tools, tracking for assessing user behaviour, the creation of motion profiles by mobile applications, or the creation of personal profiles by social networks'.[281] Targeted online advertising is a telling example. In many typical cases, a solely automated individual decision to present a targeted online advertisement to the data

---

275. G. Noto La Diega, *Against the Dehumanisation of Decision-Making*, p. 18.
276. D. Kamarinou, C. Millard, J. Singh, *Machine Learning with Personal Data*, p. 12.
277. Article 29 Data Protection Working Party, *Guidelines on Automated individual decision-making and Profiling*, p. 21. Same interpretation was repeated in Information Commissioner's Office, *Automated decision-making and profiling*, Guidelines of 5 June 2018, p. 9.
278. GDPR, Recital 71: 'The data subject should have the right not to be subject to a decision, which may include a measure, evaluating personal aspects relating to him or her which is based solely on automated processing and which produces legal effects concerning him or her or similarly significantly affects him or her, such as automatic refusal of an online credit application or e-recruiting practices without any human intervention. [...]'.
279. Article 29 Data Protection Working Party, *Guidelines on Automated individual decision-making and Profiling*, p. 22.
280. Example provided by E. Bayamlıoglu, *Transparency of Automated Decisions in the GDPR*, p. 14.
281. Article 29 Data Protection Working Party, *Opinion 01/2012 on the data protection reform proposals*, p. 14.

subject based on profiling will not meet the threshold of significance set out in Article 22 (1) of the GDPR.[282] However, the Article 29 Data Protection Working Party recognises that there may be cases where an opposite conclusion is accurate. Determining whether or not a solely automated ad targeting a particular data subject has a 'similarly significant effect' requires attention to a variety of factors including: (i) the intrusiveness of the profiling process, including the tracking of individuals across different websites, devices and services; (ii) the expectations and wishes of the individuals concerned; (iii) the way the advert is delivered; or (iv) using knowledge of the vulnerabilities of the data subjects targeted.[283]

The Article 29 Data Protection Working Party also notes that the same processing may have different implications depending upon the potential negative outcome for a particular data subject. For instance, regularly targeting the data subject, which is known or likely to be in financial difficulties, with advertisements for high interest loans may push it even further into debt.[284] This could have a significant effect on such a vulnerable individual. Similarly, solely automated individual decision-making that results in differential pricing based on personal data could also have a significant effect if, for example, prohibitively high prices effectively bar someone from certain goods or services.[285] In addition to that, significance varies on the perception of the data subject. Ultimately, it may depend on the opinion of an average data subject related to the particular decision-making process.[286] In practice, it may cause a burden for the data subject to prove that processing affects them significantly.[287]

§2.06 EXEMPTIONS FROM THE RIGHT NOT TO BE SUBJECT TO SOLELY AUTOMATED INDIVIDUAL DECISION-MAKING

Even if processing meets all of the requirements laid down in Article 22 (1) of the GDPR, there are three important exemptions from the data subject's right not to be subject to solely automated individual decision-making. Namely, if such processing is necessary for the formation or performance of a contract, authorised by the EU or Member State law or based on the data subject's explicit consent, the controller may

---

282. G. Malgieri, G. Comandé, *Why a Right to Legibility of Automated Decision-Making Exists*, p. 243; M.E. Kaminski, *The Right to Explanation, Explained*, p. 197. *See also* Article 29 Data Protection Working Party, *Guidelines on Automated individual decision-making and Profiling*, p. 22.
283. Article 29 Data Protection Working Party, *Guidelines on Automated individual decision-making and Profiling*, p. 22.
284. *Ibid.*
285. *Ibid. See also* A. Ezrachi, M.E. Stucke, *The Rise of Behavioural Discrimination*, 37 (12) European Competition Law Review (2016), pp. 485-492, who explain how profiling is used to create highly-targeted price discrimination. *See also* P.G. Picht, B. Freund, *Competition (Law) in the Era of Algorithms*, pp. 10-11, for additional remarks regarding individual price differentiation.
286. Similarly, L.A. Bygrave, *Automated Profiling: Minding the Machine*, p. 19.
287. S. Wachter, B. Mittelstadt, L. Floridi, *Why a Right to Explanation of Automated Decision-Making Does Not Exist*, p. 93.

undertake solely automated individual decision-making within the meaning of Article 22 (1) of the GDPR.[288]

Although the two provisions may seem similar, it is essential to distinguish the above exceptions set out in Article 22 (2) of the GDPR from the lawful bases for processing set out in Article 6 (1) of the GDPR. That is, solely automated individual decision-making within the meaning of Article 22 (1) is only permitted if one of the three exemptions set out in Article 22 (2) of the GDPR applies. Whereas lawful bases for processing from Article 6 (1) of the GDPR are relevant for all other automated individual decision-making and profiling.

[A]   Contract

The first possibility of solely automated individual decision-making within the meaning of Article 22 (1) allowed by the GDPR is dependent on the necessity to enter into or perform a contract between the data subject and the controller.[289] Naturally, the controller may wish to use solely automated individual decision-making processes for contractual purposes, because it believes it is the most appropriate way to achieve its business goals. In some cases, routine human involvement is impractical or even impossible due to the sheer quantity of data being processed.[290]

First and foremost, it is worth to note that the formation or performance of a contract are both broad terms, which makes them prone to abuse. Considering that the controller decides whether solely automated individual decision-making is necessary to meet its contractual obligations, the data subject may not object to it, assuming that it is aware of it at all.[291] In this scenario, the data subject may only invoke the right to contest the resulting decision, the right to express its point of view and the right to obtain human intervention, but it may not object to it being made in the first place.[292] For example, in the context of differential pricing, as the provision specifically refers to the stage prior to the conclusion of a contract, it opens the way for the solely automated individual decisions in the form of pre-contractual measures, e.g., for the purposes of offering a personalised price to the data subject.[293]

In order to rely on this exemption, one has to consider the meaning of 'necessity', which has yet to be extensively discussed in the literature. Since the interpretation of

288. GDPR, Article 22 (2): 'Paragraph 1 shall not apply if the decision: (a) is necessary for entering into, or performance of, a contract between the data subject and a data controller; (b) is authorised by Union or Member State law to which the controller is subject and which also lays down suitable measures to safeguard the data subject's rights and freedoms and legitimate interests; or (c) is based on the data subject's explicit consent'.
289. GDPR, Article 22 (2) (a): 'Paragraph 1 shall not apply if the decision is necessary for entering into, or performance of, a contract between the data subject and a data controller'.
290. Article 29 Data Protection Working Party, *Guidelines on Automated individual decision-making and Profiling*, p. 23.
291. *See* information, which must be provided to the data subject under Articles 13 (2) (f), 14 (2) (g), 15 (1) (h) of the GDPR.
292. GDPR, Article 22 (3). *See also* S. Wachter, B. Mittelstadt, L. Floridi, *Why a Right to Explanation of Automated Decision-Making Does Not Exist*, p. 94.
293. Article 29 Data Protection Working Party, *Guidelines on Automated individual decision-making and Profiling*, p. 23.

this term shapes the scope of an exception, it must be construed narrowly as in a general rule *exceptiones non sunt extendendae*.[294] One of the most influential supervisory authorities, the Information Commissioner's Office, explains that it means that solely automated individual decision-making need not be essential, but it should be a targeted and reasonable way of meeting the controller's contractual obligations.[295] Whereas, Article 29 Working Party clarifies that it should also be the least privacy-intrusive way to reasonably achieve the controller's objectives.[296]

It is rightly argued that the 'necessity' requirement should be understood as an 'enabling' requirement for the formation or conclusion of a contract.[297] Otherwise, a very strict textual interpretation of the meaning of this exception would lead to an unreasonable conclusion that solely automated individual decision is never truly indispensable for the formation or conclusion of a contract, which would render the exemption in question obsolete. As an example, if an automated assessment of a credit risk enables the conclusion of a contract on the basis of which the data subject receives a loan, it is necessary for the conclusion of such contract. Although it could be controverted that the determination of credit risk does not necessarily need to be automated, it could clearly be enabled by such measures.

Notably, the wording of the above exception implies that a decision-making process itself could potentially be carried out by a different controller than the one which is a party to the contract with the individual.[298] Although considering common business practices, if solely automated individual decision-making is outsourced to a third party, it would be a processor rather than another controller.

All in all, the extent of solely automated individual decision-making which would be necessary in a contractual context is an issue which needs to be assessed on a case-by-case basis and requires balancing of the trade-offs by the controller. As an example, the degree and intensity of profiling applied by the search engines or social networking platforms may easily fall out of the scope of contractual necessity and, therefore, may not rely on this exception.[299] Similarly, online retailers cannot argue that solely automated individual decision-making is necessary for online purchase.[300] For the most part, in order to fulfil the contract, an online retailer must process only the user's credit card information for payment purposes and the user's address to deliver

---

294. Same conclusion in E. Bayamlıoglu, *Transparency of Automated Decisions in the GDPR*, p. 35.
295. Information Commissioner's Office, *Automated decision-making and profiling*, Guidelines of 5 June 2018, p. 12.
296. Article 29 Data Protection Working Party, *Guidelines on Automated individual decision-making and Profiling*, p. 23. *See also*, European Data Protection Supervisor, *Assessing the necessity of measures that limit the fundamental right to the protection of personal data: A Toolkit*, 11 April 2017, pp. 17-19.
297. M. Brkan, *Do Algorithms Rule the World? Algorithmic Decision-Making in the Framework of the GDPR and Beyond*, p. 11.
298. Information Commissioner's Office, *Automated decision-making and profiling*, Guidelines of 5 June 2018, p. 12.
299. Article 29 Data Protection Working Party, *Opinion 06/2014 on the notion of legitimate interests of the data controller under Article 7 of Directive 95/46/EC*, adopted on 9 April 2014, pp. 16-18.
300. Article 29 Data Protection Working Party, *Guidelines on Automated individual decision-making and Profiling*, p. 13.

the goods. While building a profile of the user's tastes and lifestyle choices based on its visits to the website is not necessary for entering into, or performance of the contract.

[B]   EU or Member State Law

Second, solely automated individual decision-making could potentially take place under Article 22 (2) (b) of the GDPR, as long as the EU or Member State law to which the controller is subject, authorised it's use.[301] Seeing that safeguards set out in Article 22 (3) of the GDPR do not apply to this exemption, to mitigate this, the provision specifically mentions that the relevant law must also lay down suitable measures to safeguard the data subject's rights and freedoms and legitimate interests.[302] In connection with the above, the preamble to the GDPR provides an illustration of the EU or Member State law authorising solely automated individual decision-making for monitoring and preventing fraud and tax-evasion, or to ensure the security and reliability of a service provided by the controller.[303]

An example of EU law potentially allowing for solely automated individual decision-making is the Passenger Name Record Directive.[304] Although generally, it does not permit any decision that produces an adverse legal effect on a person or significantly affects a person only by reason of the automated processing of Passenger name record (PNR) data, it does provide for the possibility of automated matching or identification of persons who should be further examined by the competent authorities in view of potential involvement in terrorism, provided that such matching is individually reviewed by non-automated means.[305]

Some of the Member States did not provide for any exemptions under Article 22 (2) (b) of the GDPR in their law implementing the GDPR. It is the case of most countries, *videlicet* Italy, Romania, Sweden, Denmark, Poland, Finland, Greece, the Czech Republic, Estonia, Lithuania, Latvia, Portugal, Spain.[306] Nevertheless, as rightly

---

301. GDPR, Article 22 (2) (b): 'Paragraph 1 shall not apply if the decision is authorised by Union or Member State law to which the controller is subject and which also lays down suitable measures to safeguard the data subject's rights and freedoms and legitimate interests'.

302. The safeguards are explained in greater detail below in Chapter 3, §3.09.

303. GDPR, Recital 71: '[...] However, decision-making based on such processing, including profiling, should be allowed where expressly authorised by Union or Member State law to which the controller is subject, including for fraud and tax-evasion monitoring and prevention purposes conducted in accordance with the regulations, standards and recommendations of Union institutions or national oversight bodies and to ensure the security and reliability of a service provided by the controller, or necessary for the entering or performance of a contract between the data subject and a controller, or when the data subject has given his or her explicit consent. [...]'.

304. Directive (EU) 2016/681 of the European Parliament and of the Council of 27 April 2016 on the use of passenger name record (PNR) data for the prevention, detection, investigation and prosecution of terrorist offences and serious crime, Official Journal of the European Union 119, 4 May 2016, pp. 132-149.

305. Directive (EU) 2016/681, Articles 7 (6), 6 (2) (a) and 6 (5). *See* I. Mendoza, L.A. Bygrave, *The Right Not to Be Subject to Automated Decisions Based on Profiling*, p. 6.

306. G. Malgieri, *Right to Explanation and Other 'Suitable Safeguards' for Automated Decision-Making in the EU Member States Legislations*, written on 17 August 2018, available at SSRN, p. 8, Computer Law & Security Review (2019), Forthcoming. Poland is on the above list because

noted by G. Malgieri, it cannot be excluded that specific cases of solely automated individual decision-making may be permitted at the national level in future legislation, especially sectoral.

For instance, German law implementing the GDPR provides for a sectoral exemption, namely it allows solely automated individual decision-making, in certain circumstances, in the field of insurance.[307] Analogously, Polish law implementing the GDPR in sectoral law authorises solely automated individual decision-making in certain cases with regard to insurance, credit, tax, road inspection as well as professional and social rehabilitation and employment of disabled people.[308] The United Kingdom, the Republic of Ireland, the Republic of Austria and the Netherlands law implementing the GDPR present an opposite approach, as they set out generalised exemptions allowing solely automated individual decision-making under certain conditions.[309] The French and Hungarian law implementing the GDPR are considered to be the most innovative and complex regulations of solely automated individual decision-making.[310]

Although in order to rely on this exemption, solely automated individual decision within the meaning of Article 22 (1) of the GDPR has to be authorised by law, it is sometimes argued that this does not mean that there has to be a law which explicitly states that solely automated individual decision-making is authorised for a particular purpose.[311] This liberal interpretation leads to a conclusion that if a controller has a

---

Polish Ustawa o ochronie danych osobowych z dnia 10 maja 2018 r. (Dz.U. z 2018 r. poz. 1000), the Polish law implementing the GDPR did not contain any exemptions under Article 22 (2) (b) of the GDPR. Only the subsequent Polish law implementing the GDPR in sectoral laws authorises solely automated individual decision-making, in certain circumstances, as noted above.

307. § 37 des Gesetz zur Anpassung des Datenschutzrechts an die Verordnung (EU) 2016/679 und zur Umsetzung der Richtlinie (EU) 2016/680 (Datenschutz-Anpassungs- u–d -Umsetzungsgesetz EU – DSAnpUG-EU), Bundesdatenschutzgesetz vom 30. Juni 2017 (BGBl. I S. 2097).

308. Polish Ustawa o zmianie niektórych ustaw w związku z zapewnieniem stosowania rozporządzenia Parlamentu Europejskiego i Rady (UE) 2016/679 z dnia 27 kwietnia 2016 r. w sprawie ochrony osób fizycznych w związku z przetwarzaniem danych osobowych i w sprawie swobodnego przepływu takich danych oraz uchylenia dyrektywy 95/46/WE (ogólne rozporządzenie o ochronie danych) z dnia 21 lutego 2019 r. (Dz.U. z 2019 r. poz. 730).

309. Article 14 of the United Kingdom Data Protection Act 2018, (c 12); Article 57 of the Irish Data Protection Act 2018 (Number 7 of 2018); § 41 des Federal Republic of Germany Bundesgesetz, mit dem das Datenschutzgesetz 2000 geändert wird (Datenschutz-Anpassungsgesetz 2018), 1761 der Beilagen XXV. –P – Ausschussbericht NR – Gesetzestext; Artikel 40 van Dutch Uitvoeringswet Algemene verordening gegevensbescherming (UAVG), geldend van 25 mei 2018 (Stb 2018, 144).

310. French LOI n° 2018-493 du 20 juin 2018 relative à la protection des données personnelles du 20 juin 2018, JORF n°0141 du 21 juin 2018 texte n° 1; Hungarian T/623. Számú törvényjavaslat az információs önrendelkezési jogról és az információszabadságról szóló 2011. évi CXIi. törvénynek az Európai Unió adatvédelmi reformjával összefüggő módosításáról, valamint más kapcsolódó törvények módosításáról. For an outline of the Member State law referenced in this paragraph, *see* G. Malgieri, *Right to Explanation and Other 'Suitable Safeguards'*, pp. 7-21.

311. This interpretation was proposed in: Information Commissioner's Office, *Automated decision-making and profiling*, Guidelines of 5 June 2018, pp. 12-13. *See also*, K. Oastler, *GDPR Series: Automated Decisions – What Controllers Need to Know*, 18 (5) Privacy & Data Protection (2018), pp. 6-7, who wonders if it is enough for the decision not to be prohibited by law in order to be authorised within the meaning of Article 22 (2) (b) of the GDPR.

statutory power to do something, and solely automated individual decision-making is the most appropriate way to achieve this purpose, then it may be able to justify this type of processing as authorised by law and rely on Article 22 (2) (b) of the GDPR. Although in the beginning, this interpretation seems reasonable, a second look allows concluding that it opens up so many new avenues to be abused by the controllers that it may not be endorsed. Exceptions should be interpreted narrowly, otherwise high level of protection of personal data of the data subjects envisaged by the GDPR would not be maintained. To illustrate this, Polish law implementing the GDPR in sectoral law explicitly authorises solely automated individual decision-making in very clear-cut cases.[312] The scope of these exemptions is highly delimited.

Certainly, national legislation will play a major part in determining the level of protection of the data subjects with regard to solely automated individual decision-making allowed under Article 22 (2) (b) of the GDPR. This is because the Member States have broad discretionary powers in this regard, particularly as the suitable measures required to safeguard the data subjects constitute a general term. Accordingly, it would not be surprising if significant differences between the Member States' national legislative regimes emerge, thereby undermining the harmonisation aims of the regulation.[313] Although the European Data Protection Board is specifically tasked with publication of guidelines, recommendations and best practices for further specifying the criteria and conditions for automated individual decisions based on this exemption, none of those has been issued yet.[314]

[C]   Data Subject's Explicit Consent

Third, the GDPR also allows for solely automated individual decision-making within the meaning of Article 22 (1) of the GDPR, if it is based on the explicit consent of the data subject.

Unlike other exemptions from the right not to be subject to a decision based solely on automated processing, explicit consent of the data subject was not included in the prior analogue provision, i.e., Article 15 of the DPD. Although the European Parliament proposed such an amendment during the legislative process, the caveat, opposed by the European Commission, was not included in the final version of the directive. Interestingly, years later, the European Commission changed its stance and put

---

312. Polish Ustawa o zmianie niektórych ustaw w związku z zapewnieniem stosowania rozporządzenia Parlamentu Europejskiego i Rady (UE) 2016/679 z dnia 27 kwietnia 2016 r. w sprawie ochrony osób fizycznych w związku z przetwarzaniem danych osobowych i w sprawie swobodnego przepływu takich danych oraz uchylenia dyrektywy 95/46/WE (ogólne rozporządzenie o ochronie danych) z dnia 21 lutego 2019 r. (Dz.U. z 2019 r. poz. 730), Articles 43 (6), 46 (6), 60 (1) (b), 66 (1) (7), 66 (5) (5), 138 (6) (b), 147 (4).
313. I. Mendoza, L.A. Bygrave, *The Right Not to Be Subject to Automated Decisions Based on Profiling*, p. 18.
314. GDPR, Article 70 (1) (f): 'The Board shall ensure the consistent application of this Regulation. To that end, the Board shall, on its own initiative or, where relevant, at the request of the Commission, in particular: issue guidelines, recommendations and best practices in accordance with point (e) of this paragraph for further specifying the criteria and conditions for decisions based on profiling pursuant to Article 22(2)'.

forward the consent exemption already in the initial proposal for the GDPR,[315] which was successfully adopted, as it did not face any forceful opposition from the stakeholders.[316]

Meanwhile, in the literature, it is argued that the introduction of the consent exemption comes as an impairment to the essence of the data subject's right set out in Article 22 (1) of the GDPR.[317] There are concerns that the controllers will use this new caveat as a swift mechanism to deprive the data subjects of the control of their personal data and carry on with solely automated individual decision-making.[318]

Nonetheless, consent may also be construed as an advantage for transparency. Under the GDPR, the consent requirement was raised to a higher standard than in the DPD.[319] Strictly speaking, it must be a freely given, specific, informed and unambiguous affirmative indication of the individual's wishes.[320] In addition, consent does not relieve the controller from the duty of compliance with the general data

---

315. Article 20 (2) (c) (Measures based on profiling), Proposal for a Regulation the European Parliament and of the Council on the protection of individuals with regard to the processing of personal data and on the free movement of such data (General Data Protection Regulation) of 25 January 2012.

316. Opinion of the European Economic and Social Committee adopted on 23 May 2012 on the Proposal for a Regulation of the European Parliament and of the Council on the protection of individuals with regard to the processing of personal data and on the free movement of such data (General Data Protection Regulation), CES1303/2012; Position of the European Parliament adopted at first reading on 12 March 2014 with a view to the adoption of Regulation (EU) No …/2014 of the European Parliament and of the Council on the protection of individuals with regard to the processing of personal data and on the free movement of such data (General Data Protection Regulation); Position (EU) of the Council at first reading with a view to the adoption of a Regulation of the European Parliament and of the Council on the protection of natural persons with regard to the processing of personal data and on the free movement of such data, and repealing Directive 95/46/EC (General Data Protection Regulation).

317. I. Mendoza, L.A. Bygrave, *The Right Not to Be Subject to Automated Decisions Based on Profiling*, p. 19, who argue that 'the new exception for consent is likely to lower the de facto level of protection for individuals, particularly in light of the relative strength of most individuals vis-à-vis banks, insurance companies, online service providers and many other businesses. However, the GDPR tightens the assessment of what is a freely given consent and what automated decisions are necessary for the purpose of entering into or performance of a contract. The traction of this tightening will rest on how strictly the necessity criterion is interpreted'. *See also*: Amended proposal for a Council Directive on the protection of individuals with regard to the processing of personal data and on the free movement of such data, COM(92) 422 final – SYN 287, 15 October 1992, p. 27, in which the European Commission did not accept an amendment proposed by the European Parliament introducing data subject's consent as an exception allowing automated decision-making is due to similar concerns.

318. L. Naudts, *The Right Not to Be Subject to Automated Decision-Making: The Role of Explicit Consent*, 2 August 2016, available at: https://www.law.kuleuven.be/citip/blog/the-right-not-to-be-subject-to-automated-decision-making-the-role-of-explicit-consent/, accessed 1 May 2019.

319. Article 29 Data Protection Working Party, *Guidelines on Consent under Regulation 2016/679*, as last revised and adopted on 10 April 2018, p. 18.

320. GDPR, Article 4 (11): '"consent" of the data subject means any freely given, specific, informed and unambiguous indication of the data subject's wishes by which he or she, by a statement or by a clear affirmative action, signifies agreement to the processing of personal data relating to him or her'. *See also* Article 7 of the GDPR, which sets out conditions for consent. *See also* Recital 43 of the GDPR for clarification concerning burden of proof and requirements for consent and Recital 43 of the GDPR for an interpretation of a freely given consent.

protection principles provided for in Article 5 of the GDPR.[321] Although Article 22 (2) (c) of the GDPR does not specify whether such a consent can be withdrawn by the data subject, it follows from Article 7 (3) of the GDPR that any consent to the processing of personal data may be withdrawn by the data subject at any time, which presumably applies also in the context of solely automated individual decision-making.[322] Therefore, adding this exception as an additional base for solely automated individual decision-making cannot be categorically condemned.

Further, to provide even higher control over personal data, in this situation, the consent of the data subject has to be explicit. In principle, under the GDPR, such an explicit consent is required in situations where grievous data protection risks emerge, e.g., processing of special categories of personal data in Article 9 of the GDPR, transferring data to third countries or international organisations in the absence of adequate safeguards in Article 49 of the GDPR, and in the provision in question.

As this term is not defined in the GDPR, it needs to be clarified what extra efforts a controller should undertake in order to obtain an explicit consent of the data subject. According to the guidelines of the Article 29 Data Protection Working Party, the term explicit means that the data subject must give an express statement of consent, e.g., by signing a written statement, by filling in an electronic form, by sending an e-mail, by uploading a scanned document carrying the signature of the data subject or by using an electronic signature.[323] The guidelines do not rule out that oral statements could be sufficient as well, as long as the controller is able to prove that all conditions for valid explicit consent were met. The controller should consider two-stage verification to make sure explicit consent is valid. In this scenario, the data subject gives consent, which is subject to further confirmation.

There are two main challenges with regard to this particular exemption. First, the controller which wishes to rely on the consent exemption must ensure it is informed as required by Article 4 (11) of the GDPR. However, the complexity of automated individual decision-making systems hinders the data subject's capability to identify the inherent risks of such processes correctly. It is fair to wonder how an informed consent can be obtained in relation to a decision-making process that may be inherently non-transparent.[324] The extent of communication necessary to render the data subject's consent informed and thus, valid is also considered a benchmark for the minimum content of the right to be informed and the right of access, in particular, the disclosure to be made as to the logic involved and the envisaged consequences of such

---

321. Article 29 Data Protection Working Party, *Opinion 06/2014 on the notion of legitimate interests of the data controller under Article 7 of Directive 95/46/EC,* p. 13.

322. GDPR, Article 7 (3): 'The data subject shall have the right to withdraw his or her consent at any time. The withdrawal of consent shall not affect the lawfulness of processing based on consent before its withdrawal. Prior to giving consent, the data subject shall be informed thereof. It shall be as easy to withdraw as to give consent'.

323. Article 29 Data Protection Working Party, *Guidelines on Consent under Regulation 2016/679,* p. 18.

324. C. Kuner, D.J.B. Svantesson, F.H. Cate, O. Lynskey, C. Millard, *Machine Learning with Personal Data: Is Data Protection Law Smart Enough to Meet the Challenge?,* 7 (1) International Data Privacy (2017), p. 1; G. Noto La Diega, *Against the Dehumanisation of Decision-Making,* p. 20.

processing.[325] Second, the controller which wishes to rely on the consent exemption must ensure it is freely given as mandated by Articles 4 (11) and 7 (4) of the GDPR.[326] It may be problematic with regard to take-it-or-leave-it scenarios, that is, when the performance of a contract, including the provision of a service, is conditional on consent to the automated individual decision-making that is not necessary for the performance of that contract.[327]

§2.07 SOLELY AUTOMATED INDIVIDUAL DECISION-MAKING BASED ON SPECIAL CATEGORIES OF PERSONAL DATA

Unsurprisingly, Article 22 (4) of the GDPR provides an additional layer of protection for special categories of personal data.[328] In order to carry out the processing described in Article 22 (1) of the GDPR which involves special categories of personal data, the controller has to fulfil two additional conditions apart from meeting the criteria of one of the exemptions described above. First, it has to obtain an explicit consent to the processing of those personal data as in Article 9 (2) (a) of the GDPR[329] or process those personal data as it is necessary for reasons of substantial public interest as in Article 9 (2) (g) of the GDPR.[330]

Second, in both of the above cases, the controller must put in place suitable measures to safeguard the data subject's rights and freedoms and legitimate interests. Given that there is no further guidance in the GDPR, as to what such safeguards should include, it is up to the controller to consider it, depending on the circumstances of the case. Such an assessment could be a part of a DPIA, which must be conducted with regard to such processing anyway.[331]

---

325. E. Bayamlıoglu, *Transparency of Automated Decisions in the GDPR*, p. 34. *See* Chapter 3, §3.03 and §3.04.

326. GDPR, Article 7 (4): 'When assessing whether consent is freely given, utmost account shall be taken of whether, inter alia, the performance of a contract, including the provision of a service, is conditional on consent to the processing of personal data that is not necessary for the performance of that contract'.

327. For remarks on assessment of necessity, *see* §2.06[A]. *See* I. Mendoza, L.A. Bygrave, *The Right Not to Be Subject to Automated Decisions Based on Profiling*, pp. 17-18.

328. GDPR, Article 22 (4): 'Decisions referred to in paragraph 2 shall not be based on special categories of personal data referred to in Article 9(1), unless point (a) or (g) of Article 9(2) applies and suitable measures to safeguard the data subject's rights and freedoms and legitimate interests are in place'. The notion of special categories of personal data is explained in greater detail above in Chapter 1, §1.02[B].

329. GDPR, Article 9 (2) (a): 'the data subject has given explicit consent to the processing of those personal data for one or more specified purposes, except where Union or Member State law provide that the prohibition referred to in paragraph 1 may not be lifted by the data subject'.

330. GDPR, Article 9 (2) (g): 'processing is necessary for reasons of substantial public interest, on the basis of Union or Member State law which shall be proportionate to the aim pursued, respect the essence of the right to data protection and provide for suitable and specific measures to safeguard the fundamental rights and the interests of the data subject'.

331. *See* remarks in Chapter 4, §4.04.

The above requirements apply to special categories of personal data inferred from 'ordinary' personal data, in particular, through the use of profiling.[332]

§2.08   SOLELY AUTOMATED INDIVIDUAL DECISION-MAKING CONCERNING CHILDREN

The need for particular protection for children with regard to solely automated individual decision-making is enunciated in the preamble to the GDPR.[333] Despite the fact that Article 22 of the GDPR does not make a distinction between personal data concerning adults and children, Recital 71 of the GDPR says that solely automated individual decision-making, including profiling, with legal or similarly significant effects, should not apply to children.[334]

Considering that this wording is not reflected in the operative part of the GDPR, there is no absolute prohibition on this type of processing in relation to children.[335] However, in light of the above-mentioned recital, Article 29 Data Protection Working Party recommended that the controller should not rely upon the exemptions set out in Article 22 (2) of the GDPR to justify it.[336]

Notwithstanding the above, the advisory body acknowledged that it might be necessary for the controller to carry out solely automated individual decision-making, including profiling, with legal or similarly significant effects in relation to children, for example, to protect their welfare.[337] In such cases, the processing may be carried out on the basis of the exceptions in Article 22 (2) (a), (b) or (c) of the GDPR, as appropriate. Naturally, in order to protect the rights, freedoms and legitimate interests of the children, there must be fitting safeguards in place, as required by Article 22 (2) (b) and 22 (3) of the GDPR.[338]

---

332. *See* M. Veale, L. Edwards, *Clarity, Surprises, and Further Questions in the Article 29 Working Party Draft Guidance on Automated Decision-Making and Profiling*, pp. 403-404, who note that 'the rules for inferred special categories of data are likely only to become ever more controversial as the deployment of political, racial and economic modelling of data subjects through casual online exchanges, clicks and "Likes" becomes more apparent'.

333. *See*, in particular, GDPR, Recital 38: 'Children merit specific protection with regard to their personal data, as they may be less aware of the risks, consequences and safeguards concerned and their rights in relation to the processing of personal data. Such specific protection should, in particular, apply to the use of personal data of children for the purposes of marketing or creating personality or user profiles and the collection of personal data with regard to children when using services offered directly to a child. The consent of the holder of parental responsibility should not be necessary in the context of preventive or counselling services offered directly to a child'. Note also Articles 6 (1) (f), 8, 12, 40 (2) (g), 57 of the GDPR, as well as Recitals 58, 65, 71 and 75 of the GDPR.

334. GDPR, Recital 71: '[...] Such measure should not concern a child'.

335. *See* G. Noto La Diega, *Against the Dehumanisation of Decision-Making*, pp. 24-25, who rightly notes that it is an another example of poorly drafted provisions concerning automated decision-making included in the GDPR.

336. Article 29 Data Protection Working Party, *Guidelines on Automated individual decision-making and Profiling*, p. 28.

337. *Ibid.*

338. Article 40 (2) (g) of the GDPR explicitly refers to the preparation of codes of conduct incorporating safeguards for children; it may also be possible to develop existing codes. One example of a code of conduct dealing with marketing to children is that produced by FEDMA

It is considered that taking into account that children represent a vulnerable group of society, controllers should, in general, refrain from profiling them for marketing purposes.[339] Children can be particularly susceptible in the online environment and more easily influenced by behavioural advertising. For example, in online gaming, profiling can be used to target players that the algorithm considers are more likely to spend money on the game as well as providing more personalised adverts. The age and maturity of the child may affect its ability to understand the motivation behind this type of marketing or the consequences.[340]

§2.09 INTERIM CONCLUSIONS

Article 22 of the GDPR attempts to mitigate the risks to the rights and freedoms of natural persons associated with solely automated individual decision-making. At first glance, it shows much promise in terms of providing protection for the data subjects with regard to such processing. However, a closer analysis reveals that such protection is, in fact, curtailed.

Article 22 of the GDPR is not a simple provision to construe. Its scope is both narrow and vague. First of all, the right not to be subject to solely automated individual decision-making afforded to the data subject requires meeting so many criteria that it resembles a house of cards.[341] Application of Article 22 of the GDPR rests on three cumulative conditions: (i) an individual decision is made, that is (ii) based solely on automated processing, including, but not limited to profiling, and (iii) produces legal effects concerning the data subject or similarly significantly affects it. The data subject's right not to be subject to solely automated individual decision-making is contingent upon all of these conditions being satisfied. If one of them is not met, it does not apply.

Each of the above criteria involves numerous ambiguities. Specifically, in the legal doctrine, there is not even a consensus as to the legal nature of this right, as it may be read either as a right to opt out that the data subject has to actively exercise or as a

---

Code of conduct of 6 September 2000, available at: http://www.oecd.org/sti/ieconomy/2091 875.pdf, accessed 1 November 2018. *See*, in particular: '6.2 Marketers targeting children, or for whom children are likely to constitute a section of their audience, should not exploit children's credulity, loyalty, vulnerability or lack of experience; 6.8.5 Marketers should not make a child's access to a website contingent on the collection of detailed personal information. In, particular, special incentives such as prize offers and games should not be used to entice children to divulge detailed personal information'.

339. Article 29 Data Protection Working Party, *Opinion 02/2013 on apps on smart devices*, adopted on 27 February 2013, p. 26, specifies that 'data controllers should not process children's data for behavioural advertising purposes, neither directly nor indirectly, since this will be outs ide of the scope of the child's understanding and therefore exceed the boundaries of lawful processing'.

340. EU study on the impact of marketing through social media, online games and mobile applications on children's behaviour, March 2016, available at: https://ec.europa.eu/info/ publications/study-impact-marketing-through-social-media-online-games-and-mobile-applica tions-childrens-behaviour_en, accessed 1 November 2018.

341. I. Mendoza, L.A. Bygrave, *The Right Not to Be Subject to Automated Decisions Based on Profiling*, p. 19.

general prohibition that does not require any action. Obviously, each of these inter-pretations offers different protection to the interests of the data subjects and the controllers. Furthermore, given that the provision in question applies only to individual decisions, it opens the door for the controllers to circumvent the data subject's right not to be subject to solely automated individual decision-making by adopting collective automated decisions, whenever possible. Since this provision is exclusively limited in applicability to solely automated individual decisions, inconsiderable human involve-ment in the process is another potential loophole which could be abused by the controllers. Alternatively, they may also claim that a particular decision is merely an interim action in a broader process potentially involving multiple decisions and, consequently, not subject to Article 22 of the GDPR. Further, the notions of legal effects and similarly significant effects are unclear, which also contributes to legal uncertainty both for the data subject and the controller.

Besides, Article 22 (2) of the GDPR sets out three exemptions allowing the controller to undertake solely automated individual decision-making, even if it meets all of the criteria provided for in Article 22 (1) of the GDPR. These exceptions are so considerable and prone to abuse by the controllers that they erode the data subject's right not to be subject to solely automated individual decision-making to the point that the exceptions become the rule, especially considering that the controllers themselves decide whether any of the said exemptions are applicable.

Lastly, due to poor drafting of the GDPR, it is uncertain whether solely automated individual decision-making concerning children is allowed, assuming it is permitted under one of the exemptions set out in Article 22 (2) of the GDPR.

The subject matter of the right not to be subject to solely automated individual decision-making largely depends on its eventual legal interpretation. It will be deter-mined predominantly by supervisory authorities, the European Data Protection Board, the national courts, as well as the Court of Justice of the European Union. The predecessor of Article 22 of the GDPR, Article 15 of the DPD, was scarcely litigated in national courts or enforced the supervisory authorities. Because of that, it is not clear how the right not to be subject to solely automated individual decision-making provided for in the GDPR will be interpreted in the future. The Court of Justice of the European Union has yet to rule on the subject matter of Article 22 of the GDPR, and it never ruled on the subject matter of Article 15 of the DPD. However, given the growing importance of this type of processing, jurisprudence in this regard is inevitable.

Here are the key *de lege ferenda* recommendations on this subject. First of all, Article 22 (1) of the GDPR should be rephrased in order to decisively indicate whether it is intended as a right to opt out that the data subject has to actively exercise or as a general prohibition that does not require any action. Alternatively, it could be clarified in the forthcoming jurisprudence. Second, it should be explored whether collective automated individual decisions could be covered by the scope of this provision. In the literature, it is argued that recognising a decision regarding a group as actually being a bundle of individual decisions could open the door to include it in the scope of the provision in question.[342] Besides, clarifying that the notion of an individual decision should be understood broadly would also contribute to the protection of the data subjects with regard to such processing. Third, given there is much uncertainty about inconsiderable human involvement in solely automated individual decision-making, clarification should be offered by returning to the phrasing 'solely or predominantly based on' proposed by the Article 29 Data Protection Working Party and the European Parliament during the legislative process.[343] Providing specific examples or criteria of meaningful human involvement in automated decision-making that allows the controller to avoid the regime of Article 22 of the GDPR should also be considered. Alternatively, it could also be resolved in the future jurisprudence. Fourth, the scope of notions of legal effects and similarly significant effects should be explained in order not to be interpreted overly narrowly. In particular, the perspective to be taken in defining similarly significant effects should be indicated. For instance, it could be a subjective perspective of the data subject, or an external standard, such as an average data subject related to the particular decision-making process. Fifth, the notion of necessity in the entering, or performance of a contract should be delineated. Sixth, the European Data Protection Board should issue guidelines, recommendations and best practices for further specifying the criteria and conditions for automated individual decisions based on Article 22 (2) (b) of the GDPR. Seventh, the issue of solely automated individual decision-making concerning children should be resolved, as it is not clear whether, and under what criteria it is permitted.

As stressed above, the numerous ambiguities and very limited scope of Article 22 of the GDPR signal that the protection afforded to the data subject with regard to solely automated individual decision-making may be curtailed. In fact, this is only the beginning; there are further complications regarding the special rights of the data subject with regard to solely automated individual decision-making, which are examined in the following chapter.

---

342. M. Brkan, *Do Algorithms Rule the World? Algorithmic Decision-Making in the Framework of the GDPR and Beyond*, p. 9. The said view has not been substantiated besides a brief comment that teleological interpretation of the Article 22 of the GDPR, coupled with the need to guarantee the data subject a high level of safeguarding its fundamental right to data protection could lead the Court of Justice of the European Union to adopt this interpretative stance. However, the current wording of the regulation leaves collective decisions outside the scope of application of Article 22 of the GDPR.
343. *See* reference 263.

CHAPTER 3

Special Rights of the Data Subject with Regard to Solely Automated Individual Decision-Making

§3.01 INTRODUCTORY REMARKS

As explained in detail above, solely automated individual decision-making within the meaning of Article 22 (1) of the GDPR inherently entails a number of significant risks for individuals' rights and freedoms.[344] This is reflected by the data subject's right not to be subject to this type of processing. In all cases, when solely automated individual decision-making is allowed, i.e., when it is covered by one of the three exemptions set out in Article 22 (2) of the GDPR, additional safeguards apply.

Primarily, the right to be informed and the right of access apply to all of the said exemptions. In addition to that, if solely automated individual decision-making is necessary for entering into, or performance of, a contract, as well as when it is based on the data subject's explicit consent, as per Article 22 (2) (a) and 22 (2) (c) of the GDPR, respectively, the controller is required to implement, as a minimum, the following special rights of the data subject: the right to obtain human intervention; the right to contest the decision; the right to express point of view. Whereas if solely automated individual decision-making is authorised by the EU or Member State law to which the controller is subject as per Article 22 (2) (b) of the GDPR, this law must lay down suitable measures to safeguard the data subject's rights and freedoms and legitimate interests. In this case, the GDPR does not mandate any specific safeguards, as it is left to the legislators of the relevant laws. All of the above-mentioned safeguards are described in this chapter.

It is preceded by an outline of the modalities for the exercise of the rights of the data subject, which is relevant both for special rights of the data subject with regard to

---

344. *See* Chapter 1, §1.05.

solely automated individual decision-making within the meaning of Article 22 (1) of the GDPR and general rights of the data subject relevant to all automated individual decision-making systems including, but not limited to, the above-mentioned solely automated individual decision-making.[345] This chapter also includes an outline of legal limitations and technical obstacles to algorithmic transparency. Finally, interim conclusions are presented.

§3.02   MODALITIES FOR THE EXERCISE OF THE RIGHTS OF THE DATA SUBJECT

Before analysing the special rights of the data subject with regard to solely automated individual decision-making, it is important to outline several basic modalities for the exercise of these rights set out in Article 12 of the GDPR to be considered by the controller.[346] Additionally, the said provision applies also to the general rights of the data subject relevant to automated individual decision-making, outlined in Chapter 5.

First of all, as provided by Article 12 (1) of the GDPR, the controller shall take appropriate measures to provide the information to the data subject in a concise, transparent, intelligible and easily accessible form, using clear and plain language.[347] Under this provision, the controller ought to present the information efficiently and succinctly. It should be done in as simple a manner as possible, in order to avoid information fatigue of the data subject.[348] In addition to that, the information ought to be concrete and definitive instead of being phrased in abstract or ambivalent terms, which leave room for different interpretations.[349] The requirement that information is 'intelligible' means that it should be understood by an average member of the intended audience. Hence, the information should not contain, for example, exceedingly legalistic, technical or specialist language or terminology.[350] Last but not least, the data subject should not have to seek out the information, which, as a rule, must be provided

---

345. *See* Chapter 5.
346. Article 12 of the GDPR sets out the general rules which apply to: the provision of information to data subject i.e., the right to be informed (under Articles 13-14 of the GDPR); communications with data subject concerning the exercise of its rights (under Articles 15-22 of the GDPR); and communications in relation to data breaches (Article 34 of the GDPR).
347. GDPR, Article 12 (1): 'The controller shall take appropriate measures to provide any information referred to in Articles 13 and 14 and any communication under Articles 15 to 22 and 34 relating to processing to the data subject in a concise, transparent, intelligible and easily accessible form, using clear and plain language, in particular for any information addressed specifically to a child. The information shall be provided in writing, or by other means, including, where appropriate, by electronic means. When requested by the data subject, the information may be provided orally, provided that the identity of the data subject is proven by other means'.
348. *See* M.E. Kaminski, *The Right to Explanation, Explained*, p. 212, who specifies that this provision 'aims to prevent companies from flooding individuals with useless or unnecessarily complicated or time-wasting information, abusing notice requirements to create obscurity through information floods'.
349. Article 29 Data Protection Working Party, *Guidelines on Transparency under Regulation 2016/679*, as last revised and adopted on 11 April 2018, paragraph 12, pp. 8-9.
350. Article 29 Data Protection Working Party, *Guidelines on Transparency under Regulation 2016/679*, paragraph 13, p. 10.

in writing, including, where appropriate, by electronic means.[351] Contrarily, it should be immediately apparent to the data subject where and how this information can be accessed.[352] To sum up, under Article 12 (1) of the GDPR, the quality, accessibility and comprehensibility of the information, which must be provided to the data subject, is as important as its actual content.[353] Essentially, it mandates the controller to make an effort to communicate relevant information in a way that is understandable to individuals.

Of course, as rightly noted by the Article 29 Working Party, there is an inherent tension in the GDPR between the requirements to provide the comprehensive information to the data subject, which is required under the GDPR, and to do so in a form that meets all of the above prerequisites.[354] Taking that into account, and bearing in mind the fundamental principles of accountability and fairness, the controller must undertake its own analysis of the nature, circumstances, scope and context of the processing of personal data which it carries out and decide how to prioritise information, which must be provided to the data subject and what are the appropriate levels of detail and methods for conveying this information.

Article 12 (2) of the GDPR mandates the controller to facilitate the exercise of the data subject rights. In addition to that, it stipulates that the controller shall not refuse to act on the request of the data subject for exercising its right unless it demonstrates that it is not in a position to identify the data subject. This provision obliges the controller to provide a simple way for the data subject to exercise its rights, *inter alia*, these relevant to automated individual decision-making.[355] Lack of explicit obligation in the GDPR to provide the data subject with information about the right not to be subject to a solely automated individual decision set out in Article 22 (1) of the GDPR and its safeguards provided for in Article 22 (3) of the GDPR, i.e., the right to obtain human intervention, the right to contest the decision and the right to express point of view should be highly criticised.[356] Possibly, such an obligation could be derived from Article 12 (2) of the GDPR. The data subject must be informed about its rights in order to be able to exercise them. Certainly, failing to inform the data subject about its rights does not meet the obligation to facilitate their exercise. *Ergo,* the controller must inform the data subject of the above-mentioned rights to meet the said obligation. Additionally, it must provide the data subject with the necessary infrastructure for their exercise.[357]

---

351. As per Article 12 (1) of the GDPR, when requested by the data subject, the information may be provided orally, provided that the identity of the data subject is proven by other means.
352. Article 29 Data Protection Working Party, *Guidelines on Transparency under Regulation 2016/679*, paragraph 11, p. 8.
353. *Ibid.*, paragraph 4, pp. 5-6.
354. *Ibid.*, paragraph 34, p. 18.
355. Article 12 (2) *ab initio*: 'The controller shall facilitate the exercise of data subject rights under Articles 15 to 22'. *See also* Article 29 Data Protection Working Party, *Guidelines on Automated individual decision-making and Profiling*, p. 27, which underlines this obligation with regard to the rights set out in Article 22 (3) of the GDPR.
356. *See also* S. Wachter, B. Mittelstadt, C. Russell, *Counterfactual Explanations Without Opening the Black Box: Automated Decisions and the GDPR*, 31 (2) Harvard Journal of Law & Technology (2018), p. 877.
357. *Ibid.*, p. 876.

As required by Article 12 (3) of the GDPR, the controller is obliged to provide information on action taken on a such a request to the data subject without undue delay and in any event within one month of receipt of the request. That period may be extended by two further months where necessary, taking into account the complexity and number of the requests. The controller shall inform the data subject of any such extension within one month of receipt of the request, together with the reasons for the delay. Additionally, where the data subject makes the request by electronic form means, the information shall be provided by electronic means where possible unless otherwise requested by the data subject.

Article 12 (4) of the GDPR stipulates that if the controller does not take action on the request of the data subject, the controller shall inform the data subject without delay and at the latest within one month of receipt of the request of the reasons for not taking action and on the possibility of lodging a complaint with a supervisory authority and seeking a judicial remedy.

As provided for in Article 12 (5) of the GDPR, the information given to the data subject by the controller under the right to be informed and any communication and any actions taken with regard to the other rights of the data subject must be provided free of charge, as a rule.[358]

Article 12 (6) of the GDPR allows the controller to request the provision of additional information necessary to confirm the identity of the data subject where it has reasonable doubts concerning the identity of the natural person making the request referred to in Articles 15 to 21 of the GDPR.[359]

Article 12 (7) of the GDPR proposes that the information to be provided to the data subject by the controller under the right to be informed may be provided in combination with standardised icons in order to give in an easily visible, intelligible and clearly legible manner a meaningful overview of the intended processing.[360] Although the use of icons does not replace information necessary for the exercise of a data subject's rights, it may 'give in an easily visible, intelligible and clearly legible

---

358. GDPR, Article 12 (5) *in fine*:

> Where requests from a data subject are manifestly unfounded or excessive, in particular because of their repetitive character, the controller may either:
>
> (a) charge a reasonable fee taking into account the administrative costs of providing the information or communication or taking the action requested; or
> (b) refuse to act on the request.
> The controller shall bear the burden of demonstrating the manifestly unfounded or excessive character of the request.

359. GDPR, Article 12 (6): 'Without prejudice to Article 11, where the controller has reasonable doubts concerning the identity of the natural person making the request referred to in Articles 15 to 21, the controller may request the provision of additional information necessary to confirm the identity of the data subject'.
360. GDPR, Article 12 (7): 'The information to be provided to data subjects pursuant to Articles 13 and 14 may be provided in combination with standardised icons in order to give in an easily visible, intelligible and clearly legible manner a meaningful overview of the intended processing. Where the icons are presented electronically they shall be machine-readable'.

manner a meaningful overview of the intended processing'.[361] Of course, the utility of such icons to effectively convey information to the data subjects is dependent upon their standardisation, which is not in place yet.[362]

All of the above requirements aim to empower the data subject to hold the controller accountable and to exercise control over its personal data by, for example, actioning its data subject rights.[363] They are highly important to automate individual decision-making, which is ordinarily exceedingly opaque to the data subject.

§3.03 RIGHT TO BE INFORMED

First and foremost, every controller, which deploys solely automated individual decision-making, should be particularly mindful of its specific transparency obligations. Their purpose is to inform the data subject about the future solely automated individual decision-making, so it may assess its legitimacy or exercise its other special rights with regard to this type of processing.

Concretely, Articles 13 (2) (f)[364] and 14 (2) (g)[365] of the GDPR require the controller to provide the data subject with the information regarding the existence of solely automated individual decision-making and meaningful information about the logic involved, as well as the significance and the envisaged consequences of such processing for the data subject. To recapitulate, if the controller is making solely automated individual decisions within the meaning of Article 22 (1) of the GDPR it is obliged to: (i) inform the data subject that it is engaging in this type of activity; (ii)

---

361. GDPR, Recital 60.
362. GDPR, Article 12 (8): 'The Commission shall be empowered to adopt delegated acts in accordance with Article 92 for the purpose of determining the information to be presented by the icons and the procedures for providing standardised icons'.
363. *See*, for example, Opinion of Advocate General Cruz Villalón of 9 July 2015, Smaranda Bara and Others v Preşedintele Casei Naţionale de Asigurari de Sanatate, Casa Naţionala de Asigurari de Sanatate, Agenţia Naţionala de Administrare Fiscala (ANAF), Case C-201/14, ECLI: EU:C:2015:461, paragraph 74: 'the requirement to inform the data subjects about the processing of their personal data, which guarantees transparency of all processing, is all the more important since it affects the exercise by the data subjects of their right of access to the data being processed, referred to in Article 95/46, and their right to object to the processing of those data, set out in Article 14 of that directive'.
364. GDPR, Article 13 (2) (f): 'In addition to the information referred to in paragraph 1, the controller shall, at the time when personal data are obtained, provide the data subject with the following further information necessary to ensure fair and transparent processing: [...] f) the existence of automated decision-making, including profiling, referred to in Article 22(1) and (4) and, at least in those cases, meaningful information about the logic involved, as well as the significance and the envisaged consequences of such processing for the data subject. [...]'.
365. GDPR, Article 14 (2) (g): 'In addition to the information referred to in paragraph 1, the controller shall provide the data subject with the following information necessary to ensure fair and transparent processing in respect of the data subject: [...] g) the existence of automated decision-making, including profiling, referred to in Article 22(1) and (4) and, at least in those cases, meaningful information about the logic involved, as well as the significance and the envisaged consequences of such processing for the data subject. [...]'.

provide meaningful information about the logic involved; and (iii) explain the significance and envisaged consequences of the processing. It is only the first step towards protecting the data subject with regard to automated individual decision-making.[366]

The specific transparency obligations are limited to solely automated individual decision-making within the meaning of Article 22 (1) of the GDPR.[367] They do not apply to other types of automated individual decision-making. Nevertheless, the wording of both of the above provisions clearly indicates that even if the automated individual decision-making is not covered by Article 22 (1) of the GDPR, the controller should consider providing the above information anyway. It is a good practice to do this, especially if it is unlikely that the data subjects would expect that they are subject to solely automated individual decision-making.[368]

Considering that the requirement to provide the above information is contained in Articles 13 and 14 of the GDPR alike, it applies regardless of whether the personal data has been obtained directly from the data subject or not and it has to be provided at the commencement phase of the processing cycle.[369]

It is exceedingly challenging for individuals to understand how solely automated individual decision-making or profiling works. Despite that, the controller is under an obligation to provide the data subject with meaningful information about their logic. A high degree of complexity of those processes does not relieve the controller from an obligation to provide such information to the data subject. Recital 58 of the GDPR further illustrates that 'this is of particular relevance in situations where the proliferation of actors and the technological complexity of practice make it difficult for the data subject to know and understand whether, by whom and for what purpose personal data relating to him or her are being collected, such as in the case of online advertising. [...]'.

Especially considering that the word 'meaningful' means both 'intended to show the meaning' and 'useful, serious, or important'.[370] Provisions in question concern the rights of the data subject, so the notion of 'meaningful' should be interpreted in relation to the data subject, as well.[371] Hence, the literal interpretation of this provision specifies

---

366. A. Roig, *Safeguards for the Right Not to Be Subject to a Decision Based Solely on Automated Processing (Article 22 GDPR)*, 8 (3) European Journal of Law and Technology (2017), p. 6.
367. The other transparency obligations which apply to all types of automated decision-making are described below in Chapter 5, §5.02.
368. Both Article 13 (2) (f) and 14 (2) (g) of the GDPR require to the controller to provide information 'at least in those cases' i.e., at least when automated decision-making in question is covered by Article 22 (1) of the GDPR.
369. The exceptions to the obligation to provide information are described below in Chapter 5, §5.02.
370. Cambridge Dictionary, 'meaningful', available at: https://dictionary.cambridge.org/dictionary /english/meaningful, accessed 1 June 2019; G. Malgieri, G. Comandé, *Why a Right to Legibility of Automated Decision-Making Exists*, p. 257.
371. A.D. Selbst, J. Powles, *Meaningful Information and the Right to Explanation*, p. 236. *See also* Chapter III of the GDPR, which is entitled 'Rights of the data subject'.

that information about the logic involved in solely automated individual decision-making should be both understandable and significant for the data subject.[372] Presumably, in the vast majority of cases, this is an individual without particular technical expertise.

Bearing in mind the above remarks as well as the modalities for the exercise of the rights of the data subject outlined above in §3.02, from the data subject's perspective, it is not necessary to disclose the algorithms used by the controller or give an overcomplex explanation thereof.[373] To the contrary, considering the gaps in technical literacy for most individuals, this could be confusing instead of meaningful.[374] A high-level, non-technical, description of the decision-making process is more likely to be useful for the data subject.[375]

Considering that notification duties precede the decision-making process, at this point only an explanation of system functionality, as opposed to an explanation of a particular decision, could be given and this is precisely what is required by Articles 13 (2) (f) and 14 (2) (g) of the GDPR.[376] Specifically, the information provided by the controller should include details of main characteristics considered in reaching the decision and their approximate relevance, to allow the data subject to understand the reasons for the decision.[377] The language of the discussed provisions suggests that that data subjects must be provided with information about how an automated individual decision-making system works, in general, and with what predicted impact.[378] It is of vital importance that even if the controller engages processors to perform solely

---

372. G. Malgieri, G. Comandé, *Why a Right to Legibility of Automated Decision-Making Exists*, p. 257.
373. P.G. Picht, G.T. Loderer, *Framing Algorithms: Competition Law and (Other) Regulatory Tools*, 10 (5) Max Planck Institute for Innovation & Competition Research Paper No. 18-24 (2018), p. 10. This interpretation is also supported by the Article 29 Data Protection Working Party, *Guidelines on Automated individual decision-making and Profiling*, p. 25. *See also* A. Mednis, *Obowiązek informacyjny na podstawie Article 13 RODO*, 3 Informacja w Administracji Publicznej (2018), p. 12, who claims that only general rules for making solely automated individual decisions should be provided.
374. J. Burrell, *How the Machine 'Thinks': Understanding Opacity in Machine Learning Algorithms*, 3 (1) Big Data and Society (2016), p. 4. *Conferatur* G. Noto La Diega, *Against the Dehumanisation of Decision-Making*, p. 23, who submits that the data subject has a legitimate interest in asking an expert to analyse the algorithm in order to better challenge the decision, as a different interpretation would not comply with right to an effective remedy and to a fair trial under the Charter of Fundamental Rights of the European Union (Article 47) and the European Convention of Human Rights (Articles 6, 13).
375. C. Kuner, D.J.B. Svantesson, F.H. Cate, O. Lynskey, C. Millard, *Machine Learning with Personal Data: Is Data Protection Law Smart Enough to Meet the Challenge?*, p. 2.
376. In the legal doctrine, system functionality refers to 'the logic, significance, envisaged consequences, and general functionality of an automated decision-making system, e.g. the system's requirements specification, decision trees, pre-defined models, criteria, and classification structures'. *See* S. Wachter, B. Mittelstadt, L. Floridi, *Why a Right to Explanation of Automated Decision-Making Does Not Exist*, p. 78.
377. Article 29 Data Protection Working Party, *Guidelines on Automated individual decision-making and Profiling*, p. 26.
378. *See also* good practice recommendations, *ibid.*, p. 31: 'Instead of providing a complex mathematical explanation about how algorithms or machine-learning work, the controller should consider using clear and comprehensive ways to deliver the information to the data subject, for example:

automated individual decision-making on its behalf, as long as the controller is reliant upon this score it must be able to explain it and the rationale to the data subject.[379]

Such information should be meaningful to an average member of the intended audience. If the controller is uncertain about the level of intelligibility of the information, it may test it, for example, through mechanisms such as user panels, readability testing, formal and informal interactions and dialogue with industry groups, consumer advocacy groups and regulatory bodies.[380] At a minimum, the information, which must be provided by the controller should enable the data subject to exercise its other special rights with regard to solely automated decision-making under the GDPR.[381]

Aside from providing meaningful information about the logic involved, the controller is obliged to apprise the data subject of the significance and the envisaged consequences of solely automated individual decision-making. In other words, the data subject must be informed how the solely automated individual decision-making might affect it. Certainly, since the notification duties precede decision-making, the controller does not have to predict its results and inform the data subject thereof in advance. Instead, the data subject must be informed about the potential impact of such processing. In order to make this information meaningful and understandable, real, tangible examples of the type of possible consequences of such processing for the data subject should be given.[382]

As already stressed above, it should be strongly criticised that there is no explicit obligation in the GDPR to provide the data subject with information about the right not to be subject to a solely automated individual decision set out in Article 22 (1) of the GDPR and its safeguards provided for in Article 22 (3) of the GDPR, i.e., the right to obtain human intervention, the right to contest the decision and the right to express point of view.[383] The data subject must be informed about its rights in order to be able to exercise them. This is precisely why the controller is obliged to provide information to data subjects on their main rights under Articles 13 (2) (b) and 14 (2) (c) of the

---

- the categories of data that have been or will be used in the profiling or decision-making process;
- why these categories are considered pertinent
- how any profile used in the automated decision-making process is built, including any statistics used in the analysis;
- why this profile is relevant to the automated decision-making process; and
- how it is used for a decision concerning the data subject.
  Such information will generally be more relevant to the data subject and contribute to the transparency of the processing'.

379. Article 29 Data Protection Working Party, *Guidelines on Automated individual decision-making and Profiling*, pp. 24-26.
380. Article 29 Data Protection Working Party, *Guidelines on Transparency under Regulation 2016/679*, paragraph 9, p. 7.
381. A.D. Selbst, J. Powles, *Meaningful Information and the Right to Explanation*, p. 242.
382. Article 29 Data Protection Working Party, *Guidelines on Automated individual decision-making and Profiling*, p. 26.
383. *See also* S. Wachter, B. Mittelstadt, C. Russell, *Counterfactual Explanations Without Opening the Black Box*, p. 877.

GDPR.[384] Regrettably, special rights of the data subject with regard to solely automated individual decision-making are not covered by the above provisions. As mandated by Article 12 (2) of the GDPR and noted by the Article 29 Data Protection Working Party, the controller must provide a simple way for the data subject to exercise its rights laid down in Article 22 (3) of the GDPR.[385] Unquestionably, it is not easy for the data subject to use these rights if it is not even informed about them. Accordingly, it is submitted that an obligation to inform the data subject of the above-mentioned right may be potentially derived from Article 12 (2) of the GDPR. What is more, the controller must also implement the necessary infrastructure for the exercise of these rights.[386]

Admittedly, Recital 39 of the GDPR also refers to the provision of certain information which is not explicitly covered by Articles 13 and 14 of the GDPR. It states that 'natural persons should be made aware of risks, rules, safeguards and rights in relation to the processing of personal data and how to exercise their rights in relation to such processing'. Accordingly, in line with the preamble to the GDPR, the controller should determine particular risks, rules, safeguards and rights relevant to solely automated individual decision-making and bring them to the attention of data subjects, but it is not under explicit obligation to do so. Correspondingly, Recital 60 of the GDPR states: 'the controller should provide the data subject with any further information necessary to ensure fair and transparent processing taking into account the specific circumstances and context in which the personal data are processed'. This recital also reveals that the controller should give the data subject additional information if it is necessary to ensure fair and transparent processing in a given case. Unfortunately, both of the above recitals are indeterminate. In addition to that, they are not reflected in the operative part of the GDPR. This leads to conclusion that they do not create any clear-cut obligations for the controller, including an obligation to provide the data subject with information regarding its rights under Article 22 (3) of the GDPR, i.e., the right to obtain human intervention, the right to contest the decision and the right to express point of view.

Nevertheless, the above conclusion may be modified by future jurisprudence. In principle, although recitals should be taken into account when interpreting a legal act, they are not legally binding, the Court of Justice of the European Union has stated that 'whilst a recital in the preamble to a regulation may cast light on the interpretation to be given to a legal rule, it cannot in itself constitute such a rule'.[387] This gives recitals

---

384. These are: the right of access; the right to rectification; the right to erasure; the right to restriction; right to object; the right to data portability.
385. Article 12 (2) *ab initio*: 'The controller shall facilitate the exercise of data subject rights under Articles 15 to 22'. *See also* Article 29 Data Protection Working Party, *Guidelines on Automated individual decision-making and Profiling*, p. 27.
386. S. Wachter, B. Mittelstadt, C. Russell, *Counterfactual Explanations Without Opening the Black Box*, p. 876.
387. Judgment of the Court (Third Chamber) of 13 July 1989, Casa Fleischhandels-GmbH v Bundesanstalt für landwirtschaftliche Marktordnung, Case 215/88, ECLI:EU:C:1989:331, paragraph 31. *See also* Judgment of the Court (Fifth Chamber) of 19 November 1998, Gunnar Nilsson, Per Olov Hagelgren, Solweig Arrborn, Case C-162/97, ECLI:EU:C:1998:554, paragraph 54, which states that: 'the preamble to a Community act has no binding legal force and cannot be relied on as a ground for derogating from the actual provisions of the act in question'. *See also* Judgment of the Court of 15 May 1997, Textilwerke Deggendorf GmbH (TWD) v

a liminal legal status as they are not binding law, but they are often cited as authoritative interpretations where the GDPR is vague.[388] Another look at the jurisprudence of the Court of Justice of the European Union reveals that recitals cannot be used in a manner clearly contrary to their wording of EU law provisions.[389] In short, the preamble may not be used for a *contra legem* interpretation of a legal act. But this does not seem to be the case, as the wording of the GDPR does not prevent the controller from providing the above-mentioned additional information to the data subjects. Dismissing the possibility of the existence of such an obligation completely, only because recitals are not legally binding, is too formalistic, in particular, in light of the case law of the Court of Justice of the European Union which regularly uses recitals as an interpretative aid.[390] Including such wording in the preamble to the GDPR demonstrates that the legislator left the final decision on the existence of such an obligation of the controller to the Court of Justice of the European Union which is, as it has been repeatedly demonstrated in the recent case law, rather purposeful and activist when interpreting data protection legislation.[391]

§3.04   RIGHT OF ACCESS

Within the framework of the right of access, the data subject is entitled to have, *inter alia*, the exact same information about solely automated individual decision-making, including profiling, as required under Articles 13 (2) (f) and 14 (2) (g) of the GDPR.[392] Specifically, under Article 15 (1) (h) of the GDPR the controller is obliged to (i) inform the data subject that they are engaging in this type of activity; (ii) provide meaningful information about the logic involved; and (iii) explain the significance and envisaged consequences of the processing.[393]

Commission of the European Communities and Federal Republic of Germany, Case C-355/95 P, ECLI:EU:C:1997:241, paragraph 21, which states that: 'operative part of an act is indissociably linked to the statement of reasons for it, so that, when it has to be interpreted, account must be taken of the reasons which led to its adoption'.

388. M.E. Kaminski, *The Right to Explanation, Explained*, p. 194.
389. Judgment of the Court (Sixth Chamber) of 25 November 1998, Giuseppe Manfredi v Regione Puglia, Case C-308/97, ECLI:EU:C:1998:566, paragraph 3; Judgment of the Court (Fifth Chamber) of 24 November 2005, Deutsches Milch-Kontor, Case C-136/04, ECLI:EU:C:2005:716, paragraph 32.
390. Judgment of the Court (Sixth Chamber) of 9 February 2017, M. S. v P. S., Case C-283/16, ECLI:EU:C:2017:104, paragraphs 34-35; Judgment of the Court (Seventh Chamber) of 28 June 2017, Leventis and Vafias, Case C-436/16, ECLI:EU:C:2017:497, paragraph 33.
391. M. Brkan, *Do Algorithms Rule the World? Algorithmic Decision-Making in the Framework of the GDPR and Beyond*, p. 16.
392. Other information which may be obtained by the data subject under Article 15 of the GDPR is outlined below in Chapter 5, §5.03.
393. GDPR, Article 15 (1) (h): 'The data subject shall have the right to obtain from the controller confirmation as to whether or not personal data concerning him or her are being processed, and, where that is the case, access to the personal data and the following information: the existence of automated decision-making, including profiling, referred to in Article 22(1) and (4) and, at least in those cases, meaningful information about the logic involved, as well as the significance and the envisaged consequences of such processing for the data subject'.

Together, Articles 13-15 of the GDPR allow the data subject to obtain information about the personal data held about it by the controller and to scrutinise the legitimacy of data processing. In contrast to the transparency obligations of the controller set out in Articles 13-14 of the GDPR, the corresponding right of access provided for in Article 15 of the GDPR has to be invoked by the data subject. By exercising it, the data subject can become aware of a solely automated individual decision made concerning it, independently from the notification duties of the controller. Certainly, the controller should have already given the data subject this information in line with the above described transparency obligations. Nevertheless, irrespective of whether this was the case, the data subject may request this information at any time either way, including after the solely automated individual decision has been made.[394]

Given that phrasing of Article 15 (1) (h) is identical to Articles 13 (2) (f) and 14 (2) (g) of the GDPR, it is reasonable to assume that it refers to the very same scope of the information, which must be provided to the data subject.[395] Consequently, when the data subject invokes its right of access, the controller is obliged to provide the data subject only with meaningful, but properly limited information on factors taken into account for the decision-making process and on their respective 'weight' on an aggregate level, instead of an explanation of a particular decision as well.[396] It is worth to note that the implementations and interpretations of the DPD's right of access by the Member States, have mostly limited informational obligations to system functionality. If the interpretation of the GDPR follows historical precedence, its right of access is similarly confined.[397]

Recital 63 of the GDPR states that every data subject should have the right to know and obtain communication, in particular, with regard to the logic involved in any automatic personal data processing and, at least when based on profiling, the consequences of such processing.[398] Undoubtedly, the wording of this recital seems incoherent with the obligation set out in Article 15 (1) (h) of the GDPR. Concretely, it leads to three conclusions, which are divergent from the operative part of the GDPR. Firstly, it suggests that the controller should provide the data subject with information about the logic involved in any type of automated processing, even if it does not lead to solely automated individual decision-making within the meaning of Article 22 (1) of the GDPR. Second, it implies that the controller should explain the consequences of the

---

394. GDPR, Recital 63: '[...] A data subject should have the right of access to personal data which have been collected concerning him or her, and to exercise that right easily and at reasonable intervals, in order to be aware of, and verify, the lawfulness of the processing [...]'.
395. As signalled above, under Articles 13 (2) (f) and 14 (2) (g) of the GDPR the controller is not required to provide the data subject with an explanation of a particular decision already reached. *See* remarks in §3.03 above.
396. Article 29 Data Protection Working Party, *Guidelines on Automated individual decision-making and Profiling*, p. 27.
397. *See* full remarks: S. Wachter, B. Mittelstadt, L. Floridi, *Why a Right to Explanation of Automated Decision-Making Does Not Exist*, pp. 85-90.
398. GDPR, Recital 63: '[...] Every data subject should therefore have the right to know and obtain communication in particular with regard to the purposes for which the personal data are processed, where possible the period for which the personal data are processed, the recipients of the personal data, the logic involved in any automatic personal data processing and, at least when based on profiling, the consequences of such processing. [...]'.

processing at least when it is based on profiling. *A contrario*, the controller, ought not to do this when the automated processing is not based profiling, which excludes solely automated individual decision-making, which is not based on profiling. Third, it omits the controller's obligation to inform the data subject about the existence of solely automated individual decision-making. Thus, on the one hand, Recital 63 of the GDPR expands the scope of Article 15 (1) (h) of the GDPR, and on the other, it narrows it. It is submitted that these discrepancies may be considered as sloppy legislation with no bearing on the obligations of the controller.

§3.05   RIGHT TO EXPLANATION

One of the most vigorously debated questions in the academic literature regarding the GDPR is whether it gives the data subject the right to an explanation of a solely automated individual decision.[399] The purported right to an explanation would require the controllers to explain to the data subjects the reasons for a specific solely automated individual decision after it has been made. The right to explanation is viewed as a promising mechanism in the broader pursuit of accountability and transparency in solely automated individual decision-making.[400] The purported right is believed to empower the data subjects and disrupt data intensive industries, which could be forced to open their algorithmic black boxes.[401] However, in fact, there are numerous reasons to doubt both the existence of such a right in the GDPR, as well as its feasibility. Notably, the only time when the right of explanation is distinctly mentioned in the GDPR is its preamble, not the legislative provisions. The inclusion of the supposed right in the recitals and, at the same time, its omission from the operative part of the GDPR accounts for most of the discussion in the legal doctrine.

First and foremost, it has to be explained what is meant by the right in question. In the legal doctrine, the asserted right to explanation refers to the 'rationale, reasons, and individual circumstances of a specific solely automated individual decision, e.g., the weighting of features, machine-defined case-specific decision rules, information about reference or profile groups'.[402] It should permit the data subject to determine the

---

399. *See* for example: B. Goodman, S. Flaxman, *European Union Regulations on Algorithmic Decision Making and 'a Right to an Explanation'*; F. Rossi, *Artificial Intelligence: Potential Benefits and Ethical Considerations, European Parliament: Policy Department C: Citizens' Rights and Constitutional Affairs*, October 2016; L. Edwards, M. Veale, *Slave to the Algorithm?*; G. Malgieri, G. Comandé, *Why a Right to Legibility of Automated Decision-Making Exists*; S. Wachter, B. Mittelstadt, L. Floridi, *Why a Right to Explanation of Automated Decision-Making Does Not Exist*; A. Roig, *Safeguards for the Right Not to Be Subject to a Decision Based Solely on Automated Processing (Article 22 GDPR)*; G. Noto La Diega, *Against the Dehumanisation of Decision-Making*; A.D. Selbst, J. Powles, *Meaningful Information and the Right to Explanation*, pp. 233-242; IEEE Global Initiative, *Ethically Aligned Design. A Vision for Prioritizing Human Well-being with Autonomous and Intelligent Systems*, First Edition, 2019.
400. S. Wachter, B. Mittelstadt, L. Floridi, *Why a Right to Explanation of Automated Decision-Making Does Not Exist*, p. 77.
401. B. Goodman, S. Flaxman, *European Union Regulations on Algorithmic Decision Making and 'a Right to an Explanation'*, p. 50.
402. *See* S. Wachter, B. Mittelstadt, L. Floridi, *Why a Right to Explanation of Automated Decision-Making Does Not Exist*, p. 78.

extent to which a particular input was determinative or influential on the output.[403] In short, the right to an explanation would enable the data subject to obtain information about why a certain decision was taken.

There are three separate possible legal bases for the right to explanation in the GDPR. Specifically, the right to explanation may conceivably be derived from: (i) the right not to be subject to solely automated individual decision-making and safeguards enacted thereof (Article 22 of the GDPR); (ii) the right to be informed (Articles 13 (2) (f) and 14 (2) (g) of the GDPR); and (iii) the right of access (Article 15 (1) (h) of the GDPR). Each of these is considered below.

[A]   Right to Explanation Derived from the Right Not to Be Subject to Solely Automated Individual Decision-Making

First, it should be assessed whether the supposed right to explanation could be inferred from the right not to be subject to solely automated individual decision-making set out in Article 22 of the GDPR and safeguards enacted thereof. Article 22 (3) of the GDPR provides that in the cases when solely automated individual decision-making is necessary for entering into, or performance of, a contract, as well as when it is based on the data subject's explicit consent, 'the data controller shall implement *suitable measures to safeguard* the data subject's rights and freedoms and legitimate interests, at least the right to obtain human intervention on the part of the controller, to express his or her point of view and to contest the decision [italics added]'. Incontestably, the right to explanation is not explicitly mentioned in this provision. Instead, assuming that solely automated individual decision-making is allowed under Article 22 (2) (a) or 22 (2) (c) of the GDPR, the data subject is granted other rights. Under Article 22 (3) of the GDPR, the controller is obliged to implement the following suitable measures to safeguard the data subject's rights and freedoms and legitimate interests: (i) the right obtain human intervention, (ii) the right to express its point of view and (iii) the right contest the decision. They do not include the right to obtain an explanation of the decision reached.

As noted above, the purported right to explanation is mentioned only in the preamble to the GDPR. Pursuant to Recital 71 of the GDPR, which relates to the discussed provision, solely automated individual decision-making within the meaning of Article 22 (1) of the GDPR: 'should be subject to suitable safeguards, which should include specific information to the data subject and the right to obtain human intervention, to express his or her point of view, *to obtain an explanation* of the decision reached after such assessment and to challenge the decision [italics added]'.

While the preamble to the GDPR is interpretative of the operative part, it often contains language that goes well beyond it, revealing the result of political compromise during trilogue negotiations.[404] Admitting that recitals provide guidance on how to interpret a legal act, they are not legally binding. Recitals can help to clarify the intent

---

403. F. Doshi-Velez, M. Kortz, *Accountability of AI under the Law: The Role of Explanation*, p. 3.
404. M.E. Kaminski, *The Right to Explanation, Explained*, p. 194; L. Edwards, M. Veale, *Slave to the Algorithm?*, p. 50.

behind a normative instrument, but they do not have an autonomous legal effect. This means they are not enforceable as such.[405] Their role is to dispel confusion about the legislative provision to which they relate, and they cannot cause legitimate expectations to arise, even when they are drafted in normative terms.[406] The above remarks concerning the legal status of recitals are affirmed by a landmark judgment of the Court of Justice of the European Union, in the following words: 'whilst a Recital in the preamble to a regulation may cast light on the interpretation to be given to a legal rule, it cannot in itself constitute such a rule'.[407]

Sometimes a line between a valid interpretation and an invalid creation of new law can be hard to draw.[408] According to the legal doctrine, where both the operative provision and the recital are clear but inconsistent, the operative provision will control.[409] With regard to Article 22 (3) of the GDPR, it is apparent that it does not include the right to an explanation as one of the suitable measures to safeguard the data subject's rights and freedoms and legitimate interests, which have to be implemented by the controller. This provision does not require further interpretation with regard to the minimum requirements which must be fulfilled by the controller. Whereas, with respect to Recital 71 of the GDPR, it decidedly indicates that the suitable safeguards should include the right to explanation. Hence, both the operative provision and the Recital are clear but inconsistent. As a consequence, in this case, Article 22 (3) of the GDPR prevails, while Recital 71 of the GDPR does not have any positive operation of its own. Thus, the right to explanation may not be inferred from the right not to be subject to solely automated individual decision-making and safeguards enacted thereof.

Compellingly, the omission of the purported right to explanation in the wording of Article 22 (3) of the GDPR looks as if it was intentional. The initial legislative proposal put forward by the European Commission did not contain such a right at all, even in the preamble.[410] The European Parliament sought stronger protection for the data subject. As the *travaux préparatoires* show, it proposed to include the right to an explanation of the decision reached in the discussed provision, but this amendment was eventually dropped.[411] If the said amendment was adopted, it would have been

---

405. A.D. Selbst, J. Powles, *Meaningful Information and the Right to Explanation*, p. 235.
406. T. Klimas, J. Vaiciukaite, *The Law of Recitals in European Community Legislation*, 15 (1) ILSA Journal of International & Comparative Law (2008), pp. 92-93.
407. *See* reference 387.
408. M.E. Kaminski, *The Right to Explanation, Explained*, p. 194.
409. T. Klimas, J. Vaiciukaite, *The Law of Recitals in European Community Legislation*, pp. 92-93.
410. Article 20 (Measures based on profiling), Proposal for a Regulation the European Parliament and of the Council on the protection of individuals with regard to the processing of personal data and on the free movement of such data (General Data Protection Regulation) of 25 January 2012.
411. Article 20 (5) (Profiling), European Parliament Committee on Civil Liberties, Justice and Home Affairs, Report on the Proposal for a Regulation of the European Parliament and of the Council on the Protection of Individuals with Regard to the Processing of Personal Data and on the Free Movement of Such Data (General Data Protection Regulation) of 21 November 2013; Article 20 (5) (Profiling), Position of the European Parliament adopted at first reading on 12 March 2014 with a view to the adoption of Regulation (EU) No .../2014 of the European Parliament and of the Council on the protection of individuals with regard to the processing of personal data and on the free movement of such data (General Data Protection Regulation): 'Profiling which leads to measures producing legal effects concerning the data subject or does similarly significantly

part of Article 22 (3) of the GDPR, so it would be legally binding. However, the proposed safeguard was not adopted in the trilogue negotiations, which is a sign that the legislators intentionally chose to make the right to explanation non-binding by placing it in the preamble to the GDPR.

In addition to that, as S. Wachter et al. explain, rights have to be explicitly legally established prior to their enforcement.[412] As a rule, the rights of the data subject correspond with the duties of the controller. Certainly, the scope of a right is subject to interpretation; the legal basis for its existence must, however, be certain. Imposing administrative fines on the controllers without having previously clarified explicitly and beyond doubt their obligations would conflict with the principles of a fair trial.[413] Especially considering that infringement of the data subject's rights, including its rights enshrined in Article 22 (3) of the GDPR, is subject to hefty administrative fines up to EUR 20,000,000, or in the case of an undertaking, up to 4% of the total worldwide annual turnover of the preceding financial year, whichever is higher.[414]

In consideration of the foregoing, putting the right to explanation in the recitals demonstrates that the legislator did not want to drop it definitively, which allows future jurisprudence to interpret the Article 22 (3) of the GDPR to include the right to explanation. Given an activist viewpoint and efforts of the Court of Justice of the European Union to ensure a high level of data protection, it is possible that it will opt for a broad interpretation giving the data subject the right to explanation.[415] For instance, the Court of Justice of the European Union could apply a teleological interpretation of Article 22 (3) of the GDPR and recognise that the data subject requires an explanation of a given solely automated individual decision in order to be able to exercise the rights stipulated therein, in particular, to express its point of view and to contest the solely automated individual decision. It may be argued that the said rights are without use otherwise. As noted by S. Wachter et al., an argument for the right to an explanation of specific decisions could be further strengthened by relying on the rights to a fair trial and effective remedy.[416] If the data subject does not have the right to know why a certain decision was taken, it may be impossible for it to challenge the decision effectively.

The relevant jurisprudence of the Court of Justice of the European Union demonstrates that recitals cannot be used in a manner clearly contrary to their wording

---

affect the interests, rights or freedoms of the concerned data subject shall not be based solely or predominantly on automated processing and shall include human assessment, including an explanation of the decision reached after such an assessment. The suitable measures to safeguard the data subject's legitimate interests referred to in paragraph 2 shall include the right to obtain human assessment and *an explanation of the decision reached* after such assessment. [italics added]'.

412. S. Wachter, B. Mittelstadt, L. Floridi, *Why a Right to Explanation of Automated Decision-Making Does Not Exist*, p. 80.

413. *Ibid.*, p. 91. *See* European Convention on Human Rights, Article 6 and Charter of Fundamental Rights of the European Union, Article 47.

414. GDPR, Article 83 (5) (b).

415. M. Brkan, *Do Algorithms Rule the World? Algorithmic Decision-Making in the Framework of the GDPR and Beyond*, p. 17.

416. European Convention on Human Rights Articles 6 and 13, Charter of Fundamental Rights of the European Union, Article 47.

of EU law provisions.[417] Article 22 (3) of the GDPR, which is cited above, requires that the data subject is guaranteed 'at least' the safeguards listed therein. This wording implies that the list of suitable measures to safeguard the data subject's rights and freedoms and legitimate interests is non-exhaustive. Hence, adding an additional safeguard, the right to explanation, through judicial interpretation, would not amount to *contra legem* interpretation of this provision.[418] If it happened, it would likely be followed by a revision of the current version of the influential guidelines of the Article 29 Data Protection Working Party to include such a right, which currently do not include it, even as a good practice recommendation.[419]

[B]   Right to Explanation Derived from the Right to Be Informed

Second, it should be evaluated whether the asserted right to explanation could be inferred from the right to be informed provided for in Articles 13 (2) (f) and 14 (2) (g) of the GDPR. These provisions require the controller to provide the data subject with the information regarding the existence of such solely automated individual decision-making and meaningful information about the logic involved, as well as the significance and the envisaged consequences of such processing for the data subject. They do not contain any wording, which would indicate that the data subject has the right to an explanation of a particular solely automated individual decision after it has been reached.

Additionally, there is also a timeline issue that thwarts the possibility to infer the discussed right from these provisions. Depending on whether the personal data has been obtained directly from the data subject or from another source, the notification duties have to be fulfilled when the data is collected by the controller or within a reasonable period after obtaining the personal data, but at the latest within one month, depending on the circumstances of the case, respectively.[420] Since notification duties precede the decision-making process, the controller is certainly not required to give the data subject an explanation of a particular decision.[421] Logically, an explanation addressing the rationale and circumstances of a specific decision can only be given *ex post*, i.e., once a decision has been made.

Before the decision-making process, only an explanation of system functionality could be given, as required by Articles 13 (2) (f) and 14 (2) (g) of the GDPR.[422] Specifically, the information provided by the controller should include details of main

---

417. Judgment of the Court (Sixth Chamber) of 25 November 1998, Giuseppe Manfredi v Regione Puglia, Case C-308/97, ECLI:EU:C:1998:566, paragraph 3; Judgment of the Court (Fifth Chamber) of 24 November 2005, Deutsches Milch-Kontor, Case C-136/04, ECLI:EU:C:2005:716, paragraph 32.
418. M. Brkan, *Do Algorithms Rule the World? Algorithmic Decision-Making in the Framework of the GDPR and Beyond*, p. 17.
419. Article 29 Data Protection Working Party, *Guidelines on Automated individual decision-making and Profiling*, pp. 31-32.
420. GDPR, Articles 13 (1), 14 (3).
421. S. Wachter, B. Mittelstadt, L. Floridi, *Why a Right to Explanation of Automated Decision-Making Does Not Exist*, pp. 82-83.
422. *See* reference 376.

characteristics considered in reaching the decision and their approximate relevance, to allow the data subject to understand the reasons for the decision.[423] The data subject must be provided only with high profile information about how an automated individual decision-making system works in general and with what predicted impact, not an explanation of a particular decision. This interpretation is supported both by the wording of the discussed provisions and the fact that providing an explanation of a particular decision before it is actually made is simply unfeasible. Due to the above, it is unlikely that future jurisprudence will infer the right to an explanation from these provisions.

Aside from fulfilling the specific transparency requirements under Articles 13 (2) (f) and 14 (2) (g) of the GDPR, in accordance with Recital 60 of the GDPR, which relates to the above provisions, the controller ought to provide the data subject with any further information necessary to ensure fair and transparent processing taking into account the specific circumstances and context in which the personal data are processed.[424] Ultimately, the data subject should not be taken by surprise by the ways its personal data has been used.[425] That is, if the controller uses automated individual decision-making, even not covered by Article 22 of the GDPR, it should communicate additional processing details to the data subject. This, however, is neither well-defined nor a legally binding obligation of the controller. It is highly improbable that the right to explanation could be inferred from the above recital as well.

[C] Right to Explanation Derived from the Right of Access

Third, it should be discussed whether the alleged right to explanation could be inferred from the right of access stipulated in Article 15 (1) (h) of the GDPR. In contrast to the right to be informed, which precedes decision-making, the right of access allows the data subject to obtain the exact same information *ex post*, that is, after the decision-making process has been concluded. In contrast to the right to be informed, the right of access has to be invoked by the data subject. Theoretically, different timing of the right of access makes an explanation of a particular decision already reached, plausible.[426] Nevertheless, the identical wording of all of these provisions does not allow such a conclusion.

Article 15 (1) (h) of the GDPR states that the controller should apprise the data subject of the existence of solely automated individual decision-making, including profiling and provide meaningful information about the logic involved, as well as the significance and the envisaged consequences of such processing. This phrasing is identical to Articles 13 (2) (f) and 14 (2) (g) of the GDPR, which leads to an evident

---

423. *See* reference 377.
424. GDPR, Recital 60: '[...] The controller should provide the data subject with any further information necessary to ensure fair and transparent processing taking into account the specific circumstances and context in which the personal data are processed.[...]'.
425. Article 29 Data Protection Working Party, *Guidelines on Transparency under Regulation 2016/679*, paragraph 41, p. 22.
426. S. Wachter, B. Mittelstadt, L. Floridi, *Why a Right to Explanation of Automated Decision-Making Does Not Exist*, pp. 83-84.

conclusion, that it refers to the very same scope of the information, which must be provided to the data subject.[427] This is also the view of the Article 29 Data Protection Working Party.[428] *Ergo*, in case that the data subject invokes its right of access, the controller is obliged to provide the data subject only with meaningful, but suitably limited information on factors taken into account for the decision-making process and on their respective 'weight' on an aggregate level, rather than an explanation of a particular decision as well.[429] Only broadly applicable information about the logic involved in solely automated individual decision-making is required, rather than personalised disclosures.[430] Despite the different temporal context, the sameness of all of the three provisions suggests that Article 15 (1) (h) of the GDPR is not intended to introduce the purported right to explanation beyond the scope of Articles 13 (2) (f) and 14 (2) (g) of the GDPR.

This interpretation is further confirmed by the wording of the discussed provision, specifically the phrase 'envisaged consequences', which is clearly forward-looking. Such phrasing suggests that the controller is required to predict the possible consequences of the solely automated individual decision-making before such processing occurs and inform the data subject thereof. Article 15 (1) (h) of the GDPR refers to possible consequences of solely automated individual decision-making in general, not a particular decision. This interpretation follows the timeline constraints of identical provisions included in Articles 13 (2) (f) and 14 (2) (g) of the GDPR. After all, the notification duties set out therein antecede decision-making, so an obligation for the controller to predict the impact of solely automated individual decision-making for a particular data subject before the decision is actually made is unfeasible.

This indicates that the right of access, just as the right to be informed, is not addressing how a particular decision was reached, but rather the duty of the controller to provide general information about the existence, main characteristics considered in reaching the decision and consequences of such processing, which equates to the above-mentioned explanation of system functionality. This opinion is shared by the Article 29 Data Protection Working Party, which observed in its influential guidelines that 'Article 15 (1) (h) says that the controller should provide the data subject with information about the *envisaged consequences* of the processing, rather than an explanation of a *particular* decision [italics added by the Article 29 Data Protection Working Party]'.[431] As rightly observed by B. Casey et al., given that these guidelines

---

427. *See* reference 395. *Conferatur* G. Malgieri, G. Comandé, *Why a Right to Legibility of Automated Decision-Making Exists*, p. 256, who argue to the contrary.
428. Article 29 Data Protection Working Party, *Guidelines on Automated individual decision-making and Profiling*, p. 27: 'the controller should have already given the data subject this information in line with their Article 13 obligations', which clearly indicate that, according to this body, the information which must be provided under Article 15 (1) (h) of the GDPR is the same as the information which must be provided under Articles 13 (2) (f) (and 14 (2) (g)) of the GDPR.
429. *See* reference 396.
430. S. Wachter, B. Mittelstadt, C. Russell, *Counterfactual Explanations Without Opening the Black Box*, p. 865.
431. Article 29 Data Protection Working Party, *Guidelines on Automated individual decision-making and Profiling*, p. 27.

are prepared by the very same supervisory authorities on the front lines of enforcing compliance with the GDPR, their interpretation merits careful consideration.[432]

Such interpretation is also supported by the wording of Recital 71 of the GDPR, which states that solely automated individual decision-making 'should be subject to suitable safeguards, which should include specific information to the data subject and the right to obtain human intervention, to express his or her point of view, to obtain an explanation of the decision reached after such assessment and to challenge the decision'. First, the wording of this recital indicates that the right to explanation of a decision reached is out of scope of Articles 13 (2) (f), 14 (2) (g) and 15 (1) (h) of the GDPR because it is listed as a separate safeguard, other than the right to obtain specific information, which is granted by the above-mentioned provisions. Second, if the right to an explanation of a specific decision was intended to be granted, the usage of different language in the preamble and the operative part of the GDPR would be perplexing.[433]

Implementations and interpretations of the DPD's right of access by the Member States, which have mostly limited informational obligations to system functionality, uphold the above understanding of Article 15 (1) (h) of the GDPR. If the interpretation of the GDPR follows this historical precedence, its right of access is similarly limited.[434]

Notwithstanding the above, meaningful information about the logic involved in solely automated individual decision-making should enable the data subject to exercise its rights stipulated in Article 22 (3) of the GDPR, in particular, to express its point of view and to contest the solely automated individual decision.[435] In order to express its opinion or to contest a solely automated individual decision efficaciously, the data subject needs to have sufficient information about the decision-making process. If the said information is overly limited, it could deem these rights ineffective. In the academic literature, it is sometimes claimed that rights of the data subject set out in Article 22 (3) of the GDPR would be empty shells if the data subject was faced merely with a final decision without the right to explanation.[436] It is submitted that providing details of main characteristics considered in reaching the decision and their approximate relevance as required by Articles 13 (2) (f), 14 (2) (g) and 15 (1) (h) of the GDPR, as well as other information, which has to be provided to the data subject on the basis of these provisions is sufficient for the data subject to realise the above rights.[437] This view is supported by the Article 29 Data Protection Working Party in its guidelines, which also point to the right to be informed and right of access in this regard.[438]

---

432. B. Casey, A. Farhangi, R. Vogl, *Rethinking Explainable Machines*, p. 151.
433. S. Wachter, B. Mittelstadt, L. Floridi, *Why a Right to Explanation of Automated Decision-Making Does Not Exist*, p. 84.
434. *See* full remarks *ibid.*, pp. 85-90.
435. M. Brkan, *Do Algorithms Rule the World? Algorithmic Decision-Making in the Framework of the GDPR and Beyond*, p. 15.
436. *Ibid.*, p. 16; S. Wachter, B. Mittelstadt, C. Russell, *Counterfactual Explanations Without Opening the Black Box*, pp. 874-877.
437. *See* reference 377.
438. Article 29 Data Protection Working Party, *Guidelines on Automated individual decision-making and Profiling*, p. 27.

Notably, the right to explanation is not even listed therein in the 'Good practice recommendations'.[439]

This, however, will likely be established by imminent jurisprudence of the Court of Justice of the European Union. Theoretically, the broad wording of Article 15 (1) (h) of the GDPR ('meaningful information', 'logic involved', 'significance and the envisaged consequences') could allow a different reading of this provision. However, only a very extensive interpretation of Article 15 (1) (h) of the GDPR could lead to the recognition of the right to an explanation by the Court of Justice of the European Union.

§3.06   RIGHT TO EXPRESS POINT OF VIEW

Under Article 22 (3) of the GDPR, the data subject has the right to express its point of view. Therefore, the controller is recommended to consider concrete ways to allow an individual to exercise this right.[440] For instance, it could provide a link to an appeals process at the point the solely automated individual decision is delivered to the data subject, along with timescales for the review and a contact point for any queries.[441] The said process could allow the data subject to attach any evidence it believes might help the appeal and give examples of the types of information which may be useful in the review process.[442]

The GDPR does not specify any legal consequences of such an opinion.[443] It is submitted that the right in question should be interpreted together with other special rights of the data subject with regard to solely automated individual decision-making. These data subject's rights: to be informed, to access, to express data subject's point of view, to obtain human intervention and to contest the decision are all highly interconnected. This leads to two key conclusions. In the first place, the information obtained by the data subject though the right to be informed and the right of access must be sufficient for the data subject to realise the right to express its point of view.[444] Subsequently, the data subject's right to express its point of view must be looked at with the right to obtain human intervention and the right to contest the decision. If the data subject's opinion was not taken into account by the controller in the review of the decision, the right to express it would be inconsequential.

---

439. *Ibid.*, pp. 31-32.
440. Article 29 Data Protection Working Party, *Guidelines on Automated individual decision-making and Profiling*, p. 32. *See* GDPR, Article 12 (2) *ab initio*: 'The controller shall facilitate the exercise of data subject rights under Articles 15 to 22'. *See also* remarks in §3.02.
441. Article 29 Data Protection Working Party, *Guidelines on Automated individual decision-making and Profiling*, p. 32. Article 12 (2) *ab initio*: 'The controller shall facilitate the exercise of data subject rights under Articles 15 to 22'. *See also* remarks in §3.02.
442. Information Commissioner's Office, *Automated decision-making and profiling*, Guidelines of 5 June 2018, p. 17.
443. M. Brkan, *Do Algorithms Rule the World? Algorithmic Decision-Making in the Framework of the GDPR and Beyond*, p. 13.
444. With regard to the scope of these provisions, *see* remarks in §3.02 and §3.04.

§3.07 RIGHT TO OBTAIN HUMAN INTERVENTION

Another measure aimed to safeguard the data subject's rights and freedoms and legitimate interests with regard to solely automated individual decision-making introduced by Article 22 (3) of the GDPR is the right to obtain human intervention. This is especially important for those who believe that human decision-making is still better than an automated one.[445]

First and foremost, the data subject must be informed about this right in order to be able to exercise it. In spite of the fact that it is not explicitly required by the GDPR to apprise the data subject of its rights provided for in Article 22 (3) of the GDPR, the controller must provide a simple way for the data subject to exercise them, including the right to human intervention.[446] Hence, it is recommended, for example, to provide a link to an appeals process at the point a solely automated individual decision is delivered to the data subject, with timescales for the review and a contact point for any queries.[447]

Obviously, any review of such a decision must be carried out by someone who has both the authority and capability to change it. In short, human intervention must be meaningful.[448] It cannot be less than a substantial one, involving an independent judgmental assessment.[449] As recommended by the Article 29 Data Protection Working Party, the reviewer should undertake a thorough critical assessment of all the relevant data, including any additional information provided by the data subject to support the challenge.[450]

Thus the reviewer should have full access to the data in order to assess the validity of the challenge.[451] Specifically, it should be able to determine whether the profile that informs a particular decision is accurate, fair and non-discriminatory. This requires that such an individual has a sufficient level of technical understanding, particularly about the numerous ways in which profiling and automated individual decision-making can lead to inaccuracies, unfairness or discrimination.[452] In fact, as reasonably pointed out by A. Roig, in order to review a solely automated individual

---

445. K. Brennan-Marquez, S.E. Henderson, *Artificial Intelligence and Role-Reversible Judgment*, 109 (2) Journal of Criminal Law and Criminology (2019), pp. 146-148; G. Noto La Diega, *Against the Dehumanisation of Decision-Making*, p. 22. *Conferatur* D. Kamarinou, C. Millard, J. Singh, *Machine Learning with Personal Data*, p. 22.
446. GDPR, Article 12 (2) *ab initio*: 'The controller shall facilitate the exercise of data subject rights under Articles 15 to 22'. *See also* Article 29 Data Protection Working Party, *Guidelines on Automated individual decision-making and Profiling*, p. 27, which underlines this obligation with regard to the right set out in Article 22 (3) of the GDPR. *See also* remarks in §3.02.
447. Article 29 Data Protection Working Party, *Guidelines on Automated individual decision-making and Profiling*, p. 32.
448. G. Noto La Diega, *Against the Dehumanisation of Decision-Making*, p. 22.
449. G. Malgieri, G. Comandé, *Why a Right to Legibility of Automated Decision-Making Exists*, p. 252.
450. Article 29 Data Protection Working Party, *Guidelines on Automated individual decision-making and Profiling*, p. 27.
451. M.E. Kaminski, *The Right to Explanation, Explained*, p. 205.
452. Privacy International, *Data Is Power: Profiling and Automated Decision-Making in GDPR*, p. 14. *See* remarks about key concerns regarding automated individual decision-making in Chapter 1, §1.05.

decision, only a multidisciplinary team with data analysts will be able to detect false positives and discrimination resulting from profiling.[453]

It may not always be feasible for the controller to meet the above recommendations due to practical issues.[454] Human intervention cannot be meaningful if the automated individual decision-making process itself is both complex and opaque.[455] In particular, a human does not have the capacity to assess a decision which was based on large amounts of data and made with the use of highly multidimensional algorithms, such as ML ones. This is because it is simply unable to handle such an array of operational factors.[456] It also requires that the system used to make or inform a decision is sufficiently transparent.

Given that algorithms increasingly outperform humans, it seems counterproductive to put them back in the loop of the decision-making process. Especially since humans are as likely to make spur of the moment decisions as reasoned ones.[457] For these reasons, Kamarinou et al. noted that algorithms might shortly be able to overcome certain key limitations of humans and make decisions which are demonstrably fair.[458] Accordingly, these authors suggest that it might be better, not to have the appeal from a machine to a human, but to have the reverse.[459]

§3.08   RIGHT TO CONTEST THE DECISION

Finally, Article 22 (3) of the GDPR gives the data subject the right to contest a solely automated individual decision. Accordingly, the data subject can aim to reverse or nullify the decision and return to a status where no decision has been made, or to alter its result and receive an alternative decision.[460]

---

453. A. Roig, *Safeguards for the Right Not to Be Subject to a Decision Based Solely on Automated Processing (Article 22 GDPR)*, p. 6.
454. M. Brkan, *Do Algorithms Rule the World? Algorithmic Decision-Making in the Framework of the GDPR and Beyond*, p. 13.
455. Privacy International, *Data Is Power: Profiling and Automated Decision-Making in GDPR*, p. 14; C. Kuner, D.J.B. Svantesson, F.H. Cate, O. Lynskey, C. Millard, *Machine Learning with Personal Data: Is Data Protection Law Smart Enough to Meet the Challenge?*, p. 2. *See* remarks regarding lack of transparency with regard to automated individual decision-making in Chapter 1, §1.05[D].
456. L. Edwards, M. Veale, *Slave to the Algorithm?*, p. 24.
457. *Ibid.*
458. *See* D. Kamarinou, C. Millard, J. Singh, *Machine Learning with Personal Data*, p. 15, who claim that 'machine learning algorithms have the potential to achieve a high level of objectivity and neutrality, whereby learning techniques can be made to disregard factors such as age, race, ethnicity, religion, nationality, sexual orientation, etc., if instructed to do so, more effectively than humans'.
459. *Ibid.*, p. 22, where authors suggest that 'it may already in some contexts make sense to replace the current model, whereby individuals can appeal to a human against a machine decision, with the reverse model whereby individuals would have a right to appeal to a machine against a decision made by a human'.
460. S. Wachter, B. Mittelstadt, C. Russell, *Counterfactual Explanations Without Opening the Black Box*, p. 872.

Article 22 (3) of the GDPR does not specify who, on the part of the controller, should review a solely automated individual decision.[461] In fact, it does not even determine that the data subject contesting such a decision has the right to appeal to a human.[462]

How a solely automated individual decision can be contested depends on whether the safeguards set out in Article 22 (3) of the GDPR, *videlicet* the data subject's right to express its point of view, the right obtain human intervention and the right to contest the decision, are read as a unit which must be invoked together, or as individual rights which may be invoked separately or in any possible combination. As accurately outlined by S. Wachter et al., there are different models possible.[463]

First, if the safeguards are a unit which must be invoked together, human intervention is necessary to issue a new decision. Such an alternative decision could be made by a human without any help of an automated individual decision-making process. Or, a reviewer could make a new decision considering the profile that informs a particular decision supplemented by any additional information provided by the data subject to support the challenge. Given that such decisions are not based on solely automated processing within the meaning of Article 22 (1) of the GDPR, the specific rights of the data subject with regard to such processing, in particular, safeguards set out in Article 22 (3) of the GDPR, do not apply.

Alternatively, if the safeguards may be invoked separately, the data subject may exercise its right to contest the decision without invoking its right to obtain human intervention or its right express its point of view, a new decision could be issued with no human involvement.[464] It might be even appropriate for the algorithms through which decisions are made to be reviewed subsequently by other algorithms designed to facilitate auditing.[465] A human could be required only to monitor the input data and the processing leading up to the adoption of a new solely automated individual decision. Consequently, in this scenario, the specific rights of the data subject with regard to such processing, in particular, safeguards set out in Article 22 (3) of the GDPR, apply to the new decision as well.

§3.09 THE EUROPEAN UNION OR MEMBER STATE LAW SAFEGUARDS

As already outlined above, solely automated individual decision-making is allowed if it is authorised by the EU or Member State law to which the controller is subject.[466] It is important to note that safeguards set out in Article 22 (3) of the GDPR, *videlicet* the data

---

461. M. Brkan, *Do Algorithms Rule the World? Algorithmic Decision-Making in the Framework of the GDPR and Beyond*, p. 13.
462. D. Kamarinou, C. Millard, J. Singh, *Machine Learning with Personal Data*, p. 15.
463. S. Wachter, B. Mittelstadt, C. Russell, *Counterfactual Explanations Without Opening the Black Box*, p. 873.
464. *Conferatur* M. Almada., *Human Intervention in Automated Decision-Making*, pp. 1-10, who argues that 'current legislation does not allow for the complete removal of the human from the review loop, but there is no a priori ban against human-supervised use of automatic review tools, as long as the process does not become solely based on automated processing'.
465. D. Kamarinou, C. Millard, J. Singh, *Machine Learning with Personal Data*, p. 15.
466. GDPR, Article 22 (2) (b). *See* remarks in Chapter 2, §2.06[B].

subject's right to express its point of view, the right to obtain human intervention and the right to contest the decision do not apply to solely automated individual decision-making permitted under this exemption. In order to mitigate this, Article 22 (2) (b) of the GDPR mandates the law in question to lay down suitable measures to safeguard the data subject's rights and freedoms and legitimate interests.

The said provision does not specify what kind of safeguards must be included in EU or Member State law authorising solely automated individual decision-making. Hence, the law in question may lay down the exact same safeguards as those set out in Article 22 (3) of the GDPR, especially since they already considered to be 'suitable' by the legislator.

Alternatively, it may include other types of safeguards that consider the specificity of the solely automated individual decision-making that they allow. Despite this possibility, most Member States provide just the three safeguards set out in Article 22 (3) of the GDPR, that is, the data subject's right to express its point of view, the right to obtain human intervention, the right to contest the decision in law implementing the GDPR with relatively slight variations.[467] Notwithstanding the above, there are some Member States which decided to lay down different safeguards. For instance, Polish law implementing the GDPR in sectoral law includes the right to receiving appropriate explanations as to the basis of the decision taken in certain cases, in the field of credit and insurance.[468]

§3.10   LIMITATIONS TO ALGORITHMIC TRANSPARENCY

Considering that automated individual decision-making cannot be assumed to be fair and accurate, opening up its black box, or at least its lid, to substantiate its outputs is unavoidable. This is what is envisaged by algorithmic transparency. It gives the data subject insight into the internal decision-making process of algorithms. In the GDPR, it is provided, to a limited extent, by the right to be informed and the right of access. In addition to that, the purported right to explanation remains relevant to this concept as well.

Undoubtedly, it is often intentional on the part of the controller to keep its decision policy, as well as the algorithms, which implement it, undisclosed for reasons of business confidentiality or state secrecy.[469] Especially when a solely automated

---

467. For detailed analysis of Member State law which authorises solely automated individual decision-making as per Article 22 (2) (b) of the GDPR, *see* G. Malgieri, *Right to Explanation and Other 'Suitable Safeguards'*, pp. 1-21.
468. Articles 46 (4), 46 (6), 138 (6) (b), Polish Ustawa o zmianie niektórych ustaw w związku z zapewnieniem stosowania rozporządzenia Parlamentu Europejskiego i Rady (UE) 2016/679 z dnia 27 kwietnia 2016 r. w sprawie ochrony osób fizycznych w związku z przetwarzaniem danych osobowych i w sprawie swobodnego przepływu takich danych oraz uchylenia dyrektywy 95/46/WE (ogólne rozporządzenie o ochronie danych) z dnia 21 lutego 2019 r. (Dz.U. z 2019 r. poz. 730).
469. J. Burrell, *How the Machine 'Thinks'*, p. 1.

individual decision is a commercial one, there is the controller's legitimate interest in guarding the underlying decision policy or protecting the proprietary algorithms, which may be incompatible with full transparency. This can help to prevent deliberate gaming of the system by the data subjects.[470] Not to mention that the controller's competitors could gain the knowledge allowing them to reverse engineer its decision-making model otherwise.[471] Whereas in other cases, that is, when such a decision is made by a public entity, disclosure may be limited or even prohibited at all. Despite the above considerations, there is an undeniable social and ethical value of algorithmic transparency. It is submitted that algorithmic transparency to an extent it is mandated by the GDPR can be offered by the controller without completely opening the algorithmic black box.

Of course, if the controller intends to limit the information, which must be provided to the data subject as required by Articles 13 (2) (f), 14 (2) (g), 15 (1) (h) of the GDPR, it may use intellectual property rights or technical obstacles as pretexts to do so. However, if they were challenged, some of them may prove unfounded. Below, both legal limitations and technical obstacles to algorithmic transparency in the GDPR are analysed.

[A]   Intellectual Property Rights

First and foremost, among the limitations to algorithmic transparency, there are intellectual property rights. This is acknowledged in Recital 63 of the GDPR, which provides some protection for controllers concerned about revealing trade secrets or intellectual property, which may be particularly relevant in relation to profiling and subsequent automated individual decision-making. It states that the right of access can be limited by the rights of others, including the controller and concerns relating to trade secrets or intellectual property.[472] Thus, intellectual property rights allow the controller to build legal black-boxes around the algorithms used in the automated individual decision-making process.

However, the controller cannot rely on those as an excuse to deny access or refuse to provide information to the data subject. Because of this specification, the information provided to the data subject can be reduced, but never totally denied.[473]

---

470. J.A. Kroll, et al., *Accountable Algorithms*, p. 658; J. Bambauer, T. Zarsky, *The Algorithm Game*, pp. 1-47; E. Bayamlıoglu, *Contesting Automated Decisions*, p. 437.
471. J. Kingston, *Using Artificial Intelligence to Support Compliance with the General Data Protection Regulation*, p. 440.
472. GDPR, Recital 63: '[…] That right should not adversely affect the rights or freedoms of others, including trade secrets or intellectual property and in particular the copyright protecting the software. However, the result of those considerations should not be a refusal to provide all information to the data subject. […]'.
473. G. Malgieri, *Trade Secrets v Personal Data: A Possible Solution for Balancing Rights*, 6 (2) International Data Privacy Law (2016), p. 105.

[1]   Patent

Algorithms are excluded from patentability under Article 52 (2) (c) and (3) of the European Patent Convention if claimed as such.[474] It is considered that abstract algorithms do not belong to the technical field, so they are not eligible for a patent.[475] The technical character of the algorithm can only be recognised when it serves a technical purpose. Typically, automated individual decision-making does not achieve any further technical effect beyond the normal physical interactions between the algorithms used and the computer. Hence, unquestionably, patent protection may not hamper algorithmic transparency.

[2]   Copyright

Even though algorithms generally qualify as a copyrightable subject matter under the international copyright conventions, copyright protection extends only to their expression, i.e., primarily their source code and object code.[476] To the extent that algorithms comprise ideas and principles such as functions, logic, or system design, those ideas and principles are not protected. In accordance with the firmly established legislation and case law of the Member States, not to mention the international copyright

---

474. Convention on the Grant of European Patents of 5 October 1973, United Nations Treaty Series vol. 1065, pp. 199 et seq., Article 52:

   (1) European patents shall be granted for any inventions, in all fields of technology, provided that they are new, involve an inventive step and are susceptible of industrial application.

   (2) The following in particular shall not be regarded as inventions within the meaning of paragraph 1:

     (a) discoveries, scientific theories and mathematical methods;

     (b) aesthetic creations;

     (c) schemes, rules and methods for performing mental acts, playing games or doing business, and *programs for computers*;

     (d) presentations of information.

   (3) Paragraph 2 shall exclude the patentability of the subject-matter or activities referred to therein only to the extent to which a European patent application or European patent relates to such subject-matter or activities as such [italics added].

475. European Patent Office, Guidelines for Examination, point 3.6 Programs for computers, available at: https://www.epo.org/law-practice/legal-texts/html/guidelines/e/g_ii_3_6.htm, accessed 1 May 2019. *See also* European Patent Office, Opinion G 0003/08 (Programs for computers) of 12 May 2010, ECLI:EP:BA:2010:G000308.20100512, points 13.5-13.5.1, pp. 53-54.

476. Agreement on Trade-Related Aspects of Intellectual Property Rights of 15 April 1994, Marrakesh Agreement Establishing the World Trade Organization, Annex 1C, 1869 United Nations Treaty Series 299, 33 I.L.M. 1197, (hereinafter 'TRIPS'), Article 10 (1): 'Computer programs, whether in source or object code, shall be protected as literary works under the Berne Convention (1971)'; World Intellectual Property Organization Copyright Treaty, adopted in Geneva on 20 December 1996, TRT/WCT/001, (hereinafter 'WCT'), Article 4 'Computer programs are protected as literary works within the meaning of Article 2 of the Berne Convention. Such protection applies to computer programs, whatever may be the mode or form of their expression'.

conventions, only the expression of those ideas and principles is to be protected by copyright.[477]

This basic principle of copyright is echoed by Article 1 (2) and Recital 11 of Directive 2009/24 on the legal protection of computer programs, which affirm that only the expression of a computer program is protected and that ideas and principles which underlie any element of a program are not protected by copyright.[478] This leads to a conclusion that copyright is not a satisfactory form of protection where it is the idea behind the algorithm, which is the commercially valuable element.[479] Nonetheless, it allows the controllers not to disclose algorithms used in automated individual decision-making.

In addition to that, Directive 2009/24 allows a person having the right to use a computer program of a computer program 'to observe, study or test the functioning of the program in order to determine the ideas and principles which underlie any element of the program'.[480] In practice, this means that a user of a computer program is allowed to determine the functioning of the algorithm and, if it is technically possible, to reveal the importance of particular factors involved in automated individual decision-making. Nonetheless, it requires considerable skills to open the algorithmic black box by observing the software that implements it. In most cases, it would be necessary to ask a third party to do this on behalf of the lawful user of the computer program.[481] It remains to be seen whether said third parties would qualify as lawful users.[482] If not, this exception would not be useful in most of the cases.

[3]   Trade Secrets

Algorithmic transparency ought to be balanced with the trade secrets of the holders, which are protected against misappropriation by Directive 2016/943.[483] The general rule is that the unauthorised acquisition, use, or disclosure of trade secrets is

---

477. TRIPS, Article 9 (2): 'Copyright protection shall extend to expressions and not to ideas, procedures, methods of operation or mathematical concepts as such'; WCT, Article 4: 'Copyright protection extends to expressions and not to ideas, procedures, methods of operation or mathematical concepts as such'.
478. Directive 2009/24/EC of the European Parliament and of the Council of 23 April 2009 on the legal protection of computer programs, Official Journal of the European Union L 111, 5 May 2009, pp. 16-22, (hereinafter 'Directive 2009/24').
479. G. Noto La Diega, *Against the Dehumanisation of Decision-Making*, p. 14.
480. Directive 2009/24, Article 5 (3): 'The person having a right to use a copy of a computer program shall be entitled, without the authorisation of the rightholder, to observe, study or test the functioning of the program in order to determine the ideas and principles which underlie any element of the program if he does so while performing any of the acts of loading, displaying, running, transmitting or storing the program which he is entitled to do'.
481. G. Noto La Diega, *Against the Dehumanisation of Decision-Making*, p. 16.
482. This issue has not been definitively settled in jurisprudence. *See* Judgment of the Court (Grand Chamber) of 2 May 2012, SAS Institute Inc. v World Programming Ltd, Case C-406/10, ECLI:EU:C:2012:259.
483. Directive (EU) 2016/943 of the European Parliament and of the Council of 8 June 2016 on the protection of undisclosed know-how and business information (trade secrets) against their unlawful acquisition, use and disclosure (Text with EEA relevance), Official Journal of the European Union L 157, 15 June 2016, pp. 1-18, (hereinafter 'Directive 2016/943').

unlawful.[484] Under this directive, the definition of a trade secret covers any information which is secret and which derives commercial value from being secret and which has been subject to reasonable steps to maintain its secrecy.[485] Trade secrets are one of the most commonly used forms of protection of intellectual creation and innovative know-how by businesses.[486] Certainly, they have an important role in protecting an automated individual decision-making process, in particular, the proprietary algorithms, which allow the trade secret holders to achieve a competitive advantage over its competitors.[487] Classic examples of such proprietary algorithms, which are subject to trade secrecy are Google search and Facebook news feed.[488]

As a general rule, Recital 34 of Directive 2016/943 states: 'this Directive respects the fundamental rights and observes the principles recognised in particular by the Charter [of Fundamental Rights of the European Union], notably the right to respect for private and family life, the right to protection of personal data'. Moreover, Recital 35 of the said directive indicates that: 'It is important that the rights to respect for private and family life and to protection of personal data of any person whose personal data may be processed by the trade secret holder when taking steps to protect a trade secret, or of any person involved in legal proceedings concerning the unlawful acquisition, use or disclosure of trade secrets under this Directive, and whose personal data are processed, be respected. [...] Thus, this Directive should not affect the rights and obligations laid down in Directive 95/46/EC, in particular, the rights of the data subject to access his or her personal data being processed and to obtain the rectification, erasure or blocking of the data where it is incomplete or inaccurate and, where appropriate, the obligation to process sensitive data in accordance with Article 8(5) of Directive 95/46/EC'. From the above quoted recitals, it seems clear that if a conflict should arise between the privacy rights of individuals and trade secret rights of businesses, privacy rights should prevail on trade secret rights.[489]

As a matter of fact, this conclusion is premature. As already signalled, Recital 63 of the GDPR specifies that the right of access should not adversely affect the rights or freedoms of others, including trade secrets.[490] This means that, on the one hand, the prevalence of trade secrets on data protection rights is confirmed; on the other hand, the prevalence of data protection rights on trade secrets is confirmed too. This leads to

---

484. Directive 2016/943, Article 4.
485. Directive 2016/943, Article 2 (1): 'trade secret means information which meets all of the following requirements: (a) it is secret in the sense that it is not, as a body or in the precise configuration and assembly of its components, generally known among or readily accessible to persons within the circles that normally deal with the kind of information in question; (b) it has commercial value because it is secret; (c) it has been subject to reasonable steps under the circumstances, by the person lawfully in control of the information, to keep it secret'. *See also* Directive 2016/943, Recital 14.
486. Directive 2016/943, Recital 3.
487. M. Perel, N. Elkin-Koren, *Black Box Tinkering*, p. 193.
488. G. Noto La Diega, *Against the Dehumanisation of Decision-Making*, p. 12.
489. G. Malgieri, *Trade Secrets v Personal Data*, p. 104.
490. GDPR, Recital 63: '[...] That right should not adversely affect the rights or freedoms of others, including trade secrets or intellectual property and in particular the copyright protecting the software. However, the result of those considerations should not be a refusal to provide all information to the data subject. [...]'.

a conclusion that none prevails a priori over the other.[491] Such non-prevalence conclusion is not a definitive solution to balance rights, but it allows to solve conflicts between rights on a case-by-case basis.[492] Interestingly, the use of an adverb 'adversely' in the preamble to the GDPR indicates that the right of access can affect trade secrets, but not 'adversely'.[493] This itself would suggest a preference for data protection rights.

Furthermore, Article 23 (1) (i) of the GDPR provides the possibility for the EU and the Member States to restrict all the scope of *inter alia* the right of access when such a restriction respects the essence of the fundamental rights and freedoms and is a necessary and proportionate measure in a democratic society to safeguard the protection of the data subject or the rights and freedoms of others.[494] Hence, it might imply that the GDPR could accept a prevalence of trade secrets on data protection rights. Nevertheless, it has to be stressed that it is only a possibility for the EU or the Member States. Additionally, it has to be considered whether it is necessary to restrict the right of access, in particular, its provision to provide meaningful information about the logic involved in solely automated individual decision-making, to safeguard the protection of the data subject or the rights and freedoms of others.

It is argued that it is not. Transparency and trade secrets are not irreconcilable. As already stated, it is not obligatory to disclose the algorithms used in automated individual decision-making, which could constitute trade secrets. On the contrary, it is sufficient to provide the data subject with details of main characteristics considered in reaching the decision and their relevance to allow the data subject to understand the reasons for the decision. Hence, the disclosure is minimised to the general information which is not covered by trade secret protection, and it is not 'necessary' within the meaning of Article 23 (1) (i) of the GDPR to introduce any restrictions with regard to the right of access, specifically its provision to provide meaningful information about the logic involved in solely automated individual decision-making. Anyhow, any such restrictions must be necessary and also proportionate to safeguard the protection of the data subject or the rights and freedoms of others.

All in all, specific transparency provisions concerning solely automated individual decision-making contained both in the right to be informed, and the right of access should not be subject to any restrictions because they do not adversely affect the trade secrets of the controllers, as per Recital 63 of the GDPR. The above rights should

---

491. G. Malgieri, G. Comandé, *Why a Right to Legibility of Automated Decision-Making Exists*, p. 263.
492. *See* detailed discussion: G. Malgieri, *Trade Secrets v Personal Data*, pp. 102-116.
493. *Ibid.*, p. 104.
494. GDPR, Article 23 (1) (i): 'Union or Member State law to which the data controller or processor is subject may restrict by way of a legislative measure the scope of the obligations and rights provided for in Articles 12 to 22 and Article 34, as well as Article 5 in so far as its provisions correspond to the rights and obligations provided for in Articles 12 to 22, when such a restriction respects the essence of the fundamental rights and freedoms and is a necessary and proportionate measure in a democratic society to safeguard: (i) the protection of the data subject or the rights and freedoms of others'.

be interpreted in the spirit of general legal favour for data protection rights that should reduce the impact of trade secrets protection.[495]

[B]   Technical Obstacles

Besides the legal constraints described above, there are also technical obstacles to algorithmic transparency. They relate preeminently to the right to explanation, assuming that the GDPR mandates it at all, but they remain relevant to the right to be informed and the right of access, as well.

Solely automated individual decision-making processes are increasingly complex, especially when they use ML algorithms, which work fundamentally differently from simple algorithms with hand-written linear decision-making rules.[496] Automated individual decision-making systems which use ML algorithms are uniquely in danger of defying any human understanding.[497] Even 'ordinary' algorithms may be intricate and practically inscrutable for an average data subject.[498] Because of high-dimensionality of data and complexity of the algorithms, it is inherently problematic to interpret how each of the numerous, sometimes even innumerable, data points contributes to a particular decision, as it could be required by the purported right to explanation.[499] Automated individual decision-making systems, which use ML algorithms, are opaque instead of transparent. In some cases, it may even be difficult to provide the data subject the meaningful information about the logic involved in the solely automated individual decision-making process in general, as required by Articles 13 (2) (f), 14 (2) (g) and Article 15 (1) (h) of the GDPR.

Besides this lack of transparency, there is also a lack of predictability and uniformity of the decision policy implemented by ML algorithms. As a matter of fact, such algorithms can find patterns in the available dataset and develop a suitable reaction or strategy with regard to these patterns autonomously, without any further programming.[500] They are able to make solely automated individual decisions independently of pre-set rules and parameters, which is especially useful when there is a lot of personal data to be analysed but makes them unforeseeable at the same time.[501] ML algorithms build their own knowledge, and they produce their own decision-making rules, which may be reconfigured by the algorithms themselves, without human intervention. As a result, automated individual decisions produced by ML algorithms are challenging to predict beforehand, as well as to explain afterwards. Use of ML

---

495. G. Malgieri, G. Comandé, *Why a Right to Legibility of Automated Decision-Making Exists*, pp. 243, 264.
496. The notion of ML is explained in greater detail above in Chapter 1, §1.02[H][3]. *See also* Chapter 1, §1.05[A].
497. A.D. Selbst, J. Powles, *Meaningful Information and the Right to Explanation*, p. 233. *See also* detailed analysis in: J. Burrell, *How the Machine 'Thinks'*, pp. 1-12.
498. R. Kitchin, *Thinking Critically about and Researching Algorithms*, pp. 20-21; D. Kamarinou, C. Millard, J. Singh, *Machine Learning with Personal Data*, p. 19.
499. B. Mittelstadt, P. Allo, M. Taddeo, S. Wachter, L. Floridi, *The Ethics of Algorithms: Mapping the Debate*, p. 6.
500. J. Kingston, *Using Artificial Intelligence to Support Compliance with the General Data Protection Regulation*, p. 432.
501. M. Perel, N. Elkin-Koren, *Black Box Tinkering*, p. 181.

algorithms, which operate with some degree of autonomy, makes the rationale of decision-making intrinsically opaque, even for those who develop and employ them.[502] The research on interpretable ML algorithms in the context of automated individual decision-making is only in the early stages.[503]

Moreover, ML algorithms are inherently based on discovering reliable associations and correlations to aid in accurate out-of-sample prediction, with no concern for causal reasoning or explanation beyond the statistical sense.[504] There is a clear mismatch between mathematical optimisation in the high-dimensionality characteristic of ML algorithms and the demands of human scale reasoning and styles of semantic interpretation.[505] This inherent feature of ML algorithms can thus severely inhibit the use of special rights of the data subject with regard to solely automated individual decision-making, not to mention the purported right to explanation.[506]

§3.11 INTERIM CONCLUSIONS

Specific provisions of the GDPR aimed at the protection of natural persons with regard to solely automated individual decision-making reflect European scepticism towards this type of processing. Therefore, they establish several special rights of the data subject, which aim to address concerns regarding automated individual decision-making, notably the right to be informed, the right of access, the right to express a point of view, the right to human intervention and the right to contest the decision. The purpose of these special rights is to create a version of an algorithmic due process that protects the data subject.[507]

---

502. M. Hildebrandt, *The New Imbroglio: Living with Machine Algorithms*, [in:] *The Art of Ethics in the Information Society*, L.A.W. Janssens (ed.), Amsterdam University Press 2016, p. 57.
503. *See* for example: D.K. Citron, F. Pasquale, *The Scored Society*, pp. 1-33; A. Datta, S. Sen, Y. Zick, *Algorithmic Transparency via Quantitative Input Influence*, paper presented at the 37th IEEE Symposium on Security and Privacy, San Jose, United States of America, published by IEEE Symposium on Security and Privacy, 23-25 May 2016, pp. 598-617; S. Wachter, B. Mittelstadt, C. Russell, *Counterfactual Explanations Without Opening the Black Box*, pp. 841-887; M. Gleicher, *A Framework for Considering Comprehensibility in Modeling*, 4 (2) Big Data (2016), pp. 75-88; L. Edwards, M. Veale, *Slave to the Algorithm?*, pp. 18-84; J. Burrell, *How the Machine 'Thinks'*, pp. 1-12; R. Kitchin, *Thinking Critically about and Researching Algorithms*, pp. 14-29; B. Cowgill, C. Tucker, *Algorithmic Bias: A Counterfactual Perspective*, Working Paper: NSF Trustworthy Algorithms, December 2017; Information Commissioner's Office, *Big data, artificial intelligence, machine learning and data protection*, Guidelines of 1 March 2017, version 2.2, paragraphs 189-197, pp. 86-89; N. Diakopoulos, S. Friedler, *How to Hold Algorithms Accountable*, MIT Technology Review, available at: https://www.technologyreview.com/s/602933/how-to-hold-algorithms-accountable/, accessed 1 June 2019.
504. B. Goodman, S. Flaxman, *European Union Regulations on Algorithmic Decision Making and 'a Right to an Explanation'*, p. 55; J. Kingston, *Using Artificial Intelligence to Support Compliance with the General Data Protection Regulation*, p. 432.
505. J. Burrell, *How the Machine 'Thinks'*, p. 1.
506. *See* reference 116.
507. *See* M.E. Kaminski, *The Right to Explanation, Explained*, p. 198. *See also* D.K. Citron, F. Pasquale, *The Scored Society*, pp. 1-33, who accentuate the importance of due process in automated decision-making.

However, they do not build a forceful fortress, which could care for individuals with regard to this type of processing.[508] These special rights are applicable to a very narrow range of cases meeting all of the requirements set out in Article 22 (1) of the GDPR. Vice versa, if an automated individual decision does not meet all of the above criteria, it is not constrained by the provisions on special rights of the data subject. Additionally, Article 22 (3) of the GDPR specifies that the preeminent safeguards apply only if the processing is conducted under Article 22 (2) (a) or (c) of the GDPR.[509] Thus, if solely automated individual decision-making is authorised by the EU or Member State law to which the controller is subject, the data subject does not have the said rights.[510] Although the law in question must lay down suitable measures to safeguard the data subject's rights and freedoms and legitimate interests, in these cases, the level of protection of the data subject may significantly diverge.

The scope of the special rights of the data subject is far from explicit. The information which must be provided to the data subject's under the right to be informed and the right of access, that is, meaningful information about the logic involved in solely automated individual decision-making, as well as the significance and the envisaged consequences of such processing for the data subject, is vague and, likely, limited. Although to some extent it may be useful for the data subject to invoke its special rights, in particular, the right to human intervention or the right to contest the decision, it is unlikely to provide significant remedial utility in instances where the discrimination involved is only observable at a statistical scale. Although the data subject must be informed about its rights in order to be able to exercise them, there is no explicit obligation of the controller to inform the data subject about the right not to be subject to a solely automated individual decision and its safeguards, that is the right express point of view, the right to human intervention and the right to contest the decision. Not to mention that, despite much debate, a consensus has not yet emerged in the legal doctrine concerning the supposed right to an explanation of a particular solely automated individual decision. In addition to that, some of the special rights of the data subject, in particular, the right to be informed and the right of access, may be limited by intellectual property rights. Even though in some cases such claims of the controllers may be unfounded, it should be noted that questioning them by the data subject could be both time consuming and costly. This means that they may prove to be effective limitations to algorithmic transparency in spite of lack of their legitimacy. In practice, these special rights of the data subject are further weakened also by technical obstacles to their effective implementation, particularly when applied to complex solely automated individual decision-making systems.

As the ambiguities outlined in this chapter indicate, the special rights of the data subjects with regard to solely automated individual decision-making can be a weak or powerful mechanism depending on its eventual legal interpretation. The effectiveness

---

508. M. Brkan, *Do Algorithms Rule the World? Algorithmic Decision-Making in the Framework of the GDPR and Beyond*, pp. 1, 7.

509. That is the right express point of view, the right to human intervention and the right to contest the decision. Whereas the right to be informed and the right of access apply to all three exemptions allowing solely automated individual decision-making.

510. GDPR, Article 22 (2) (b).

of the new framework will largely be determined by supervisory authorities, the European Data Protection Board, national courts as well as the Court of Justice of the European Union and their future judgments. As it stands, transparent and accountable automated individual decision-making is not yet guaranteed by the GDPR, nor is the right to an explanation of specific decisions forthcoming.[511]

Having in mind the above, here are the key *de lege ferenda* recommendations that could offer the data subjects greater protection with regard to solely automated individual decision-making. First, one of the main transparency gaps should be closed, meaning the controllers should be under an explicit obligation to inform the data subject about the right not to be subject to a solely automated individual decision and its safeguards, that is, the right express point of view, the right to human intervention and the right to contest the decision. Second, the scope of the information which must be provided to the data subject by the controller under the right to be informed and the right of access, that is meaningful information about the logic involved in solely automated individual decision-making, as well as the significance and the envisaged consequences of such processing for the data subject, should be clarified to ensure that information provided to the data subjects by the controllers is useful and not overly vague. At a minimum, it should include factors taken into account for the decision-making process and on their respective 'weight' on an aggregate level. Otherwise, the rights to contest a decision, to obtain human intervention or to express views granted in Article 22 (3) of the GDPR may be meaningless.[512] Third, if a right to explanation is intended as suggested in Recital 71 of the GDPR, it should be explicitly added to a legally binding Article 22 (3) of the GDPR.[513] Fourth, the European Data Protection Board should issue guidelines, recommendations and best practices for further specifying the criteria and conditions for automated individual decisions based on Article 22 (2) (b) of the GDPR in order to ensure that protection of the data subjects with regard to solely automated individual decision-making is as consistent as possible. Finally, the research on interpretable algorithms, in particular, ML ones, in the context of automated individual decision-making should be supported. It should enable the controllers to provide meaningful information about the logic involved in such processing to the data subjects without adversely affecting its rights, especially intellectual property rights.

While the special rights of the data subject give rise to the discussion concerning the protection of natural persons with regard to solely automated individual decision-making, currently there is no guarantee that the protection thus provided will be extensive.[514] Reliance on the individual rights of the data subject places a primary and heavy onus on them to challenge bad decisions.[515] In particular, discrimination may only become apparent when looking at the corpus of the decisions as a whole, something that will not happen by virtue of individual rights invoked by the data

---

511. S. Wachter, B. Mittelstadt, L. Floridi, *Why a Right to Explanation of Automated Decision-Making Does Not Exist*, p. 47.
512. *Ibid.*, p. 31.
513. *Ibid.*, p. 43.
514. R. Williams, *Rethinking Deference for Algorithmic Decision-Making*, p. 17.
515. L. Edwards, M. Veale, *Enslaving the Algorithm*, pp. 50-51.

subjects.[516] For these reasons, the next chapter explores general provisions of the GDPR, which are relevant to automated individual decision-making and could provide protection to individuals with regard to such processing.

---

516. *Ibid. See also* S. Wachter, B. Mittelstadt, C. Russell, *Counterfactual Explanations Without Opening the Black Box*, p. 853, who explain that the best tools for uncovering systematic biases are likely to be based upon large-scale statistical analysis and not upon explanations of individual decisions.

CHAPTER 4

General Provisions Relevant to Automated Individual Decision-Making

§4.01 INTRODUCTORY REMARKS

General provisions of the GDPR play an important role in governing automated individual decision-making.[517] Therefore, this chapter contains an analysis of the fundamental data protection principles, which are the most relevant to such processing. These are lawfulness, fairness and transparency; purpose limitation; data minimisation; accuracy and storage limitation principles. These universal principles stood the test of time for decades, and they can be applied in different technical, economic and social contexts.[518] Subsequently, they remain pertinent to automated individual decision-making.[519]

Furthermore, this chapter elaborates on a number of general provisions of the GDPR which aim to aid the controller in building better processing operations, *inter alia*, automated individual decision-making systems, from the beginning, as opposed to remodeling them afterwards. These are provisions on data protection by design and by default; DPIA; certification and codes of conduct. Although they do not give the data subject any individual rights, they protect it nonetheless, and they may even do so more effectively.

As already stressed above, the specific provisions outlined in Chapter 2 apply only to solely automated individual decision-making within the meaning of Article 22 (1) of the GDPR. Whereas this is an overview of the general provisions which are the

---

517. *See also* L. Edwards, M. Veale, *Slave to the Algorithm?*, p. 19; M.E. Kaminski, *The Right to Explanation, Explained*, p. 197.
518. *See,* in particular, Article 5 of the GDPR of the Convention for the Protection of Individuals with regard to Automatic Processing of Personal Data of 28 January 1981, European Treaty Series No. 108, which establishes largely analogous principles relating to processing of personal data.
519. C. Kuner, D.J.B. Svantesson, F.H. Cate, O. Lynskey, C. Millard, *Machine Learning with Personal Data: Is Data Protection Law Smart Enough to Meet the Challenge?*, p. 1.

most relevant to automated individual decision-making and apply to all such systems. Finally, this chapter contains interim conclusions.

§4.02   DATA PROTECTION PRINCIPLES

[A]   Lawfulness, Fairness and Transparency Principle

The first fundamental data protection principle that 'personal data shall be processed lawfully, fairly and in a transparent manner in relation to the data subject' is set out in Article 5 (1) (a) of the GDPR. As commented by L. Bygrave, this principle 'embraces and generates the other core principles of data protection laws'.[520] Having regard to the concerns regarding automated individual decision-making, this principle is particularly important in relation to such processing.[521] Its meaning as well as its significance to this type of processing are explained below.

First of all, personal data must be processed lawfully. This requirement is interpreted extensively, which means that the controller, which processes personal data, must respect all applicable legal requirements, including, but not limited to, data protection law.[522]

Second, personal data must be processed fairly. The notion of fairness is also understood broadly, and it refers to the criterion of social acceptance of personal data processing operations, which cannot be equated with lawfulness.[523] Therefore, it implies contemplating the legitimate expectations of the data subject.[524]

Third, this principle mandates the controller to process personal data in a transparent manner in relation to the data subject. The meaning of transparency is delineated in Recital 39 of the GDPR. It clarifies that it should be transparent to natural persons that personal data concerning them is collected, used, consulted or otherwise processed and to what extent the personal data is or will be processed. It further states that the principle of transparency requires that any information and communication relating to the processing of that personal data be easily accessible and easy to understand, and that clear and plain language be used. It also adds that this principle concerns, in particular, information to the data subjects on the identity of the controller and the purposes of the processing and further information to ensure fair and transparent processing in respect of the natural persons concerned and their right to

---

520. L. Bygrave, *Data Protection Law: Approaching Its Rationale, Logic and Limits*, Kluwer Law International 2002, p. 58.
521. *See* extensive remarks in Chapter 1, §1.05.
522. *See*, in particular, Article 6 of the GDPR, which states that processing shall be lawful only if and to the extent that at least one of the hypotheses it lists applies.
523. P. Drobek, *Commentary on Article 5 of the GDPR*, [in:] *RODO. Ogólne rozporządzenie o ochronie danych. Komentarz*, E. Bielak-Jomaa, D. Lubasz (eds), Warsaw 2018, LEX.
524. Information Commissioner's Office, *Automated decision-making and profiling*, Guidelines of 5 June 2018, p. 20. Therein, the Information Commissioner's Office recommends the controller to consider what do people reasonably expect it to do with their data. It provides an example of a retailer analysing loyalty card data to decide what new products to suggest to a customer, which might be an expected activity and an example of analysing someone's social media posts to reject them for a job, refuse a loan, or increase their insurance, which might not be.

obtain confirmation and communication of personal data concerning them which is being processed. Last but not least, it recommends that natural persons should be made aware of risks, rules, safeguards and rights in relation to the processing of personal data and how to exercise their rights in relation to such processing.

Accordingly, transparency concerns three central areas: (i) provision of information to the data subject related to fair processing; (ii) how the controller communicates with the data subject in relation to its rights under the GDPR; and (iii) how the controller facilitates the exercise by the data subject of its rights.[525] The wording of the preamble referred to above clearly indicates that the transparency principle is further developed in other provisions of the GDPR, in particular, the right to be informed and the right of access, as well as the general provision concerning transparent information, communication and modalities for the exercise of the rights of the data subject.[526] All in all, transparency is considered to be an overreaching obligation under the GDPR aiming to engender the trust of the data subject in the processing of its personal data by enabling it to understand and, if necessary, challenge these processes by exercising its data subject's rights.[527]

Generally, the processes of profiling and the subsequent automated individual decision-making are far from transparent for the data subject, which may find it challenging to understand the complex techniques involved in such processing.[528] Although to a certain extent, it is mitigated by the aforesaid provisions concerning the right to be informed and the right of access and modalities for the exercise of the rights of the data subject, lack of transparency of automated individual decision-making remains a serious concern.[529] Accordingly, such processes are problematic to factor in the transparency principle.

In addition to that, under Article 5 (1) (a) of the GDPR, processing does not only have to be transparent but also lawful and fair. Despite that, it is widely acknowledged that automated individual decision-making systems can be discriminatory for numerous reasons.[530] In particular, profiling, which often precedes automated individual decision-making, can be discriminatory, and as a result lead to denying individuals access to employment opportunities, credit or insurance, or targeting them with excessively risky or costly financial products.[531] Such systems do not meet the requirement of lawfulness or fairness.

It could be argued that whether the decision is ultimately fair for the data subject is a question for antidiscrimination laws and not, principally, for data protection law. However, automated individual decision-making involves the processing of personal data, so data protection law applies as well and, consequently, its fundamental

---

525. Article 29 Data Protection Working Party, *Guidelines on Transparency under Regulation 2016/679*, paragraph 1, p. 4.
526. GDPR, Articles 12-15.
527. M. Brkan, *Do Algorithms Rule the World? Algorithmic Decision-Making in the Framework of the GDPR and Beyond*, p. 14.
528. Lack of transparency of automated decision-making is described in Chapter 1, §1.05[D].
529. *See* reference 526.
530. *See* remarks in Chapter 1, §1.05[C].
531. Article 29 Data Protection Working Party, *Guidelines on Automated individual decision-making and Profiling*, pp. 9-10.

principle of fairness must be complied with by the controller.[532] The above conclusion is confirmed by the wording of Recital 71 of the GDPR, which provides guidelines on how automated individual decision-making should be conducted in order to fulfil the fairness principle. Markedly, it states that that the controller should use appropriate mathematical or statistical procedures for the profiling along with other measures, in a manner that takes account of the potential risks involved for the interests and rights of the data subject, and prevent, *inter alia*, discriminatory effects on natural persons.[533] Therefore, the GDPR, to a certain extent, assumes the role of antidiscrimination law and accepts it may protect the data subjects from discrimination.

Currently, creating automated individual decision-making systems as to which there is no risk of discrimination is problematic. Even assuming that algorithms do not take into account personal data regarding legally protected characteristics in the automated individual decision-making process, they may still discriminate based on their correlative proxies instead.[534] Therefore, this solution is ineffective, as it does not provide sufficient protection of individuals against discrimination. Whereas assuming that algorithms omit not only personal data regarding legally protected characteristics but also any variables with which they are correlated may make the resulting automated individual decision-making systems virtually useless.[535] As explained by B. Goodman and S. Flaxman, this is because of the fact that correlations can become increasingly complex and difficult to detect in large datasets, which makes the task of exhaustively identifying and disregarding personal data correlated with legally protected characteristics a priori may be unfeasible.[536] Accordingly, the problem of algorithmic discrimination requires further research in order to find appropriate solutions.[537]

Besides, to ensure that the automated individual decisions are fair, they should be made under the same decision policy consistently applied in each case.[538] Such a decision policy should be determined before knowing the inputs and each decision is reproducible from the particular decision policy and the inputs for that decision. This stands in contradiction with the use of ML algorithms, whose decision-making logic is

---

532. D. Kamarinou, C. Millard, J. Singh, *Machine Learning with Personal Data*, p. 11.
533. GDPR, Recital 71: '[…] In order to ensure fair and transparent processing in respect of the data subject, taking into account the specific circumstances and context in which the personal data are processed, the controller should use appropriate mathematical or statistical procedures for the profiling, implement technical and organisational measures appropriate to ensure, in particular, that factors which result in inaccuracies in personal data are corrected and the risk of errors is minimised, secure personal data in a manner that takes account of the potential risks involved for the interests and rights of the data subject, and prevent, inter alia, discriminatory effects on natural persons on the basis of racial or ethnic origin, political opinion, religion or beliefs, trade union membership, genetic or health status or sexual orientation, or processing that results in measures having such an effect'.
534. K. Wiedemann, *Automated Processing of Personal Data for the Evaluation of Personality Traits*, p. 14.
535. B. Goodman, S. Flaxman, *European Union Regulations on Algorithmic Decision Making and 'a Right to an Explanation'*, pp. 53-55.
536. *Ibid.*
537. The research is still at an early stage, *see* reference 503.
538. *See* remarks on procedural regularity: J.A. Kroll, et al., *Accountable Algorithms*, pp. 637-638, 656-657.

changeable and difficult to predict. Of course, ensuring that a decision procedure is well justified or relies on sound reasoning, and as a result, fair, is a separate challenge from achieving procedural regularity.

Despite the above-mentioned issues, the controller remains under the obligation to process personal data lawfully and fairly. Therefore, it has to ensure that its automated individual decision-making system is not merely efficient but also compliant with the aforementioned principles. Hence, it should aim to reduce the risk of unlawful or unfair processing, which could, *inter alia*, result in discrimination. For example, as advised by the Article 29 Working Party, the controller should carry out frequent assessments on the data sets it processes to check for any bias, and develop ways to address any prejudicial elements, including any over-reliance on correlations.[539] It also urges the controller to introduce appropriate procedures and measures to prevent errors, inaccuracies or discrimination on the basis of special categories of personal data.[540] It also notes that these measures should be used on a cyclical basis, not only at the design stage but also continuously and the outcome of such testing should feed back into the system design. As another example of good practice recommendations, the controller is advised by the Information Commissioner's Office to introduce sample quality checks on the results from its automated individual decision-making systems to remove any bias or discriminatory effects and audit its ML algorithms to check for decision-making rationale and consistency.[541] Also, the European Parliament recommends the business to conduct regular assessments into the representativeness of data sets, consider whether data sets are affected by biased elements, and develop strategies to overcome those biases and highlights the need to review the accuracy and meaningfulness of data analytics predictions on the basis of fairness and ethical concerns.[542] While, as proposed by J. A. Kroll et al., compliance with this principle could be verified, for example, through the use of technical tools that allow checking whether the automated individual decision-making system is blind to a particular attribute.[543]

---

539. Article 29 Data Protection Working Party, *Guidelines on Automated individual decision-making and Profiling*, p. 28. *See also* p. 32 of the above guidelines, where the Article 29 Working Party lists, *inter alia*: (i) algorithmic auditing – testing the algorithms used and developed by ML systems to prove that they are actually performing as intended, and not producing discriminatory, erroneous or unjustified results and (ii) ethical review boards to assess the potential harms and benefits to society of particular applications for profiling as good practice recommendations.
540. GDPR, Recital 71.
541. Information Commissioner's Office, *Automated decision-making and profiling*, Guidelines of 5 June 2018, p. 18.
542. European Parliament resolution of 14 March 2017 on fundamental rights implications of big data: privacy, data protection, non-discrimination, security and law-enforcement, paragraph 22.
543. J.A. Kroll, et al., *Accountable Algorithms*, p. 637.

[B]   Purpose Limitation Principle

Purpose limitation is also among the key data protection principles to be taken into account by the controller, which deploys an automated individual decision-making system. It is set out in Article 5 (1) (b) of the GDPR, which mandates the controller to collect personal data for specified, explicit and legitimate purposes and not further process it in a manner that is incompatible with those purposes.[544] As explained by the Article 29 Working Party, the purpose limitation principle is designed to offer a balanced approach that aims to reconcile the need for predictability and legal certainty regarding the purposes of the processing on the one hand, and the pragmatic need for some flexibility on the other.[545] Beyond the GDPR, it is also enshrined in the primary law, the Charter of Fundamental Rights of the European Union.[546] There are two main aspects of the purpose limitation principle, purpose specification and compatible use.[547]

The first aspect of the principle implies that the purposes of processing personal data must be specified from the very beginning, at the time of collection of personal data. Conversely, processing of personal data for unspecified purposes is unlawful because it does not allow to delimit the scope of the processing precisely. In addition to that, the said purposes of data processing must be explicit, that is sufficiently unambiguous and clearly expressed. They must also be legitimate, which means that they may not entail a disproportionate interference with the rights, freedoms and interests at stake, in the name of the interests of the controller. The requirement of legitimacy is understood broadly. It goes beyond the requirement for the processing to be based on at least one of the lawful grounds provided for in Article 6 of the GDPR. It also requires that the purposes are in accordance with data protection law, as well as other applicable laws, such as employment law, contract law or consumer protection law.[548]

The second aspect of the principle indicates that the processing of personal data for purposes other than those for which the personal data were initially collected is only allowed where the processing is compatible with the purposes for which the personal data were initially collected. Further processing of personal data that is incompatible with the purposes of the original processing is, therefore, prohibited. Recognising that the notion of compatible is vague, to provide more legal certainty, the Article 6 (4) of

---

544. GDPR, Article 5 (1) (b): 'Personal data shall be collected for specified, explicit and legitimate purposes and not further processed in a manner that is incompatible with those purposes; further processing for archiving purposes in the public interest, scientific or historical research purposes or statistical purposes shall, in accordance with Article 89(1), not be considered to be incompatible with the initial purposes ("purpose limitation")'.
545. Article 29 Data Protection Working Party, *Opinion 03/2013 on purpose limitation*, p. 5.
546. Charter of Fundamental Rights of the European Union, Article 8 (2): 'Such data must be processed fairly *for specified purposes* and on the basis of the consent of the person concerned or some other legitimate basis laid down by law. Everyone has the right of access to data which has been collected concerning him or her, and the right to have it rectified [italics added]'.
547. Article 29 Data Protection Working Party, *Opinion 03/2013 on purpose limitation*, pp. 11-13.
548. Article 29 Data Protection Working Party, *Opinion 03/2013 on purpose limitation*, pp. 12, 19-20.

the GDPR establishes a list of criteria to be considered in order to ascertain whether processing for another purpose is compatible with the purpose for which the personal data are initially collected. The controller, after having met all the requirements for the lawfulness of the original processing, should take into account, *inter alia*: (i) any link between both purposes; (ii) the context in which the personal data have been collected, in particular, regarding the relationship between data subjects and the controller; (iii) the nature of the personal data, in particular, whether special categories of personal data or personal data related to criminal convictions and offences are processed; (iv) the possible consequences of the intended further processing for data subjects; and (v) the existence of appropriate safeguards, which may include encryption or pseudonymisation.[549]

Whether further processing is compatible with the original purposes for which the data was collected has to be assessed *ad casum*, taking into account the range of factors mentioned above, including what information the controller initially provided to the data subject.[550] There are only two exceptions to the above-mentioned rule, that is if the data subject consents to the new incompatible purpose or if the processing is based on the EU or Member State law. In addition to that, further processing for archiving purposes in the public interest, scientific or historical research purposes or statistical purposes is recognised as compatible provided certain GDPR requirements are met.[551]

Profiling can involve the use of personal data that was originally collected for something else.[552] In particular, ML algorithms and big data are fundamentally based around the idea of repurposing data, which is, in principle, contrary to the purpose

---

549. GDPR, Article 6 (4):

> Where the processing for a purpose other than that for which the personal data have been collected is not based on the data subject's consent or on a Union or Member State law which constitutes a necessary and proportionate measure in a democratic society to safeguard the objectives referred to in Article 23 (1), the controller shall, in order to ascertain whether processing for another purpose is compatible with the purpose for which the personal data are initially collected, take into account, inter alia:
>
> (a) any link between the purposes for which the personal data have been collected and the purposes of the intended further processing;
> (b) the context in which the personal data have been collected, in particular regarding the relationship between data subjects and the controller;
> (c) the nature of the personal data, in particular whether special categories of personal data are processed, pursuant to Article 9, or whether personal data related to criminal convictions and offences are processed, pursuant to Article 10;
> (d) the possible consequences of the intended further processing for data subjects;
> (e) the existence of appropriate safeguards, which may include encryption or pseudonymisation.
>
> *See also* GDPR, Recital 50.

550. Article 29 Data Protection Working Party, *Guidelines on Automated individual decision-making and Profiling*, p. 11.
551. GDPR, Article 89 (1).
552. Article 29 Data Protection Working Party, *Guidelines on Automated individual decision-making and Profiling*, p. 11.

limitation principle.[553] In these cases, consent would almost always be required; otherwise, further use of personal data cannot be considered compatible.[554]

[C]   Data Minimisation Principle

Data minimisation is another key data protection principle, which must be considered by the controller which deploys an automated individual decision-making system. Pursuant to Article 5 (1) (c) of the GDPR, 'personal data shall be adequate, relevant and limited to what is necessary in relation to the purposes for which they are processed'.[555] Recital 39 of the GDPR further explains that personal data should only be processed if the purpose of the processing could not reasonably be fulfilled by other means. In other words, the controller should not have more personal data than it needs to achieve the purpose of the processing.

As interpreted by the Information Commissioner's Office, personal data is adequate when it is sufficient to properly fulfil the particular purpose of the processing stated by the controller and relevant when it has a rational link to that purpose.[556] Whereas, the requirement to limit the personal data to what is necessary does not only refer to the quantity, but also to the quality of it. Accordingly, the controller may not process an excessively large number of data, as well as it may not process a single piece of data in relation to the purposes for which they are processed if it would entail a disproportionate interference in the data subject's rights and interests. Besides, this requirement also entails 'ensuring that the period for which the personal data are stored is limited to a strict minimum'.[557]

Of course, because of numerous business opportunities created by the significant growth in computing power, availability of data, cheaper storage costs and progress in algorithms, the controllers collect more personal data than they actually need, on the assumption that it will prove useful in the future.[558] In particular, big data, which may also be processed in a way that directly affects the data subjects, encourages limitless collection and retention of all the data which stands in contradiction to the data minimisation principle, as well as the storage limitation principle outlined below in §4.02[E]. ML algorithms also need large datasets in order to develop their own decision-making rules. A typical example of the use of big data and ML algorithms is profiling, which often precedes automated individual decision-making.

---

553. C. Kuner, D.J.B. Svantesson, F.H. Cate, O. Lynskey, C. Millard, *Machine Learning with Personal Data: Is Data Protection Law Smart Enough to Meet the Challenge?*, p. 32.
554. Article 29 Data Protection Working Party, *Opinion 03/2013 on purpose limitation*, p. 46.
555. This principle is also reflected in data protection by design and by default principles set out in Article 25 of the GDPR. *See* remarks in §4.03.
556. Information Commissioner's Office, Principle (c): Data minimisation, available at: https://ico.org.uk/for-organisations/guide-to-data-protection/guide-to-the-general-data-protection-regulation-gdpr/principles/data-minimisation/, accessed 1 July 2019.
557. GDPR, Recital 39. *See also* remarks about storage limitation principle in §4.02[E].
558. Article 29 Data Protection Working Party, *Guidelines on Automated individual decision-making and Profiling*, p. 11.

Nevertheless, the controller must comply with the data minimisation principle. Accordingly, the controller must be able to demonstrate compliance with the said principle and justify that the processed personal data is adequate, relevant and limited to what is necessary in relation to the purposes for which it is processed. In particular, the controller must ensure that any special category of personal data that may have been inferred as a result of profiling is deleted if it is not needed.[559] Alternatively, the controller may consider using anonymised or, assuming it provides sufficient protection, pseudonymised data for profiling.[560] However, this solution is only partial. At the moment, such data is used for decision-making regarding specific individuals; it is no longer anonymous, so all of the GDPR requirements, including the data minimisation principle, apply.

As pragmatically argued by G. Noto La Diega, the data minimisation principle does not mean that the controller must always collect as little personal data as possible.[561] It means that the quantity must be related to the purpose, provided that the personal data is adequate and relevant. For instance, the application of big data and ML algorithms to make solely automated individual decisions within the meaning of Article 22 (1) of the GDPR can justify the processing of large amounts of personal data, for at least two reasons. Firstly, the more personal data is used to train ML algorithms, the more accurate the decisions may be, so it is still limited to what is necessary within the meaning of Article 5 (1) (c) of the GDPR for the functioning of such automated individual decision-making systems.[562] Second, the processing of small amounts of personal data, leading to inaccurate decisions, would be inadequate within the meaning of this provision, as such decisions produce legal effects concerning the data subject or similarly significantly affect it.

Lastly, the controller must make sure that the personal data is relevant within the meaning of Article 5 (1) (c) of the GDPR, so it has a rational link to the purpose of a particular case of solely automated individual decision-making. Of course, in certain circumstances, collecting or inferring more personal data is not preferable because it is particularly sensitive, irrelevant or because it reveals patterns that are unsuitable for decision-making, for instance, if they are discriminatory.[563] However, this issue is connected to a greater extent with the lawfulness, fairness and transparency principle described above in §4.02[A].

---

559. Information Commissioner's Office, *Automated decision-making and profiling,* Guidelines of 5 June 2018, p. 18.
560. Article 29 Data Protection Working Party, *Guidelines on Automated individual decision-making and Profiling,* p. 11. The GDPR does not apply to anonymised data, but pseudonymised data remains within its scope. For additional remarks in this regard *see* Chapter 1, §1.02[A].
561. G. Noto La Diega, *Against the Dehumanisation of Decision-Making,* p. 25. *Conferatur* D. Kamarinou, C. Millard, J. Singh, *Machine Learning with Personal Data,* p. 18, who argue that the controller may provide the algorithm with only the data that is strictly necessary for the specific profiling purpose, even if that leads to a narrower representation of the data subject and possibly a less fair decision for it.
562. I. Žliobaitė, B. Custers, *Using Sensitive Personal Data May Be Necessary,* p. 197.
563. Processing of special categories of personal data within the meaning of Article 9 (1) of the GDPR is subject to a general prohibition, unless one of the exceptions applies.

[D]   Accuracy Principle

Accuracy is another fundamental data protection principle relevant to automated individual decision-making. Article 5 (1) (d) of the GDPR stipulates that 'personal data shall be accurate and, where necessary, kept up to date; every reasonable step must be taken to ensure that personal data that are inaccurate, having regard to the purposes for which they are processed, are erased or rectified without delay'.[564]

During the profiling process or the subsequent automated individual decision-making, inaccurate personal data may be blindingly applied to an individual.[565] Certainly, if personal data used in such processes is inaccurate, any ensuing profile or decision will be erroneous as well. Exceptionally, solely automated individual decision-making within the meaning of Article 22 (1) of the GDPR carries a high risk for the data subject, because such a decision, even if it is faulty, produces legal effects concerning the data subject or similarly significantly affects it. In this case, for the data subject, crucial opportunities are usually at stake, including the ability to get credit, insurance, a job, or even receive medical treatment.

Hence, according to the guidelines of the Article 29 Working Party, the controller which deploys an automated individual decision-making system, including profiling, should consider accuracy at all stages of the process, specifically when: (i) collecting data; (ii) analysing data; (iii) building a profile for an individual; and (iv) applying a profile to make a decision affecting the individual.[566] In particular, the controller needs to introduce measures to verify and ensure on an ongoing basis that personal data re-used or obtained indirectly is accurate and up to date.[567] This obligation applies to all automated individual decision-making systems including, but not limited to, the above-mentioned solely automated individual decision-making systems.

There is also a risk that automated individual decision-making is based on inconclusive personal data.[568] As already explained above, profiling, which often precedes automated individual decision-making, may use personal data from various different sources in order to infer something about an individual based on qualities of other individuals who are statistically similar.[569] This means that the new personal data has not been collected but calculated using algorithms. Hence, inevitably, profiling produces uncertain knowledge and involves some margin of error, as it based on a process of statistical extrapolation producing partially accurate and partially inaccurate results.[570]

---

564. This principle is also reflected in data protection by design and by default principles set out in Article 25 of the GDPR. *See* remarks in §4.03.
565. *See* remarks in Chapter 1, §1.05[A].
566. Article 29 Data Protection Working Party, *Guidelines on Automated individual decision-making and Profiling*, p. 12.
567. Information Commissioner's Office, *Automated decision-making and profiling*, Guidelines of 5 June 2018, p. 18; Article 29 Data Protection Working Party, *Guidelines on Automated individual decision-making and Profiling*, p. 12.
568. *See* remarks in Chapter 1, §1.05[A].
569. Article 29 Data Protection Working Party, *Guidelines on Automated individual decision-making and Profiling*, p. 7. *See also* remarks in Chapter 1 §1.02[H][3] above.
570. *See* reference 164.

Accordingly, the controller may also consider setting a high threshold of probability as a requirement for any automated individual decision, especially if it produces legal effects concerning the data subject or similarly significantly affects it. Besides, it should be taken into account that the accuracy principle is further strengthened by the data subject's right to rectification, which allows it to improve the quality of the data, as well as the right to be informed, which mandates the controller to provide the data subject with information about the existence of this right.[571] The controller must fulfil these obligations as well.

[E]   Storage Limitation Principle

Another important data protection principle which must be taken into consideration by the controller that deploys an automated individual decision-making system is storage limitation. It is set out in Article 5 (1) (e) of the GDPR, which says that 'personal data shall be kept in a form which permits the identification of data subjects for no longer than is necessary for the purposes for which the personal data are processed'.[572] In addition to that, Recital 39 of the GDPR prescribes that, in order to fulfil the above obligation, time limits should be established by the controller for erasure or for a periodic review. Of course, they could differ for each category of personal data.

On first sight, the use of big data and ML algorithms, enabled by the maximised retention of all the data, in the process of profiling, which often precedes automated individual decision-making clearly contradicts with the storage limitation principle. Although the controller may, to a certain point, consider using anonymised or, assuming it provides sufficient protection, pseudonymised data for such processing, at the moment such data is used for decision-making regarding specific individuals, it is no longer anonymous, so all of the GDPR requirements, including the storage limitation principle, apply.[573]

Nonetheless, the storage limitation principle may be interpreted flexibly. The controller's retention policy may take into account that accuracy of some of the automated individual decision-making systems may require that personal data that is stored for longer periods.[574] However, the time limit must still be narrowed to what is necessary within the meaning of Article 5 (1) (e) of the GDPR. Especially considering that the controller must also make sure that the data remains updated throughout the

---

571. GDPR, Articles 16, 13 (2) (b) and 14 (2) (c), respectively. *See* remarks in Chapter 5, §5.04 and §5.02.
572. Notwithstanding the above, Article 5 (1) (e) of the GDPR allows personal data to be stored for longer periods insofar as the personal data will be processed solely for archiving purposes in the public interest, scientific or historical research purposes or statistical purposes in accordance with Article 89 (1) of the GDPR subject to implementation of the appropriate technical and organisational measures required by the Regulation in order to safeguard the rights and freedoms of the data subject. This principle is also reflected in data protection by design and by default principles set out in Article 25 of the GDPR. *See* remarks in §4.03.
573. Article 29 Data Protection Working Party, *Guidelines on Automated individual decision-making and Profiling*, p. 11. The GDPR does not apply to anonymised data, but pseudonymised data remains within its scope. For additional remarks in this regard, *see* Chapter 1, §1.02[A].
574. *See* remarks in §4.02[E] above, which analogously apply to the storage limitation principle.

retention period to reduce the risk of inaccuracies, which is more difficult for longer storage periods.[575]

As justly noted by L. Edwards, M. Veale, there is a widely held societal value to being able to 'make a fresh start', which is challenged by the technological change.[576] The Information Commissioner's Office also succinctly remarks that just because the systems allow the controllers to retain vast quantities of data, does not mean they should.[577] Although in certain cases, the storage limitation principle may be interpreted flexibly, the necessity requirement contained therein must not be read overly broadly. While preparing a retention policy, the controllers ought to have in mind the overall purpose of the GDPR, that is, the protection of natural persons with regard to the processing of personal data.

§4.03   DATA PROTECTION BY DESIGN AND BY DEFAULT

Data protection by design and by default are some of the key obligations relevant for the controller which deploys an automated individual decision-making system.[578] These principles exemplify the increased emphasis on making the controller account-able and responsible for its data processing operations embodied by the GDPR.[579] They recognise that a regulator cannot do everything by top-down control, but that the controller must itself be involved in the design of less privacy-invasive systems.[580] The controller's obligations arising from these two different principles are described in brief below.

The principle of data protection by design set out in Article 25 (1) of the GDPR mandates the controller to put in place technical and organisational measures that are designed to implement the data protection principles effectively and to integrate the necessary safeguards into the processing of personal data so that the processing meets the requirements of the GDPR and otherwise ensures protection of the rights of data subjects.[581] Article 25 (1) of the GDPR references pseudonymisation as an example of

---

575. GDPR, Article 5 (1) (d). *See also* Article 29 Data Protection Working Party, *Guidelines on Automated individual decision-making and Profiling*, p. 12; Information Commissioner's Office, *Automated decision-making and profiling*, Guidelines of 5 June 2018, p. 20.
576. L. Edwards, M. Veale, *Slave to the Algorithm?*, p. 31. *See also* J.-F. Blanchette, D.G. Johnson, *Data Retention and the Panoptic Society: The Social Benefits of Forgetfulness*, 18 (1) The Information Society (2002), pp. 33-45.
577. Information Commissioner's Office, *Automated decision-making and profiling*, Guidelines of 5 June 2018, p. 20.
578. *Conferatur* L. Edwards, *Data Protection: Enter the General Data Protection Regulation*, [in:] *Law, Policy and the Internet*, p. 111, who wrongly claims that Article 25 of the GDPR is advisory.
579. GDPR, Articles 5 (2) and 24.
580. L. Edwards, M. Veale, *Enslaving the Algorithm*, pp. 51-52.
581. GDPR, Article 25 (1): 'Taking into account the state of the art, the cost of implementation and the nature, scope, context and purposes of processing as well as the risks of varying likelihood and severity for rights and freedoms of natural persons posed by the processing, the controller shall, both at the time of the determination of the means for processing and at the time of the processing itself, implement appropriate technical and organisational measures, such as pseudonymisation, which are designed to implement data-protection principles, such as data minimisation, in an effective manner and to integrate the necessary safeguards into the

a suitable measure enabling privacy by design. It is supplemented by other examples listed in Recital 78 of the GDPR.[582]

The said measures must receive proper consideration of the controller throughout the cycle of the processing of personal data, especially in the early design stage, not just added at its end. Moreover, this obligation extends until the very end of the processing. As expressly indicated by the wording of Article 25 of the GDPR, the measures in question must be not only technical but also organisational. This means that they do not encompass just the design and operation of software or hardware, they also extend to business strategies and other organisational practices, for instance, rules determining which and under what circumstances employees in an organisation are authorised to access or otherwise process certain categories of personal data.

At the same time, Article 25 (1) of the GDPR acknowledges that the controller's efforts to move towards data protection by design may be limited by the state of the art, the cost of implementation and the nature, scope, context and purposes of processing, as well as the risks that it poses for the rights and freedoms of the data subjects. Hence, the principle of data protection by design is qualified by an extensive list of contextual factors, which demonstrate a risk-based approach to assessing what measures are necessary.

Whereas the principle of data protection by default set out in Article 25 (2) of the GDPR requires the controller to implement appropriate technical and organisational measures for ensuring that, by default, only personal data which are necessary for each specific purpose of the processing are processed.[583] That obligation applies to the amount of personal data collected, the extent of their processing, the period of their storage and their accessibility. The provision stipulates that such measures shall ensure by default that personal data is not made accessible without the individual's intervention to an indefinite number of natural persons. Comparing both of the above provisions, the principle of data protection by design covers a potentially broader range of data protection measures than the principle of data protection by default, which

---

processing in order to meet the requirements of this Regulation and protect the rights of data subjects'. For the data protection principles, *see* Article 5 of the GDPR.

582. GDPR, Recital 78: '[...] Such measures could consist, inter alia, of minimising the processing of personal data, pseudonymising personal data as soon as possible, transparency with regard to the functions and processing of personal data, enabling the data subject to monitor the data processing, enabling the controller to create and improve security features. When developing, designing, selecting and using applications, services and products that are based on the processing of personal data or process personal data to fulfil their task, producers of the products, services and applications should be encouraged to take into account the right to data protection when developing and designing such products, services and applications and, with due regard to the state of the art, to make sure that controllers and processors are able to fulfil their data protection obligations'.

583. GDPR, Article 25 (2): 'The controller shall implement appropriate technical and organisational measures for ensuring that, by default, only personal data which are necessary for each specific purpose of the processing are processed. That obligation applies to the amount of personal data collected, the extent of their processing, the period of their storage and their accessibility. In particular, such measures shall ensure that by default personal data are not made accessible without the individual's intervention to an indefinite number of natural persons'.

centres on data minimisation and confidentiality. Also, the former principle is process-oriented, while the latter is concerned mostly with results that ensure data minimisation and confidentiality.

The controller which intends to use an automated individual decision-making system must adhere to both of the principles described above. Enabling the data subject to effectively exercise its special rights with regard to solely automated individual decision-making must not be seen as an afterthought but as one of the conditions for accepting and using such a system. Based on Article 25 (1) of the GDPR the controller is obliged to implement measures that allow the data subject to effectively exercise its special rights with regard to solely automated individual decision-making, even if it is not explicitly demanded by the relevant provisions. By way of illustration, the controller must put in place adequate channels for the data subject to invoke the right of access, the right to express its point of view, the right to obtain human intervention and the right to contest the decision. It must also establish internal procedures to be able to handle such requests.[584]

§4.04   DATA PROTECTION IMPACT ASSESSMENT

DPIA is another crucial obligation of the controller which deploys an automated individual-decision-making system. It is a process designed to describe the envisaged processing, assess its necessity and proportionality and manage the risks to the rights and freedoms of natural persons associated with the processing of personal data by assessing them and determining the measures to address them. Thus, it is considered an important tool for accountability, as it supports the controller in complying with the GDPR requirements and demonstrating that appropriate measures have been taken to ensure it.[585] In short, as aptly summarised by the Article 29 Working Party, it is 'a process for building and demonstrating compliance'.[586] Of course, a DPIA is not intended as a tool to stop the processing, but rather as a way to refine it.[587]

584. For further remarks concerning data protection by design and by default, *see* Information Commissioner's Office, *Big data, artificial intelligence, machine learning and data protection*, Guidelines of 1 March 2017, version 2.2, pp. 72-74; M. Almada, *Human Intervention in Automated Decision-Making*, pp. 1-10.

585. Article 29 Data Protection Working Party, *Guidelines on Data Protection Impact Assessment (DPIA) and determining whether processing is 'likely to result in a high risk' for the purposes of Regulation 2016/679*, as last revised and adopted on 4 October 2017, p. 4; Article 29 Data Protection Working Party, *Guidelines on Automated individual decision-making and Profiling*, pp. 29-30. Accountability is an explicit requirement of the controller under Article 5 (2) of the GDPR. The obligation of the controller to conduct a DPIA in certain circumstances should also be understood against the background of Article 24 of the GDPR concerning the responsibility of the controller.

586. Article 29 Data Protection Working Party, *Guidelines on Data Protection Impact Assessment (DPIA)*, p. 4.

587. L. Edwards, M. Veale, *Enslaving the Algorithm*, p. 52.

In line with the risk-based approach embodied by the GDPR, carrying out a DPIA is not mandatory for every processing operation.[588] According to Article 35 (1) of the GDPR, a DPIA is only required when the processing, in particular, using new technologies, is likely to result in a high risk to the rights and freedoms of natural persons.[589] It is up to the controller to assess whether there is a need to conduct a DPIA. Notwithstanding the above, a DPIA is considered to be the required norm for an automated individual decision-making system.[590]

First, such a system commonly uses new technologies, which, as reflected by Article 35 (1) of the GDPR, increases the probability that the processing in question is likely to result in a high risk to the rights and freedoms of natural persons and, thus, requires a DPIA. As already characterised above, automated individual decision-making systems ordinarily employ new technologies or novel applications of existing technologies, such as AI, ML and big data.[591]

Second, it goes without saying that an automated individual decision-making system is generally likely to result in a high risk to the rights and freedoms of natural persons as per Article 35 (1) of the GDPR.[592] Especially considering that the reference to the rights and freedoms of natural persons concerns the rights to data protection and privacy, but it may also involve other fundamental rights such as freedom of speech, freedom of thought, freedom of movement, the prohibition of discrimination, right to liberty, conscience and religion.[593] In connection with the above, automated individual decision-making systems pose a high risk to not only the rights to data protection and privacy but also other fundamental rights.

Third, a DPIA is expressly required in the case of a systematic and extensive evaluation of personal aspects relating to natural persons which is based on automated processing, including profiling, and on which decisions are based that produce legal effects concerning the natural person or similarly significantly affect the natural person under Article 35 (3) (a) of the GDPR.[594] This provision is relevant to many automated

---

588. For further remarks on the risk-based approach, *see* Article 29 Working Party, *Statement on the role of a risk-based approach in data protection legal frameworks*, adopted on 30 May 2014, pp. 1-4.
589. GDPR, Article 35 (1): 'Where a type of processing in particular using new technologies, and taking into account the nature, scope, context and purposes of the processing, is likely to result in a high risk to the rights and freedoms of natural persons, the controller shall, prior to the processing, carry out an assessment of the impact of the envisaged processing operations on the protection of personal data. A single assessment may address a set of similar processing operations that present similar high risks'.
590. L. Edwards, M. Veale, *Slave to the Algorithm?*, p. 78.
591. P.G. Picht, G.T. Loderer, *Framing Algorithms*, p. 12. *See* remarks in Chapter 1, §1.02[F], §1.02[G] and §1.02[H].
592. *See* remarks in Chapter 1, §1.05.
593. Article 29 Working Party, *Statement on the role of a risk-based approach*, p. 4.
594. GDPR, Article 35 (3) (a). *See also* Recital 91 of the GDPR. Two other cases which require a DPIA under Article 35 (3) (b) and (c) of the GDPR are, respectively: (i) processing on a large scale of special categories of data, or of personal data relating to criminal convictions and offences; (ii) systematic monitoring of a publicly accessible area on a large scale. These cases may be relevant to automated decision-making systems as well. Given that the list provided for in Article 35 (3) of the GDPR is non-exhaustive, any other automated individual decision-making system that is likely to result in such a high risk to the rights and freedoms of natural persons is also subject to a DPIA, depending upon the specifics of the case.

individual decision-making systems, including, but not limited to, solely automated individual decision-making systems within the meaning of Article 22 (1) of the GDPR. Markedly, Article 35 (3) (a) refers to evaluations including profiling and decisions that are based on automated processing, rather than solely automated processing. As a consequence, Article 35 (3) (a) of the GDPR also applies in the case of decision-making including profiling with legal or similarly significant effects, that is, not solely auto-mated within the meaning of Article 22 (1) of the GDPR.[595] By way of illustration, the controller may envisage an automated individual decision-making system with a significant degree of human involvement. Nevertheless, such processing could still present a high risk to the rights and freedoms of natural persons, so it remains subject to an obligation to carry out a DPIA.

Fourth, automated individual decision-making system normally requires a DPIA to be carried out, because it meets the criteria of processing operations which are likely to result in a high risk outlined by the highly influential Article 29 Working Party. Concretely, the Article 29 Working Party guidelines elaborate on the particular elements of Articles 35 (1) of the GDPR, as well as the list provided for in Article 35 (3) of the GDPR by enumerating nine criteria for determining whether the processing operations are likely to result in a high risk and, as a result, subject to an obligation to carry out a DPIA.[596] These include instances where processing involves: (1) evaluating or scoring, (2) automated individual decision-making with legal or similarly significant effects, (3) systematic monitoring, (4) sensitive data or data of a highly personal nature, (5) data processed on a large scale, (6) datasets are matched or combined, (7) data concerning vulnerable data subjects, (8) innovative use or applying technological or organisational solutions, (9) processing that inherently prevents data subjects from exercising a right or using a service or a contract. The body concludes that, in most cases, the controller can assume that a processing meeting two of the above criteria requires a DPIA to be carried out. Considering that basically all of the nine criteria are relevant to automated individual decision-making systems, the said threshold is usually met.

Fifth, automated individual decision-making system requires a DPIA to be carried out as it meets the criteria of processing operations which are likely to result in a high risk established by the supervisory authorities. By way of explanation, under Article 35 (4) of the GDPR, the supervisory authorities are required to establish and make public a list of the kinds of processing operations which are subject to the requirement for a DPIA. These kinds of processing operations are largely analogous to the aforesaid criteria indicated by the Article 29 Working Party, as they are subject to the consistency mechanism of the GDPR.[597]

---

595. Article 29 Data Protection Working Party, *Guidelines on Automated individual decision-making and Profiling*, pp. 29-30.
596. *See* Article 29 Data Protection Working Party, *Guidelines on Data Protection Impact Assessment (DPIA)*, pp. 9-12, for a detailed description of the criteria.
597. GDPR, Article 63. *See*, for instance, Komunikat Prezesa Urzędu Ochrony Danych Osobowych z dnia 17 czerwca 2019 r. w sprawie wykazu rodzajów operacji przetwarzania danych osobowych wymagających oceny skutków przetwarzania dla ich ochrony, (Monitor Polski 2019 Poz. 666). *See also* Information Commissioner's Office, Examples of processing 'likely to

Last but not least, in cases where it is still unclear whether the prospective automated individual decision-making system operation requires a DPIA, carrying out a preliminary DPIA to assess the risks may be the best means of ensuring compliance.[598] In other words, demonstrating that a DPIA is not necessary will, in many instances, itself require a DPIA. This circular causation is likely to incentivise companies to be especially cautious when deciding if a DPIA is required.[599]

Given that a DPIA is meant as a tool for helping decision-making concerning the envisaged processing, the GDPR mandates that it must be carried out prior to its deployment.[600] It may even begin as early as is feasible in the design of the processing operations, even if some of the processing operations remain undeveloped.[601] Besides, considering that compliance is an ongoing process, a DPIA must be reviewed where necessary, at least when there is a change of the risk represented by processing operations underlying a DPIA in question.[602]

The controller is ultimately responsible for ensuring that the DPIA is carried out, but it is free to involve anybody inside or outside the organisation. Specifically, besides involving its own business units, the controller may consider seeking advice from independent experts of different professions, such as lawyers, academics, IT experts, security experts, sociologists, ethics.[603] In complex cases, only a multidisciplinary team will be able to conduct a proper DPIA. If the processing is wholly or partly performed by a data processor, the processor must also assist the controller in carrying out the DPIA and provide any necessary information.[604] The controller is also mandated to seek the advice of the data protection officer, where designated and views of data subjects or their representatives on the intended processing, where appropriate.[605]

Article 35 (7) of the GDPR specifically enumerates four basic features that a DPIA must contain, at a minimum: (i) a systematic description of the envisaged processing operations and the purposes of the processing, including, where applicable, the legitimate interest pursued by the controller; (ii) an assessment of the necessity and proportionality of the processing operations in relation to the purposes; (iii) an assessment of the risks to the rights and freedoms of data subjects; (iv) the measures

---

result in high risk', available at: https://ico.org.uk/for-organisations/guide-to-data-protection/guide-to-the-general-data-protection-regulation-gdpr/data-protection-impact-assessments-dpias/examples-of-processing-likely-to-result-in-high-risk/, accessed 1 July 2019.

598. Article 29 Data Protection Working Party, *Guidelines on Data Protection Impact Assessment (DPIA)*, p. 8.
599. B. Casey, A. Farhangi, R. Vogl, *Rethinking Explainable Machines*, p. 175.
600. GDPR, Article 35 (1), 35 (10), Recitals 90, 93. This is coherent with the data protection by design and by default principles set out in Article 25 of the GDPR.
601. Article 29 Data Protection Working Party, *Guidelines on Data Protection Impact Assessment (DPIA)*, p. 14.
602. GDPR, Article 35 (11).
603. Article 29 Data Protection Working Party, *Guidelines on Data Protection Impact Assessment (DPIA)*, p. 15.
604. Article 28 (3) (f) of the GDPR.
605. GDPR, Article 35 (1), 35 (9). Though GDPR does not specify which cases are considered as 'appropriate', so it is up to the controller to determine these cases. Also, the GDPR allows the controller to seek these views through variety of means, depending on the context.

envisaged to address the risks, including safeguards, security measures and mechanisms to ensure the protection of personal data and to demonstrate compliance with the GDPR taking into account the rights and legitimate interests of data subjects and other persons concerned.[606] The GDPR provides the controller with the flexibility to determine the precise structure and form of the DPIA in order to allow for this to fit with existing working practices.[607] However, it must choose a methodology which is sufficiently comprehensive to comply with the GDPR.[608]

If a DPIA reveals that the processing would result in a high risk in the absence of measures taken by the controller to mitigate the risk, the controller is required to seek consultation from the supervisory authority prior to the deployment of an automated individual decision-making system.[609] As explained by the Article 29 Data Protection Working Party, whenever the controller cannot find sufficient measures to reduce the risks to an acceptable level, consultation with the supervisory authority is mandatory.[610] This involves, *inter alia*, providing a complete DPIA to the supervisory authority, which, in turn, may provide its written advice where it is of the opinion that the intended processing would infringe the GDPR.[611]

A DPIA does not have to be publicly available, although it is considered a good practice by the Article 29 Data Protection Working Party to do so, at least in parts, such as a summary of the main findings, a conclusion, or even just a statement that a DPIA has been carried out.[612] This is because publishing a DPIA helps foster trust in the controller's processing operations, and demonstrates accountability and transparency. It may be of great value in order to build better automated individual decision-making systems overall.[613]

As advised by the Article 29 Working Party, apart from addressing any other risks connected with automated individual decision-making, a DPIA can be particularly useful for the controller which is unsure whether the prospective automated individual

---

606. *See also* GDPR, Article 35 (8): 'Compliance with approved codes of conduct referred to in Article 40 by the relevant controllers or processors shall be taken into due account in assessing the impact of the processing operations performed by such controllers or processors, in particular for the purposes of a data protection impact assessment'. For further guidance *see*, in particular GDPR, Recitals 84, 91.
607. Article 29 Data Protection Working Party, *Guidelines on Data Protection Impact Assessment (DPIA)*, p. 17.
608. Examples of a DPIA methodology: Information Commissioner's Office, Guidance on DPIAs, available at: https://ico.org.uk/for-organisations/guide-to-data-protection/guide-to-the-gene ral-data-protection-regulation-gdpr/data-protection-impact-assessments-dpias/, accessed 1 July 2019. For criteria which should be met by any DPIA methodology, *see* Article 29 Data Protection Working Party, *Guidelines on Data Protection Impact Assessment (DPIA)*, p. 22.
609. GDPR, Article 36 (1). Based on Article 36 (5) of the GDPR, Member State law may additionally require controllers to consult with, and obtain prior authorisation from, the supervisory authority in relation to processing by a controller for the performance of a task carried out by the controller in the public interest, including processing in relation to social protection and public health.
610. Article 29 Data Protection Working Party, *Guidelines on Data Protection Impact Assessment (DPIA)*, p. 19.
611. GDPR, Article 36 (2), 36 (3).
612. Article 29 Data Protection Working Party, *Guidelines on Data Protection Impact Assessment (DPIA)*, p. 18.
613. L. Edwards, M. Veale, *Enslaving the Algorithm*, pp. 51-52.

decision-making system falls within the scope of Article 22 (1) of the GDPR, and, if one of the exemptions from the data subject's right not to be subject to such processing applies, what safeguards are required.[614] For example, such safeguards may include appropriate contractual commitments from the designers and service providers offering ML components and capabilities, and the implementation of practical measures to ensure that data subjects' personal data, including any profiles created from the use of such data, are inaccessible to service providers except where strictly necessary.[615] The controller may also consider setting a high threshold of probability as a requirement for any automated individual decision, especially if it produces legal effects concerning the data subject or similarly significantly affects it.

Finally, yet importantly, it has to be acknowledged that techniques of the type envisioned by a DPIA already have a well-documented track record of detecting and combating algorithmic discrimination in otherwise opaque systems. As Sandvig et al. describe, audit studies are the most prevalent social scientific methods for the detection of discrimination in complex computational systems.[616] In recent years, such techniques have been used to successfully detect and document algorithmic bias across diverse industry sectors and social domains.[617]

Hence, an obligation of the controller to conduct a DPIA of an automated individual decision-making system is likely to provide more effective protection with regard to such processing to the data subject than its individual rights.[618] It is performed prior to the processing, so it aids building a better system from the beginning as opposed to remodeling it *post factum*, for instance, as a reaction to individual rights invoked by the data subjects. Moreover, it gives the controller access to the whole picture of the processing operations. Some of the risks to the rights and freedoms of natural persons may only be detected then. Special rights of the data subject with regard to solely automated individual decision-making are unlikely to provide significant remedial utility in instances where the discrimination involved is only observable at a statistical scale.[619] Providing limited information to the data subject, as required under Articles 13 (2) (f), 14 (2) (g), 15 (1) (h) of the GDPR, may give the data subject a false impression that the controller remains in line with the GDPR, even when, in fact,

---

614. Article 29 Data Protection Working Party, *Guidelines on Automated individual decision-making and Profiling*, p. 20.

615. D. Kamarinou, C. Millard, J. Singh, *Machine Learning with Personal Data*, p. 14; Article 29 Data Protection Working Party, *Guidelines on Automated individual decision-making and Profiling*, p. 32.

616. C. Sandvig, K. Hamilton, K. Karahalios, C. Langbort, *Auditing Algorithms: Research Methods for Detecting Discrimination on Internet Platforms*, Paper presented to Data and Discrimination: Converting Critical Concerns into Productive Inquiry, a preconference at the 64th Annual Meeting of the International Communication Association on 22 May 2014 Seattle, United States of America, p. 5.

617. F. Pasquale, *The Black Box Society*.

618. For further remarks concerning a DPIA, *see also* Information Commissioner's Office, *Big data, artificial intelligence, machine learning and data protection*, Guidelines of 1 March 2017, version 2.2, pp. 70-71; G. Noto La Diega, *Against the Dehumanisation of Decision-Making*, p. 24; B. Casey, A. Farhangi, R. Vogl, *Rethinking Explainable Machines*, pp. 169-183; L. Edwards, M. Veale, *Slave to the Algorithm?*, pp. 77-78; D. Kamarinou, C. Millard, J. Singh, *Machine Learning with Personal Data*, pp. 13-14.

619. B. Casey, A. Farhangi, R. Vogl, *Rethinking Explainable Machines*, p. 181.

its processing operations may be discriminatory.[620] In such cases, a DPIA may be much more useful for the controller to refine the processing, so it meets the GDPR requirements.

§4.05   CERTIFICATION

Certification plays an important role in the accountability framework for data protection, and it could be particularly useful for the controller which deploys automated individual-decision-making systems or the processor involved in this process.[621] Certification is a way for the controller to demonstrate compliance with the GDPR to the regulators, the public and in business to business relationships. Thus, certification enhances transparency, as, in theory, it allows the data subject to quickly assess the level of data protection of relevant products and services.[622] However, in practice, there is little proof that the data subjects regard certification as an indication of trust, so the controllers may be unwilling to incur its costs or make an effort to obtain it unless by doing so they can avoid more stringent top-down regulation.[623]

Articles 42 and 43 of the GDPR provide a legal basis for the establishment of data protection certification mechanisms and of data protection seals and marks. The GDPR does not define 'certification'. According to the guidelines of the European Data Protection Board, it means third-party attestation related to processing operations by controllers and processors.[624] Whereas a seal or a mark may be used to signify the successful completion of the certification procedure. With regard to an entity issuing certifications, the GDPR allows for a number of different models.[625] All of them are subject to the control of the competent supervisory authorities and the European Data Protection Board in order to ensure good quality of the services and a level playing field.[626]

---

620. *Ibid.*
621. Article 29 Working Party, *Opinion 3/2010 on the principle of accountability*, adopted on 13 July 2010, paragraphs 66-71, pp. 17-18.
622. GDPR, Article 42 (1): 'The Member States, the supervisory authorities, the Board and the Commission shall encourage, in particular at Union level, the establishment of data protection certification mechanisms and of data protection seals and marks, for the purpose of demonstrating compliance with this Regulation of processing operations by controllers and processors […]'. *See also* GDPR, Recital 100: 'In order to enhance transparency and compliance with this Regulation, the establishment of certification mechanisms and data protection seals and marks should be encouraged, allowing data subjects to quickly assess the level of data protection of relevant products and services'.
623. L. Edwards, M. Veale, *Enslaving the Algorithm*, pp. 52-53.
624. European Data Protection Board, *Guidelines 1/2018 on certification and identifying certification criteria in accordance with Articles 42 and 43 of the Regulation*, Version 3.0, 4 June 2019, paragraphs 17-18, p. 8. *See also* the universal definition of International Organization for Standardization: 'Certification – the provision by an independent body of written assurance (a certificate) that the product, service or system in question meets specific requirements', available at: https://www.iso.org/certification.html, accessed 1 July 2019.
625. GDPR, Article 42 (5). For further information, *see* European Data Protection Board, *Guidelines 1/2018 on certification and identifying certification criteria*.
626. It has to be noted that voluntary self- or co-regulation has a bad track record, also with regard to data protection, which causes scepticism about its effectiveness. *See* Article 29 Working

Although certification is voluntary, it is encouraged by the GDPR.[627] For example, the regulation expressly indicates that certification may be used to demonstrate compliance: (i) with the obligations of the controller; (ii) with the provisions on data protection by design and by default; (iii) with the obligations of the processor; (iv) with the provisions on appropriate technical and organisational measures to ensure a level of security appropriate to the risk.[628] Furthermore, the adherence to an approved certification mechanism is a factor, which supervisory authorities must consider when deciding to impose an administrative fine and deciding on its amount.[629] Of course, certification in itself does not prove compliance with the GDPR or reduce the responsibility of the controller or the processor for it.[630]

The GDPR allows a broad scope of what can be certified, as long as the focus remains on demonstrating compliance of the processing operation of the controller or the processor with the GDPR.[631] Thus, certification may relate to a specific personal data processing operation or set of operations, which, for example, constitute an automated individual decision-making system. At any instance, for the reasons of clarity, it must be precisely described which processing operations are included in the object of certification and then the core components, *videlicet* which personal data, processes or procedures related to the processing operation(s) and technical infrastructure are subject to an assessment and which are not.[632]

Universally, certification criteria should reflect all of the relevant compliance aspects in support of the assessment of the processing operation, *inter alia*, where applicable: (i) the lawfulness of processing pursuant to Article 6 of the GDPR; (ii) the principles of data processing pursuant to Article 5 of the GDPR; (iii) the data subjects'

Party, *Opinion 3/2010 on the principle of accountability*, paragraph 69, p. 18: 'Because the quality of the services and the need for them to operate in the internal market are a key criterion, the law will have to set up the conditions that will serve to achieve such quality. It does not seem possible to leave this to the market. Experience in other areas such as in certification of goods has shown a tendency towards the bottom. Competition among service providers may lead to a reduction of prices and also to certain flexibility or relaxation of the procedures'. *See also* L. Edwards, M. Veale, *Enslaving the Algorithm*, pp. 52-53, who note: 'Certification scheme and trust seals have to make money to survive, which can only be obtained by asking fees from members. Given this self-interest, it is hard to punish members too hard when they breach the rules of the seal or certificate, for fear they will leave, either altogether or for a less demanding trust seal (in a plural market, which is generally what is envisaged)' recalling as an example the Safe Harbor agreement between the EU and the United States of America (Commission Decision 2000/520/EC of 26 July 2000 pursuant to Directive 95/46/EC of the European Parliament and of the Council on the adequacy of the protection provided by the safe harbour privacy principles and related frequently asked questions issued by the US Department of Commerce, Official Journal of the European Union L 215, 25 August 2000 pp. 7-47), which envisaged self-certification, but as it was ineffective in ensuring an adequate level of protection for the data subjects, was considered invalid in Judgment of the Court (Grand Chamber) of 6 October 2015, Maximillian Schrems v Data Protection Commissioner, joined party: Digital Rights Ireland Ltd, Case C-362/14, ECLI:EU:C:2015:650.

627. GDPR, Article 35 (3).
628. GDPR, Articles 24 (3), 25 (3), 28 (5) and 32 (3), respectively.
629. GDPR, Article 83 (2) (j).
630. GDPR, Article 42 (4).
631. European Data Protection Board, *Guidelines 1/2018 on certification and identifying certification criteria*, paragraph 50, p. 15.
632. *Ibid.*, paragraph 58, p. 17.

rights pursuant to Articles 12-23 of the GDPR; (iv) the obligation to notify data breaches pursuant to Article 33 of the GDPR; (v) the obligation of data protection by design and by default, pursuant to Article 25; (vi) whether a DPIA, pursuant to Article 35 (7) (d) of the GDPR has been conducted, if applicable; and (vii) the technical and organisational measures put in place pursuant to Article 32 of the GDPR.[633] In short, since the GDPR is directed at the protection of fundamental rights of natural persons, this perspective must be apparent in the certification criteria.

With regard to automated individual decision-making systems, more concrete certification criteria could be developed. This is because a notable advantage of certification is that standards could be set on a per-sector basis.[634] Of course, the certification bodies or the competent supervisory authorities must be able to understand the systems that they are certifying. Accordingly, they could engage multidisciplinary teams including lawyers, academics, IT experts, security experts, sociologists, ethics, in particular with sector-specific experience. Possibly, hitherto research on interpretable ML algorithms in the context of automated individual decision-making could be helpful in determining such concrete criteria with regard to such systems, as well.[635]

Any automated individual decision-making may be subject to certification. Notably, it is available to the controllers or the processors which deploy systems which remain outside the narrow scope of the definition set out in Article 22 (1) of the GDPR. In spite of the fact that specific provisions on solely automated individual decision-making, in particular, special rights of the data subjects, do not apply to such systems, they remain subject to general GDPR requirements and face similar challenges. Consequently, it is reasonable to assume that certification criteria developed principally for solely automated individual decision-making systems could be valuable for systems which are not wholly automated alike.

As proposed by L. Edwards and M. Veale, certification could be focused on two main aspects of an automated individual decision-making system. Firstly, it could pertain to the algorithm as a software object by (i) directly specifying either its design specifications or the process of its design, such as the expertise involved (technology-based standards), or (ii) specifying output-related requirements that can be monitored and evaluated (performance-based standards). Second, it could apply to the controller or the system, which would consider the algorithm as situated in the context of their use.[636]

Pursuant to Article 42 (6) of the GDPR, the controller or processor which submits its processing to the certification mechanism must provide the certification body, or where applicable, the competent supervisory authority, with all information and access to its processing activities which are necessary to conduct the certification procedure. This obligation may be contrasted with the limited information, which must be

---

633. *Ibid.*, paragraph 48, p. 15.
634. L. Edwards, M. Veale, *Slave to the Algorithm?*, p. 80.
635. *See* reference 503.
636. L. Edwards, M. Veale, *Enslaving the Algorithm*, pp. 52-53.

provided to the data subject with regard to solely automated individual decision-making under Articles 13 (2) (f), 14 (2) (g), 15 (1) (h) of the GDPR. Because of the latter, it is not always feasible for the data subject to effectively protect its interests. Certification may balance the controller's interests, in particular, the need for business confidentiality, with the protection of the data subject with regard to automated individual decision-making.[637] Providing all relevant information and access to its processing activities, which are subject to certification, to the certification body or the competent supervisory authority, instead of the data subject allows the controller to preserve the confidentiality of the system while ensuring that it remains compliant with the GDPR.[638]

Certification, although voluntary, could provide measures for addressing the some of the shortcomings of the specific provisions on solely automated individual decision-making provided for in the GDPR. Especially assuming that certification criteria go beyond the expressed GDPR requirements. On the other hand, as accurately noted by T. Henderson, if the purpose of certification is to indicate compliance with the relevant law, then it is possible that all of the failings of the other provisions of the GDPR are simply reiterated by certification.[639]

Last but not least, it may be anticipated that some of the controllers and processors will obtain certification in order to differentiate themselves on the market and gain a competitive advantage. For the reason of compliance comfort, data subjects may favour the controllers which are certified, similarly in business to business relationships.[640]

---

637. As already outlined in Chapter 3, §3.10[A], in some cases, intellectual property rights may limit the algorithmic transparency. *See also* T. Henderson, *Does the GDPR Help or Hinder Fair Algorithmic Decision-Making?*, written on 21 August 2017, LLM dissertation, Innovation, Technology & The Law, University of Edinburgh 2017, available at SSRN, p. 24.

638. GDPR, Article 54 (2): 'The member or members and the staff of each supervisory authority shall, in accordance with Union or Member State law, be subject to a duty of professional secrecy both during and after their term of office, with regard to any confidential information which has come to their knowledge in the course of the performance of their tasks or exercise of their powers. During their term of office, that duty of professional secrecy shall in particular apply to reporting by natural persons of infringements of this Regulation'. *See* Article 43 (3) of the GDPR, which stipulates that where accreditation of certification bodies is carried out by national accreditation bodies, these must meet the requirements of Regulation (EC) No. 765/2008 of the European Parliament and of the Council of 9 July 2008 setting out the requirements for accreditation and market surveillance relating to the marketing of products and repealing Regulation (EEC) No. 339/93, Official Journal of the European Union L 218, 13 August 2008, pp. 30-47, which include 'adequate arrangements to safeguard the confidentiality of the information obtained' (Article 8 (4)). *See also* T. Henderson, *Does the GDPR Help or Hinder Fair Algorithmic Decision-Making?*, p. 24, who observes that 'flexibility in choosing EU-level and national bodies means that this may not be the case for all certifications, and so further legislation may still be needed for data controllers to trust the certification bodies'.

639. T. Henderson, *Does the GDPR Help or Hinder Fair Algorithmic Decision-Making?*, p. 24.

640. *See also* Article 29 Working Party, *Opinion 3/2010 on the principle of accountability*, paragraph 67, p. 17.

§4.06   CODES OF CONDUCT

Codes of conduct are another voluntary accountability tool provided for in the GDPR, which may be useful for the controller which conducts automated individual decision-making. Like a DPIA and certification, it is a mechanism which can be used to assist the controller or the processor in building and demonstrating its compliance with the GDPR.[641] Adherence to a code of conduct is also taken into consideration by supervisory authorities when imposing an administrative fine.[642]

In the opinion of the European Data Protection Board, codes of conduct represent a practical, potentially cost effective and meaningful method to achieve greater levels of consistency of protection for data protection rights.[643] Notably, given that they involve a degree of co-regulation, they provide an opportunity for particular sectors or even different sectors, which conduct a common processing activity with the same processing characteristics, such as automated individual decision-making, to find practical solutions to problems identified by the particular sector or in relation to common processing activities, as well as to consolidate best practice processing operations in this regard.[644] In other words, codes of conduct give operational meaning to the GDPR requirements.[645] Such codes of conduct are subject to the approval of the competent supervisory authority and monitoring by an accredited monitoring body as per Articles 40-41 of the GDPR.

Codes of conduct could aid the controller or the processor to comply with the GDPR by governing areas such as, *inter alia*: fair and transparent processing; legitimate interests pursued by controllers in specific contexts; the collection of personal data; the information provided to the public and to data subjects; the exercise of the rights of data subjects; data protection by design and default measures, all of which are challenging with regard to automated individual decision-making, including profiling.[646]

Given that automated individual decision-making raises many concerns with regard to the protection of individuals, and it is challenging to implement it in a way

---

641. GDPR, Articles 24 (3); 28 (5) and 32 (3).
642. GDPR, Article 83 (2) (j).
643. European Data Protection Board, *Guidelines 1/2019 on Codes of Conduct and Monitoring Bodies under Regulation 2016/679*, Version 2.0, 4 June 2019, paragraph 1, p. 5. Codes do not necessarily need to be confined or limited to a specific sector. For example, a code could apply to separate sectors who have a common processing activity which share the same processing characteristics and needs. Where a code is cross-sectoral in its application, more than one monitoring body may be appointed under that code. However, where this is the case the code should make it absolutely clear as to the scope of that monitoring body's functions, in other words by specifying the sectors in respect of which each monitoring body will perform its functions under Article 41 and the oversight mechanisms available to each monitoring body. In this regard, the relevant sections of these guidelines which set out the responsibilities, obligations and accreditation requirements in relation to monitoring bodies apply individually to each such monitoring body appointed under the code.
644. European Data Protection Board, *Guidelines 1/2019 on Codes of Conduct and Monitoring Bodies*, paragraphs 13-15, p. 9.
645. *Ibid.*, paragraph 7, p. 7.
646. GDPR, Article 40 (2).

that meets the GDPR requirements, associations and other bodies representing categories of controllers or processors which conduct such processing, should seriously
consider preparing a code of conduct in this regard. For example, as advised by the
Article 29 Working Party, controllers could consider it for auditing processes involving
ML algorithms.[647]

It is important to note that such codes of conduct would need to specify the
practical application of the GDPR and accurately reflect the nature of automated
individual decision-making or sector which deploys it. They should be able to provide
unambiguous, concrete, attainable and enforceable (testable), sector or common
processing activity specific improvements in terms of compliance with data protection
law, not just re-state the GDPR.[648]

Since algorithms used in automated individual decision-making systems are
complex, opaque and, above all else, proprietary, formulating codes of conduct by the
controllers or processors which are involved in such processing constitutes a great
added value. This is because they have a deep understanding of the underlying
processing operations and their limitations. On the other hand, for the same reasons,
they may be unwilling to share their knowledge, if only for the reasons of business
confidentiality. In particular, considering that such an exercise is voluntary.

§4.07   INTERIM CONCLUSIONS

Given that the specific provisions dedicated to solely automated individual decision-
making may not provide sufficient protection for the data subject, supplementarily,
general provisions of the regulation relevant to such processing are examined. The
provisions in question are fundamental data protection principles, which are the most
relevant to such processing, *videlicet* lawfulness, fairness and transparency; purpose
limitation; data minimisation; accuracy and storage limitation principles, as well as
provisions on data protection by design and by default; DPIA; certification and codes of
conduct. In this chapter, it is shown that these general provisions play a major role with
regard to automated individual decision-making, and they can aid the controller in
deploying better such systems.[649]

There are many advantages of shifting the dialogue from one focusing on narrow
and ambiguous Article 22 of the GDPR and the special rights of the data subjects with
regard to solely automated individual decision-making systems to one concentrated on
general provisions of the GDPR.[650] Crucially, they apply to all cases of automated
individual decision-making, and they are not restricted by the narrow scope of Article
22 of the GDPR. Moreover, they do not require any action of individuals, which relieves
the latter of an undue burden. In some cases, these special rights may even not be fit

---

647. Article 29 Data Protection Working Party, *Guidelines on Automated individual decision-making and Profiling*, p. 32.
648. European Data Protection Board, *Guidelines 1/2019 on Codes of Conduct and Monitoring Bodies*, paragraphs 36-37, p. 15.
649. B. Casey, A. Farhangi, R. Vogl, *Rethinking Explainable Machines*, p. 183.
650. *Ibid.*, p. 180.

for purpose. For instance, as already noted above, the right to be informed or the right of access is unlikely to be useful for individuals in instances where the discrimination present in automated individual decision-making is only observable at a statistical scale.[651]

Having regard to the concerns regarding automated individual decision-making, the lawfulness, fairness and transparency principle is particularly important in relation to such processing. Given that all of these notions are understood broadly, fulfilling this principle may constitute a challenge and, ultimately, a valuable exercise for the controller who conducts automated individual decision-making. Likewise, the purpose limitation principle is particularly important, as it allows the data subject to delimit the scope of automated individual decision-making concerning it and to make sure it is legitimate. This is because according to this principle, personal data must be collected for specified, explicit and legitimate purposes and not further processed in a manner that is incompatible with those purposes. Hence, it offers a balanced approach that aims to reconcile the need for predictability and legal certainty regarding the purposes of the processing on the one hand and the pragmatic need for some flexibility on the other. In turn, the data minimisation principle requires that the personal data used in automated individual decision-making must be adequate, relevant and limited to what is necessary, which is particularly demanding in case of systems which use large datasets. Also, the accuracy principle offers protection to the data subject in case of automated individual decision-making based on inaccurate or incomplete personal data, including the data obtained through profiling. This is particularly important with regard to solely automated individual decision-making within the meaning of Article 22 (1) of the GDPR which carries a high risk for the data subject because such a decision, even if it is faulty, produces legal effects concerning the data subject or similarly significantly affects it. Finally, the storage limitation principle prevents the controller from maximising retention of all personal data, as it requires that the personal data must be kept in a form which permits the identification of data subjects for no longer than is necessary for the purposes for which it is processed. Although in certain cases, the storage limitation principle may be interpreted flexibly, the necessity requirement contained therein must not be read overly broadly.

Whereas, data protection by design and by default, DPIA, certification and codes of conduct all recognise that a regulator cannot do everything by top-down control, but that the controller must itself be involved in the design of less privacy-invasive systems. The first two of the above are mandatory for the controllers which deploy automated individual decision-making systems. They are intended to ensure that the GDPR requirements are effectively implemented in such systems already at their design stage. Importantly, such techniques have a well-documented track record of detecting and combating algorithmic discrimination, even in complex and opaque individual decision-making systems. In spite of the fact that the other two of the above-mentioned tools, that is certification and codes of conduct, are voluntary, they may provide great added value. *Inter alia*, they may be used by the controllers to demonstrate compliance

---

651. *Ibid.*, p. 181.

with the GDPR requirements. Another notable advantage of certification and codes of conduct is that standards could be set by properly selected, multidisciplinary teams on a per-sector basis or with regard to similar processing operations, in this case, automated individual decision-making. Certification could provide measures for addressing the some of the shortcomings of the specific provisions on solely automated individual decision-making provided for in the GDPR. In particular, it allows for a proper examination of automated individual decision-making systems by a trusted third party. This allows the controllers to limit the risk of exposing their proprietary algorithms protected by copyright law or trade secrets, while also providing an oversight mechanism, which ensures that the data subject's rights and freedoms are protected as well. Finally, given that automated individual decision-making process raises many concerns with regard to the protection of individuals and it is challenging to implement it in a way that meets the GDPR requirements, associations and other bodies representing categories of controllers or processors which conduct such processing should seriously consider preparing codes of conduct in this regard. Markedly, such codes of conduct could be valuable for the controllers, as they aim to set out the practical application of the GDPR with regard to such processing instead of just re-stating the regulation.

In view of the above, here are the key recommendations that could offer the data subjects greater protection with regard to automated individual decision-making. Firstly, the fundamental GDPR principles relevant to such processing should be thoughtfully considered by the controllers which deploy such processing. Additionally, the European Data Protection Board could issue further guidelines, recommendations and best practices concerning application of these principles in the context of automated individual decision-making. This could raise awareness of the controllers as to their obligations with regard to individual decision-making under principles relating to the processing of personal data. Secondly, certification and codes of conduct that specifically concern automated individual decision-making should be prepared. In particular, methods and ethical requirements for auditing automated individual decision-making systems should be developed, both as standalone accountability tools and as mechanisms to provide information to the data subjects, as required under Articles 13 (2) (f), 14 (2) (g), 15 (1) (h) of the GDPR.[652] Last but not least, further research concerning the general provisions of the GDPR against the backdrop of automated individual decision-making should be encouraged.

The next chapter focuses on the general rights of the data subject relevant to automated individual decision-making, as they could be more useful for individuals than the special rights discussed above.

---

652. S.Wachter, B. Mittelstadt, L. Floridi, *Why a Right to Explanation of Automated Decision-Making Does Not Exist*, pp. 46-47. *See also* B. Mittelstadt, *Auditing for Transparency in Content Personalization Systems*, 10 International Journal of Communication 2016, pp. 4991-5002.

CHAPTER 5

Rights of the Data Subject Relevant to Automated Individual Decision-Making

§5.01 INTRODUCTORY REMARKS

The GDPR establishes various general rights of the data subject, some of which are particularly relevant to automated individual decision-making. These are the right to be informed; the right of access; the right to rectification; the right to erasure and the right to object. Although they are not specifically designed to protect individuals with regard to automated individual decision-making, they can play an important role in relation to such processing. These rights are actionable against the controller conducting the profiling process and the controller making an automated individual decision about a data subject if these entities are not the same.[653] Of course, it is up to individuals to exercise their rights which may put an excessive burden on them.[654]

As already stressed above, the special rights of the data subject outlined in Chapter 3 apply only to solely automated individual decision-making within the meaning of Article 22 (1) of the GDPR. Whereas, this is an overview of the general rights of the data subject which are the most relevant to automated individual decision-making and apply to all such systems. Finally, this chapter contains interim conclusions.

---

653. Article 29 Data Protection Working Party, *Guidelines on Automated individual decision-making and Profiling*, pp. 15-16.
654. L. Edwards, M. Veale, *Slave to the Algorithm?*, p. 67, B. Casey, A. Farhangi, R. Vogl, *Rethinking Explainable Machines*, p. 180; F. Pasquale, *The Black Box Society*, pp. 3-4; J.A. Kroll, et al., *Accountable Algorithms*, pp. 633, 638; L. Edwards, M. Veale, *Enslaving the Algorithm*, p. 51.

§5.02   RIGHT TO BE INFORMED

Articles 13 and 14 of the GDPR oblige the controller to inform the data subject about the details of the processing at its commencement regardless of whether the controller collects personal data directly from the data subject or not. These provisions develop further the transparency principle, which is intrinsically linked to the lawfulness and fairness principles, all three of them being enclosed in Article 5 (1) (a) of the GDPR.[655]

While transparency can be achieved in various ways, it is considered that its most important building block is the information given to the data subject at the beginning of the processing activity, which should then be made easily accessible throughout the processing operation. This is because the right to be informed empowers the data subject to hold the controller accountable and to exercise control over its personal data by, for example, actioning the rights of the data subject.[656] In general, the data subject is unable to exercise these rights, if it is unaware of the existence of the processing activity and its details in the first place. Therefore, the right to be informed is paramount among the rights of the data subject. It is all the more important with regard to automated individual decision-making systems, which ordinarily lack transparency.[657]

The right to be informed applies to all processing activities of the controller, irrespective of the lawful ground for processing upon which they are based.[658] Therefore, it applies to all cases of automated individual decision-making, including profiling and not only solely automated individual decision-making within the meaning of Article 22 (1) of the GDPR.

The detailed information to be provided to the data subject by the controller should be specific to the processing in question and, to the extent possible, it should not cover disparate processing activities collectively. Because of that, the controller which deploys an automated individual decision-making system should consider preparing a separate notice containing the details of such processing. Of course, given that the right to be informed applies not only at the point of collection of personal data, but throughout the processing cycle, the controller must comply with the same requirements when communicating any subsequent material changes to the initial notice provided to the data subject.

The scope of the right to be informed is extensive. Article 13 of the GDPR applies where the personal data is provided by the data subject or observed by the controller, while Article 14 of the GDPR applies where the personal data is otherwise obtained by

---

655. M.E. Kaminski, *The Right to Explanation, Explained*, p. 209. This principle is described in Chapter 4, §4.02[A].
656. *See* reference 363.
657. *See* remarks in Chapter 1, §1.05[D].
658. Solely automated individual decision-making within the meaning of Article 22 (1) of the GDPR is only permitted if one of the three exemptions set out in Article 22 (2) of the GDPR applies. Whereas lawful grounds for the processing relevant for all other automated individual decision-making and profiling are set out in Articles 6 (1) and 9 (2) of the GDPR.

the controller (e.g., from third-party controllers; publicly available sources; data brokers; or other data subjects[659]).

As for timing for the provision of the information, the notice must be provided at the time when personal data are obtained and not *post factum*.[660] Whereas in the case of indirectly obtained personal data, the general requirement is that the information must be provided within a reasonable period after obtaining the personal data and no later than one month.[661]

The information which must be provided by the controller to the data subject is quite comprehensive and it includes the following details: the identity and contact details of the controller and, where applicable, of the controller's representative; the contact details of the data protection officer, where applicable; the purposes of the processing for which the personal data are intended as well as the legal basis for the processing; the categories of personal data concerned (required only where personal data have not been obtained from the data subject); where the processing is based on Article 6 (1) (f) of the GDPR, the legitimate interests pursued by the controller or by a third party; the recipients or categories of recipients of the personal data if any; where applicable, the fact that the controller intends to transfer personal data to a third country or international organisation and the existence or absence of an adequacy decision by the European Commission, or in the case of transfers referred to in Article 46 or 47 or 49 (1) (2) of the GDPR, reference to the appropriate or suitable safeguards and the means by which to obtain a copy of them or where they have been made available; the period for which the personal data will be stored, or if that is not possible, the criteria used to determine that period; the existence of the rights of the data subject: the right of access, the right to rectification, the right to erasure, the right to restriction of processing, the right to object, as well as the right to data portability; where the processing is based on Article 6 (1) (a) or 9 (2) (a) of the GDPR, the existence of the right to withdraw consent at any time; the right to lodge a complaint with a supervisory authority; whether providing the personal data is compulsory and if so, which are the possible consequences of not providing it (required only where personal data have been obtained from the data subject); the source from which the personal data originate, and if applicable, whether it came from a publicly accessible source (required only where personal data have not been obtained from the data subject); the existence of automated individual decision-making, including profiling, and at least in the cases regulated by Article 22 (1) and (4) of the GDPR, meaningful information about the logic involved, as well as the significance and the envisaged consequences of such processing for the data subject.[662]

---

659. Article 29 Data Protection Working Party, *Guidelines on Transparency under Regulation 2016/679*, paragraph 26, pp. 15-16.
660. GDPR, Article 13 (1).
661. GDPR, Article 14 (3) (a). The general time limit of one month for provision of the information may be further curtailed under Article 14 (3) (b) and 14 (3) (a) of the GDPR. Namely, if the personal data is to be used for communication with the data subject, it must be provided at the latest at the time of the first communication to that data subject and if a disclosure to another recipient is envisaged, it must be provided at the latest when the personal data are first disclosed.
662. GDPR, Articles 13 (1)-(2) and 14 (1)-(2).

If the controller intends to further process the personal data for a purpose other than that for which it was collected or obtained, it must also provide the data subject prior to that further processing with information on that other purpose and with any relevant further information as referred to in Article 13 (2) or 14 (2) of the GDPR, respectively.[663] Although Article 13 (3) or 14 (4) of the GDPR do not distinguish between a further, completely different purpose and a further compatible purpose, these provisions only refer to processing the personal data for compatible purposes. This follows from the purpose limitation principle set out in Article 5 (1) (b) of the GDPR, which prohibits the processing of personal data for further purposes that are not compatible with the initial one.[664] Hence, if the controller intends to process the personal data for a new, compatible purpose, the notice to the data subject must be updated to include additional details of the processing with regard to this new purpose. It must be provided to the data subject by the controller prior to the new processing taking place. Ultimately, the data subject should not be taken by surprise by the ways its personal data has been used.[665]

Apart from the content, the form and the manner in which the details of the processing must be provided to the data subject, are also important. It is up to the controller to decide upon the appropriate way to meet this obligation.[666] Notably, it should take into consideration Article 12 of the GDPR, which concerns transparent information, communication and modalities for the exercise of the rights of the data subject.[667]

The controller is exempted from providing the above information where and insofar as the data subject already has the information.[668] Additionally, Article 14 (5) of the GDPR, applicable where personal data has not been obtained from the data subject, envisages a broader set of exceptions to the right to be informed. It does not apply where an insofar as (i) the provision of such information proves impossible or would involve a disproportionate effort, in particular, for processing for archiving purposes in the public interest, scientific or historical research purposes or statistical purposes, subject to the conditions and safeguards referred to in Article 89 (1) of the GDPR or in so far as the obligation referred to in Article 14 (1) of the GDPR is likely to render impossible or seriously impair the achievement of the objectives of that processing. In such cases, the controller shall take appropriate measures to protect the data subject's rights and freedoms and legitimate interests, including making the information publicly available; (ii) obtaining or disclosure is expressly laid down by the EU or Member State law to which the controller is subject and which provides appropriate measures to protect the data subject's legitimate interests; or (iii) where

---

663. GDPR, Articles 13 (3) and 14 (4), which are expressed in identical terms, apart from the word 'collected', which is used in Article 13, and which is replaced with the word 'obtained' in Article 14.
664. *See* Chapter 4, §4.02[B].
665. Article 29 Data Protection Working Party, *Guidelines on Transparency under Regulation 2016/679*, paragraph 45, pp. 23-24.
666. For further guidance as to how provide details of the processing to the data subject, *see* Article 29 Data Protection Working Party, *Guidelines on Transparency under Regulation 2016/679*.
667. *See* Chapter 3, §3.02.
668. GDPR, Article 13 (4).

the personal data must remain confidential subject to an obligation of professional secrecy regulated by the EU or Member State law, including a statutory obligation of secrecy.[669] Although any of the above exemptions from the right to be informed could be relevant to automated individual decision-making, the controller ought to take into account that exceptions should, as a general rule, be interpreted and applied narrowly. Nonetheless, if it seeks to rely on one of the exemptions from the right to be informed, it must be able to demonstrate that the relevant conditions are met in accordance with the principle of accountability set out in Articles 5 (2) and 24 (1) of the GDPR.

Markedly, solely automated individual decision-making within the meaning of Article 22 (1) of the GDPR is subject to an additional special right to be informed.[670] Nonetheless, with regard to automated individual decision-making, including profiling, even if it is not caught by Article 22 (1) of the GDPR, the data subject must be informed about details of such processing. In particular, it must be apprised of the purposes of both (i) automated individual decision-making and (ii) profiling.[671] Especially this information could allow the data subject to better understand the underlying system.[672] This, in turn, could enable the data subject to exercise its rights under the GDPR and gain control of its personal data used in an automated individual decision-making process.

§5.03 RIGHT OF ACCESS

The right of access established in Article 15 of the GDPR allows the data to obtain details of the processing, which are largely analogous to those, which must be provided to it by the controller under the right to be informed.[673] However, in contrast to the

---

669. GDPR, Article 14 (5) (a)-(d).
670. GDPR, Articles 13 (2) (f) and 14 (2) (g), which mandate the controller to inform the data subject about the existence of automated decision-making, including profiling, referred to in Article 22 (1) and (4) and, at least in those cases, meaningful information about the logic involved, as well as the significance and the envisaged consequences of such processing for the data subject. This obligation of the controller is described in Chapter 3, §3.02.
671. GDPR, Articles 13 (1) (c) and 14 (1) (c). Article 29 Data Protection Working Party, *Guidelines on Automated individual decision-making and Profiling*, pp. 16-17. *See also* Recital 60 of the GDPR, which states that the data subject should be informed of the existence of profiling and the consequences of such profiling.
672. E. Bayamlıoğlu, *Transparency of Automated Decisions in the GDPR*, pp. 24-26.
673. GDPR, Article 15 (1)-(2):

> 1. The data subject shall have the right to obtain from the controller confirmation as to whether or not personal data concerning him or her are being processed, and, where that is the case, access to the personal data and the following information: (a) the purposes of the processing; (b) the categories of personal data concerned; (c) the recipients or categories of recipient to whom the personal data have been or will be disclosed, in particular recipients in third countries or international organisations; (d) where possible, the envisaged period for which the personal data will be stored, or, if not possible, the criteria used to determine that period; (e) the existence of the right to request from the controller rectification or erasure of personal data or restriction of processing of personal data concerning the data subject or to object to such processing; (f) the right to lodge a complaint with a supervisory authority; (g) where the personal data are not collected from the data subject, any available information as to their source; (h) the existence of automated decision-making, including profiling, referred

transparency obligations set out in Articles 13-14 of the GDPR, the complementary right of access has to be invoked by the data subject, which may be done at any time throughout the processing cycle.

Identically to the right to be informed, solely automated individual decision-making within the meaning of Article 22 (1) of the GDPR is subject to an additional special right of access.[674] Besides, by exercising the right of access, the data subject may obtain details of the processing with regard to any automated individual decision-making, including profiling, including the categories of data used in such a process, as well as the purposes of such processing. This information could be useful for the data subject for the same reasons as indicated above in §5.02.

Furthermore, pursuant to Article 15 (3) of the GDPR, the controller must provide a copy of the personal data undergoing processing. This allows the data subject to detect any inaccuracies in the personal data used by the controller, which could be subsequently corrected under the right to rectification. However, in some cases, this would require reviewing huge amounts of personal data, which places a significant burden on the data subject. According to the Article 29 Working Party, under this provision, the controller has a duty to make available the data used as an input to create the profile as well as access to information on the profile and details of which segments the data subject has been placed into.[675] However, it is highly questionable that a copy of the personal data undergoing processing must be structured in such a way, as this conclusion does not follow from the wording of this provision.[676]

§5.04   RIGHT TO RECTIFICATION

Article 16 of the GDPR gives that the data subject the right to obtain from the controller the rectification of inaccurate personal data concerning it, as well as the right to have incomplete personal data completed.[677] If the data subject exercises this right, the controller must restrict the processing under Article 18 (1) (a) of the GDPR for a period

---

      to in Article 22(1) and (4) and, at least in those cases, meaningful information about the logic involved, as well as the significance and the envisaged consequences of such processing for the data subject.

   2. Where personal data are transferred to a third country or to an international organisation, the data subject shall have the right to be informed of the appropriate safeguards pursuant to Article 46 relating to the transfer.

674. GDPR, Article 15 (1) (h), which mandates the controller to inform the data subject about the existence of automated decision-making, including profiling, referred to in Article 22 (1) and (4) and, at least in those cases, meaningful information about the logic involved, as well as the significance and the envisaged consequences of such processing for the data subject. This obligation of the controller is described in Chapter 3, §3.04.

675. Article 29 Data Protection Working Party, *Guidelines on Automated individual decision-making and Profiling*, pp. 16, 31.

676. With regard to the right of access, *see also* remarks concerning limitations to algorithmic transparency in Chapter 3, §3.10.

677. GDPR, Article 16: 'The data subject shall have the right to obtain from the controller without undue delay the rectification of inaccurate personal data concerning him or her. Taking into account the purposes of the processing, the data subject shall have the right to have incomplete personal data completed, including by means of providing a supplementary statement'.

enabling it to verify the accuracy of the personal data. This right is particularly useful with regard to profiling, which often precedes automated individual decision-making.

Any conclusions resulting from the profiling process which, subsequently, constitute the basis for an automated individual decision, can only be as reliable as the personal data they are based on. Thus, if the personal data is inaccurate or irrelevant, or taken out of context, the risk of rendering a wrong decision is inevitable. Even assuming that the personal data used in such processing is accurate, as profiling can involve an element of prediction, it produces partially accurate and partially inaccurate results.[678]

The right to rectification applies both to the personal data used to create the profile of the data subject, regardless if it was provided by the data subject, observed or otherwise obtained by the controller and to the profile itself, that is, any category assigned to the data subject.[679] Therefore, it allows the data subject to challenge the accuracy of the personal data used by the controller, as well as the profile, that is, any category that has been applied to it as a result of the profiling process. Additionally, the right to rectification allows the data subject to complement incomplete personal data with additional information.

As described above, the controller is obliged to provide the data subject with access to its personal data and its profile under Article 15 of the GDPR. This right of access enables the data subject to exercise the right to rectification. Additionally, the right to rectification is closely related to the accuracy principle set out in Article 5 (1) (d) of the GDPR, and it supports the controller as to compliance with it.[680]

With regard to solely automated individual decision-making within the meaning of Article 22 of the GDPR, the controller is required to provide the data subject with meaningful information about the logic involved in such processing under Articles 13 (2) (f) and 14 (2) (g) 15 (1) (h) of the GDPR. This information is currently interpreted to include the details of main characteristics considered in reaching the decision and their approximate relevance, to allow the data subject to understand the reasons for the decision.[681] Consequently, the right to rectification could be useful for the data subject

---

678. *See* remarks about profiling in Chapter 1, §1.02[F] and §1.05[A].

679. Article 29 Data Protection Working Party, *Guidelines on Automated individual decision-making and Profiling*, pp. 17-18; Privacy International, *Data Is Power: Profiling and Automated Decision-Making in GDPR*, p. 16.

680. GDPR, Article 5 (1) (d): 'Personal data shall be accurate and, where necessary, kept up to date; every reasonable step must be taken to ensure that personal data that are inaccurate, having regard to the purposes for which they are processed, are erased or rectified without delay'. For further remarks about the accuracy principle *see* Chapter 4, §4.02[D]. *See also* Article 29 Data Protection Working Party, *Guidelines on Automated individual decision-making and Profiling*, pp. 31-32, which recommends the controllers to consider introducing online preference management tools such as a privacy dashboard, which gives data subjects the option of managing what is happening to their information across a number of different services allowing them to alter settings, update their personal details, and review or edit their profile to correct any inaccuracies.

681. *See* reference 377.

attempting to correct inaccuracies in these most important characteristics and subsequently to contest such a decision under Article 22 (3) of the GDPR.[682]

§5.05   RIGHT TO ERASURE

Pursuant to Article 17 (1) of the GDPR, the data subject has the right to erasure (so-called right to be forgotten). It can be invoked by the data subject against any controller which processes personal data concerning it if one of the hypotheses listed therein applies.[683] Some of the various grounds for the right to erasure overlap. Specifically, if the personal data is no longer necessary for the purpose for which it was collected or otherwise processed or consent on which the processing is withdrawn, the personal data is also unlawfully processed. As a matter of fact, Article 17 (1) (d) of the GDPR is a general clause which applies where the processing of the personal data does not otherwise comply with the GDPR.[684] Whereas other grounds for the right to erasure concern the following different scenarios: (i) the data subject invokes its right to object under Article 21 GDPR; (ii) the personal data has to be erased for compliance with a legal obligation; (iii) the personal data has been collected in relation to the offer of information society services referred to in Article 8 (1) of the GDPR.[685]

---

682. S. Wachter, B. Mittelstadt, C. Russell, *Counterfactual Explanations Without Opening the Black Box*, p. 872. The authors note that if large amounts of personal data are held by the controller, then the subject may have to check tens of thousands of items for inaccuracies.
683. GDPR, Article 17 (1):

> The data subject shall have the right to obtain from the controller the erasure of personal data concerning him or her without undue delay and the controller shall have the obligation to erase personal data without undue delay where one of the following grounds applies:
>
> (a) the personal data are no longer necessary in relation to the purposes for which they were collected or otherwise processed;
> (b) the data subject withdraws consent on which the processing is based according to point (a) of Article 6(1), or point (a) of Article 9(2), and where there is no other legal ground for the processing;
> (c) the data subject objects to the processing pursuant to Article 21(1) and there are no overriding legitimate grounds for the processing, or the data subject objects to the processing pursuant to Article 21(2);
> (d) the personal data have been unlawfully processed;
> (e) the personal data have to be erased for compliance with a legal obligation in Union or Member State law to which the controller is subject;
> (f) the personal data have been collected in relation to the offer of information society services referred to in Article 8(1)'.

684. GDPR, Recital 65.
685. GDPR, Article 8 (1): 'Where point (a) of Article 6(1) applies, in relation to the offer of information society services directly to a child, the processing of the personal data of a child shall be lawful where the child is at least 16 years old. Where the child is below the age of 16 years, such processing shall be lawful only if and to the extent that consent is given or authorised by the holder of parental responsibility over the child. Member States may provide by law for a lower age for those purposes provided that such lower age is not below 13 years'. *See also* Recital 65 of the GDPR which states that right is relevant in particular where the data subject has given its consent as a child and is not fully aware of the risks involved by the

Furthermore, as per Article 17 (2) of the GDPR, where the controller is obliged to erase the personal data, which it has made public, the controller, taking account of available technology and the cost of implementation, must take reasonable steps, including technical measures, to inform other controllers which are processing the personal data that the data subject has requested the erasure by such controllers of any links to, or copy or replication of, those personal data. Considering that these controllers are not explicitly obliged to do anything with this information, the data subject may have to invoke the right erasure request to these controllers as well, unless they chose to erase the personal data voluntarily.[686]

Last but not least, it follows from Article 17 (3) of the GDPR that the right to erasure is not absolute, and it does not apply in certain cases.[687] Namely, the further retention of the personal data is lawful where it is necessary, for exercising the right of freedom of expression and information, for compliance with a legal obligation, for the performance of a task carried out in the public interest or in the exercise of official authority vested in the controller, on the grounds of public interest in the area of public health, for archiving purposes in the public interest, scientific or historical research purposes or statistical purposes, or for the establishment, exercise or defence of legal claims.

The right to erasure may be invoked by the data subject on any of the above-mentioned grounds, as any of them may be relevant to automated individual decision-making, including profiling. Notably, this right applies to the personal data used in such processing, regardless if it was provided by the data subject, observed or otherwise obtained by the controller and to the profile itself, that is any category assigned to the data subject.[688] Such broad scope of the personal data which may be erased under this right is particularly important with regard to automated individual

---

processing, and later wants to remove such personal data, especially on the internet and remarks that the data subject should be able to exercise that right notwithstanding the fact that he or she is no longer a child.

686. L. Edwards, M. Veale, *Slave to the Algorithm?*, p. 72.

687. GDPR, Article 17 (3):

Paragraphs 1 and 2 shall not apply to the extent that processing is necessary:

(a) for exercising the right of freedom of expression and information;
(b) for compliance with a legal obligation which requires processing by Union or Member State law to which the controller is subject or for the performance of a task carried out in the public interest or in the exercise of official authority vested in the controller;
(c) for reasons of public interest in the area of public health in accordance with points (h) and (i) of Article 9(2) as well as Article 9(3);
(d) for archiving purposes in the public interest, scientific or historical research purposes or statistical purposes in accordance with Article 89(1) in so far as the right referred to in paragraph 1 is likely to render impossible or seriously impair the achievement of the objectives of that processing; or
(e) for the establishment, exercise or defence of legal claims'.

688. Article 29 Data Protection Working Party, *Guidelines on Automated individual decision-making and Profiling*, pp. 17-18.

decision-making systems, which use ML algorithms allowing the controller to make heavy use of personal data, which is not explicitly provided by the data subject.[689]

§5.06   RIGHT TO OBJECT

Pursuant to Article 21 (1) of the GDPR, the data subject has the right to object to the processing of personal data concerning it, including profiling, on grounds relating to its particular situation.[690] This right applies to cases where processing is based on Article 6 (1) (e) or (f) of the GDPR, that is when it is (i) necessary for the performance of a task carried out in the public interest or in the exercise of official authority vested in the controller, or (ii) necessary for the purposes of the legitimate interests pursued by the controller or by a third party.[691] In accordance with the right to object, the controller shall no longer process the personal data unless the controller demonstrates compelling legitimate grounds for the processing which override the interests, rights and freedoms of the data subject or for the establishment, exercise or defence of legal claims.

Additionally, Article 21 (2) of the GDPR grants the data subject an unconditional right to object to the processing of personal data concerning it for direct marketing purposes, including profiling to the extent that it is related to such direct marketing.[692]

If the data subject exercises the right to object pursuant to Article 21 (1) of the GDPR, the controller must restrict the processing under Article 18 (1) (d) of the GDPR until the moment it demonstrates that there are overriding legitimate grounds for the processing.[693] If the controller does not demonstrate that or the data subject exercises this right pursuant to Article 21 (2) of the GDPR, the controller is under obligation to no longer process the personal data for such purposes Article 21 (3) of the GDPR or, if there are no other purposes for processing the data, to erase it under Article 17 (1) (c) of the GDPR.

The right to object has to be explicitly brought to the attention of the data subject and presented clearly and separately from other information at the latest at the time of

---

689. L. Edwards, M. Veale, *Slave to the Algorithm?*, pp. 68-69.
690. GDPR, Article 21 (1): 'The data subject shall have the right to object, on grounds relating to his or her particular situation, at any time to processing of personal data concerning him or her which is based on point (e) or (f) of Article 6(1), including profiling based on those provisions. The controller shall no longer process the personal data unless the controller demonstrates compelling legitimate grounds for the processing which override the interests, rights and freedoms of the data subject or for the establishment, exercise or defence of legal claims'.
691. As per Article 6 (1) (f) of the GDPR, except where such legitimate interests are overridden by the interests or fundamental rights and freedoms of the data subject which require protection of personal data, in particular where the data subject is a child.
692. GDPR, Article 21 (2): 'Where personal data are processed for direct marketing purposes, the data subject shall have the right to object at any time to processing of personal data concerning him or her for such marketing, which includes profiling to the extent that it is related to such direct marketing'. *See also* Recital 70 of the GDPR, which states that this right may be exercised by the data subject with regard to initial or further processing, at any time and free of charge.
693. *See also* Recital 69 of the GDPR, which states that it should be for the controller to demonstrate that its compelling legitimate interest overrides the interests or the fundamental rights and freedoms of the data subject.

the first communication with the data subject.[694] This right is useful for the data subject which does not want to be subject to automated individual decision-making, regardless of whether it includes profiling or not, as long as it is based on two of the above-mentioned lawful bases for processing of personal data set out in Article 6 (1) (e) and (f) of the GDPR. However, it may not be invoked by the data subject which is subject to solely automated individual decision-making within the meaning of Article 22 (1) of the GDPR, as the lawful bases for processing of personal data are not relevant to this type of processing which is subject to special provisions of Article 22 of the GDPR.[695]

§5.07 INTERIM CONCLUSIONS

The GDPR establishes various general rights of the data subject, some of which are particularly relevant to automated individual decision-making. These are the right to be informed; the right of access; the right to rectification; the right to erasure and the right to object. Although they are not specifically designed to afford the data subjects protection with regard to automated individual decision-making, they can play an important role in relation to such processing. As underlined above, they do not apply only to solely automated individual decision-making within the meaning of Article 22 (1) of the GDPR, but to all such systems. Notwithstanding the above, it remains up to the individuals to exercise their rights which may put an excessive burden on them.

In accordance to the right to be informed, the controller is required to inform the data subject about numerous details of the processing at its commencement regardless whether the controller collects personal data directly from the data subject or not. This right is especially important with regard to automated individual decision-making, which ordinarily lacks transparency. As a result, this obligation of the controller empowers the data subject to hold the controller accountable and to exercise control over its personal data used in such processing by, for example, actioning one of the rights of the data subject. Especially the information about the purposes of automated individual decision-making could allow the data subject to better understand the underlying system. Furthermore, the right of access allows the data to obtain details of the processing, which are largely analogous to those, which must be provided to it by the controller under the right be informed, at its own request. Additionally, this right allows the data subject to obtain a copy of the personal data undergoing processing, which enables it to detect any inaccuracies or incompletions in the personal data used by the controller. Any inaccurate personal data could be subsequently corrected or completed by the data subject under the right to rectification. Markedly, this right also applies to the profile, that is any category assigned to the data subject in the process of profiling. By invoking this right, individuals may ensure the accuracy of the personal data concerning them, which is obviously reflected in more accurate decisions in their cases. In certain cases, the right to erasure (so-called right to be forgotten) could also be exercised by the data subject, which wishes that the controller erases some of the

---

694. GDPR, Article 21 (4).
695. Solely automated individual decision-making within the meaning of Article 22 (1) of the GDPR is only permitted if one of the three exemptions set out in Article 22 (2) of the GDPR applies.

personal data. As the right to rectification, the right to erasure also applies to the profile, that is any category assigned to the data subject. Finally, in some cases, the data subject has also the right to object to processing, including automated individual decision-making, on grounds relating to its particular situation. Though, there may occur cases when the controller is allowed to process the personal data in spite of the data subject invoking this right. However, with regard to automated individual decision-making conducted for direct marketing purposes, this right is unconditional, so the controller may no longer conduct such processing. Notwithstanding the above, this particular right may not be invoked by the data subject which is subject to solely automated individual decision-making within the meaning of Article 22 (1) of the GDPR, as the lawful bases for processing of personal data are not relevant to this type of processing which is subject to special provisions of Article 22 of the GDPR.

In view of the above, here are the key recommendations that could offer the data subjects greater protection with regard to automated individual decision-making. First, the general rights of the data subject relevant to such processing should be thoughtfully considered by the controllers which deploy such processing. Second, the European Data Protection Board could issue further guidelines, recommendations and best practices concerning application of these rights in the context of automated individual decision-making. Additionally, supervisory authorities could take action to raise awareness of the data subjects as to their rights which could be invoked with regard to automated individual decision-making. Last but not least, further research concerning the general rights of the data subject against the backdrop of automated individual decision-making should be encouraged.

CHAPTER 6
Conclusions

Given that the automation of individual decision-making processes is omnipresent, the GDPR aims to make sure that society can take full advantage of the capabilities of such processing while minimising the possible undesired consequences for individuals. To recapitulate the key concerns with regard to such processing, first of all, it is common knowledge that most databases contain inaccurate or incomplete data, which may be blindingly applied to individuals in the process of automated individual decision-making. Moreover, the use of profiling in such processing unavoidably involves a margin of error and it may lead to inaccurate predictions about individuals. In addition, algorithms are designed by humans, and they are unavoidably value-laden and may contain latent bias, which may lead to discrimination. Even self-learning ML algorithms are likely to repeat or even aggravate discrimination present in the past decision-making because they are trained on historical data. Most of all, automated individual decision-making is ordinarily non-transparent, which makes the capacity of individuals to examine and understand such process and its results largely subdued.

In view of the above, the purpose of this doctoral dissertation is to describe and analyse the GDPR framework aimed at protecting natural persons with regard to automated individual decision-making. Its main objective is to examine whether this legislative act affords sufficient protection of natural persons with regard to such processing. In addition to that, the focus of the thesis is to identify the loopholes that hinder or prevent the above. Above all, this doctoral dissertation is aimed at identifying *de lege lata* rules and *de lege ferenda* postulates that could provide individuals with effective protection in relation to automated individual decision-making. Due to the above, this thesis contributes to the ongoing discussion on algorithmic accountability.

To achieve the said ambitions, this thesis first analyses the key provision of the GDPR, which attempts to mitigate the risks to the rights and freedoms of natural persons associated with solely automated individual decision-making, *videlicet* the right not to be subject to solely automated decision-making set out in Article 22 of the regulation. It is shown that it is narrow, vague and full of potential loopholes, which may be abused by the controllers. In fact, even the legal nature of this right is uncertain,

137

as it may be read either as a right to opt out that the data subject has to actively exercise or as a general prohibition that does not require any action. Besides, it envisages three exceptions, which are so considerable and prone to abuse by the controllers, that they erode the data subject's right not to be subject to solely automated individual decision-making to the point that the exceptions become the rule.

Subsequently, the doctoral dissertation examines several special rights of the data subject, which aim to address concerns regarding automated individual decision-making, notably the right to be informed, the right of access, the right to express a point of view, the right to human intervention and the right to contest the decision. These special rights are applicable to a very narrow range of cases meeting all of the requirements set out in Article 22 (1) of the GDPR. Additionally, the preeminent safeguards apply only if the processing is conducted under Article 22 (2) (a) or (c) of the GDPR, that is, if it is necessary for the formation or performance of a contract or based on the data subject's explicit consent.[696] Thus, if solely automated individual decision-making is authorised by the EU or Member State law to which the controller is subject, the data subject does not have the said rights.[697] Although the law in question must lay down suitable measures to safeguard the data subject's rights and freedoms and legitimate interests, in these cases, the level of protection of the data subject may significantly diverge.

The scope of the above-mentioned rights is very vague. Not to mention that the data subject may even not be aware of them, as there is no explicit obligation of the controller to inform the data subject about the right not to be subject to a solely automated individual decision and its safeguards, that is, the right express point of view, the right to human intervention and the right to contest the decision. Despite much debate, a consensus has not yet emerged in the legal doctrine concerning the supposed right to an explanation of a particular solely automated individual decision. In addition to that, some of the special rights of the data subject, in particular, the right to be informed and the right of access, may be limited by intellectual property rights. Aside from that, these special rights of the data subject are further weakened also by technical obstacles to their effective implementation, particularly when applied to complex solely automated individual decision-making systems.

Consequently, given that the GDPR provisions dedicated to solely automated individual decision-making may not provide sufficient protection for the data subject, supplementarily, general provisions of the regulation relevant to such processing are examined. The provisions in question are fundamental data protection principles, which are the most relevant to such processing, *videlicet* lawfulness, fairness and transparency; purpose limitation; data minimisation; accuracy and storage limitation principles, as well as provisions on data protection by design and by default; DPIA; certification and codes of conduct.

---

696. That is the right express point of view, the right to human intervention and the right to contest the decision. Whereas the right to be informed and the right of access apply to all three exemptions allowing solely automated individual decision-making.

697. GDPR, Article 22 (2) (b).

It is established that these general provisions play a major role with regard to automated individual decision-making, and they can aid the controller in deploying better such systems. Strikingly, they apply to all cases of automated individual decision-making, and they are not restricted by the narrow scope of Article 22 (1) of the GDPR. Moreover, they do not require any action of individuals, which relieves the latter of an undue burden. These principles may address some of the key concerns with regard to automated individual decision-making, such as discrimination, which are difficult, if not impossible to tackle with the use of specific provisions dedicated to solely automated individual decision-making.

While data protection by design and by default, DPIA, certification and codes of conduct all force the controller to be involved in the design of less privacy-invasive systems. The first two provisions are mandatory for the controllers, which deploy automated individual decision-making. They are intended to ensure that the GDPR requirements are effectively implemented in such systems already at their design stage. The latter two provisions are voluntary, but they may provide great added value, as standards could be set by properly selected, multidisciplinary teams on a per-sector basis or with regard to similar processing operations, in this case, automated individual decision-making. In addition to that, certification could provide measures for addressing the some of the shortcomings of the specific provisions on solely automated individual decision-making provided for in the GDPR. Notably, it allows for a proper examination of automated individual decision-making systems by a trusted third party. This allows the controllers to limit the risk of exposing their proprietary algorithms protected by copyright law or trade secrets, while also providing an oversight mechanism, which ensures that the data subject's rights and freedoms are protected as well.

Given that automated individual decision-making process raises many concerns with regard to the protection of individuals and it is challenging to implement it in a way that meets the GDPR requirements, associations and other bodies representing categories of controllers or processors which conduct such processing should seriously consider preparing codes of conduct in this regard. Markedly, such codes of conduct could be valuable for the controllers, as they aim to set out the practical application of the GDPR with regard to such processing instead of just re-stating the regulation.

Lastly, the general rights of the data subject relevant to automated individual decision-making are taken under the loop, and it is shown they could be more useful for individuals than the special rights discussed above. These are the right to be informed; the right of access; the right to rectification; the right to erasure and the right to object. As underlined above, they do not apply only to solely automated individual decision-making within the meaning of Article 22 (1) of the GDPR, but to all such systems.

In light of foregoing considerations, although the GDPR may appear to give strong protection against automated individual decision-making, as it currently stands, it may prove ineffectual. It is submitted that the protection afforded to the data subject by the specific provisions dedicated to solely automated individual decision-making is curtailed. Accordingly, it is argued that general provisions of the regulation play a major role with regard to automated individual decision-making, and they could provide individuals with more effective protection in relation to automated individual decision-making. Having in mind the above, the key *de lege ferenda* postulates, and recommendations that could offer the data subjects greater protection with regard to solely automated individual decision-making are also presented in the above chapters.[698]

Presently, the research is limited by lack of jurisprudence. Certainly, it is difficult to form conclusions based on the uncertain and ambiguous legal framework. It requires a certain amount of speculation. The application of the discussed provisions remains open to judicial and regulator's discretion. Specifically, it will be determined predominantly by supervisory authorities, the European Data Protection Board, the national courts, as well as the Court of Justice of the European Union. The predecessor of Article 22 of the GDPR, Article 15 of the DPD, was rarely litigated in national courts or enforced the supervisory authorities. Because of that, it is not clear how the right not to be subject to solely automated individual decision-making provided for in the GDPR will be interpreted in the future. The Court of Justice of the European Union has yet to rule on the subject matter of Article 22 of the GDPR, and it never ruled on the subject matter of Article 15 of the DPD. However, given the growing importance of this type of processing, jurisprudence in this regard is inevitable. In particular, further research will need to focus on first jurisprudential applications of the EU and Member State law authorising solely automated individual decision-making.

---

698. *Vide* interim conclusions in Chapter 2, §2.09; Chapter 3, §3.11; Chapter 4, §4.07; Chapter 5, §5.07, respectively.

Bibliography

Papers of Data Protection Authorities

Article 29 Data Protection Working Party, *Advice paper on essential elements of a definition and a provision on profiling within the EU General Data Protection Regulation*, adopted on 13 May 2013.

Article 29 Data Protection Working Party, *Guidelines on Automated individual decision-making and Profiling for the purposes of Regulation 2016/679*, as last revised and adopted on 6 February 2018.

Article 29 Data Protection Working Party, *Guidelines on Consent under Regulation 2016/679*, as last revised and adopted on 10 April 2018.

Article 29 Data Protection Working Party, *Guidelines on Data Protection Impact Assessment (DPIA) and determining whether processing is 'likely to result in a high risk' for the purposes of Regulation 2016/679*, as last revised and adopted on 4 October 2017.

Article 29 Data Protection Working Party, *Guidelines on transparency under Regulation 2016/679*, as last revised and adopted on 11 April 2018.

Article 29 Data Protection Working Party, *Opinion 01/2012 on the data protection reform proposals*, adopted on 23 March 2012.

Article 29 Data Protection Working Party, *Opinion 02/2013 on apps on smart devices*, adopted on 27 February 2013.

Article 29 Data Protection Working Party, *Opinion 03/2013 on purpose limitation*, adopted on 2 April 2013.

Article 29 Data Protection Working Party, *Opinion 05/2014 on Anonymisation Techniques*, adopted on 10 April 2014.

Article 29 Data Protection Working Party, *Opinion 06/2014 on the notion of legitimate interests of the data controller under Article 7 of Directive 95/46/EC*, adopted on 9 April 2014.

Article 29 Data Protection Working Party, *Opinion 4/2007 on the concept of personal data*, adopted on 20 June 2007.

Article 29 Data Protection Working Party, *Update of Opinion 8/2010 on applicable law in light of the CJEU judgement in Google Spain*, adopted on 16 December 2015.

Article 29 Working Party, *Opinion 1/2010 on the concepts of 'controller' and 'processor'*, adopted on 16 February 2010.

Article 29 Working Party, *Opinion 3/2010 on the principle of accountability*, adopted on 13 July 2010.

Article 29 Working Party, *Statement on the role of a risk-based approach in data protection legal frameworks*, adopted on 30 May 2014.

European Data Protection Board, *Guidelines 1/2018 on certification and identifying certification criteria in accordance with Articles 42 and 43 of the Regulation*, Version 3.0, adopted on 4 June 2019.

European Data Protection Board, *Guidelines 1/2019 on Codes of Conduct and Monitoring Bodies under Regulation 2016/679*, Version 2.0, adopted on 4 June 2019.

European Data Protection Board, *Guidelines 3/2018 on the territorial scope of the GDPR (Article 3) – Version for public consultation*, adopted on 16 November 2018.

European Data Protection Supervisor, *Assessing the necessity of measures that limit the fundamental right to the protection of personal data: A Toolkit*, adopted on 11 April 2017.

European Data Protection Supervisor, *Opinion 3/2015 (with addendum). Europe's big opportunity. Recommendations on the EU's options for data protection reform*, adopted on 27 July 2015 (updated with addendum, 9 October 2015), (2015/C 301/01).

European Data Protection Supervisor, *Opinion 3/2018 on online manipulation and personal data*, adopted on 19 March 2018.

European Data Protection Supervisor, *Opinion 7/2015 Meeting the challenges of big data*, adopted on 19 November 2015.

Information Commissioner's Office, *Automated decision-making and profiling*, Guidelines of 5 June 2018.

Information Commissioner's Office, *Big data, artificial intelligence, machine learning and data protection*, Guidelines of 1 March 2017, version 2.2.

Information Commissioner's Office, *Examples of processing 'likely to result in high risk'*, available at: https://ico.org.uk/for-organisations/guide-to-data-protection/guide-to-the-general-data-protection-regulation-gdpr/data-protection-impact-assessments-dpias/examples-of-processing-likely-to-result-in-high-risk/, accessed 1 July 2019.

Information Commissioner's Office, Feedback request – profiling and automated decision-making of 6 April 2017.

Information Commissioner's Office, *Guidance on Data Protection Impact Assessments (DPIAs)*, available at: https://ico.org.uk/for-organisations/guide-to-data-protection/guide-to-the-general-data-protection-regulation-gdpr/data-protection-impact-assessments-dpias/, accessed 1 July 2019.

Information Commissioner's Office, *Guide to data protection*, available at: https://ico.org.uk/for-organisations/guide-to-data-protection/guide-to-the-general-data-protection-regulation-gdpr/, accessed 1 July 2019.

Documents of International Organisations

Council of Europe, *Explanatory Report to the Protocol amending the Convention for the Protection of Individuals with regard to Automatic Processing of Personal Data*, Council of Europe Treaty Series No. 223, Strasbourg, 10 October 2018.

Council of Europe, *Recommendation CM/Rec(2010)13 of the Committee of Ministers to member states on the protection of individuals with regard to automatic processing of personal data in the context of profiling*, 23 November 2010.

European Patent Office, *Guidelines for Examination, Programs for computers*, available at: https://www.epo.org/law-practice/legal-texts/html/guidelines/e/index.htm, accessed 1 May 2019.

European Patent Office, Opinion G 0003/08 (Programs for computers) of 12 May 2010, ECLI:EP:BA:2010:G000308.20100512.

Decision of the EEA Joint Committee No. 154/2018 of 6 July 2018 amending Annex XI (Electronic communication, audiovisual services and information society) and Protocol 37 (containing the list provided for in Article 101) to the EEA Agreement [2018/1022], Official Journal of the European Union L 183, 19 July 2018, pp. 23-26.

Academic Writings

Acemoglu D., Restrepo P., *Artificial Intelligence, Automation and Work*, National Bureau of Economic Research Working Paper 24196, January 2018.

Aletras N., Tsarapatsanis D., Preoţiuc-Pietro D., Lampos V., *Predicting Judicial Decisions of the European Court of Human Rights: A Natural Language Processing Perspective*, 2 (e93) PeerJ Computer Science (2016), pp. 1-19.

Almada M., *Human Intervention in Automated Decision-Making: Toward the Construction of Contestable Systems*, written on 23 April 2019, preprint available at SSRN: https://papers.ssrn.com/sol3/papers.cfm?abstract_id = 3264189, accessed 1 October 2019, pp. 1-10, 17th International Conference on Artificial Intelligence and Law (ICAIL), 17-21 June 2019, Montréal, Canada, Forthcoming.

Bambauer J., Zarsky T., *The Algorithm Game*, 94 (1) Notre Dame Law Review (2018), pp. 1-46; Arizona Legal Studies Discussion Paper No. 18-09, March 2018, pp. 1-47.

Bayamlıoğlu E., *Contesting Automated Decisions: A View of Transparency Implications*, 4 (4) European Data Protection Law Review (2018), pp. 433-446.

Bayamlıoğlu E., *Transparency of Automated Decisions in the GDPR: An Attempt for Systemization*, Privacy Law Scholars Conference (PLSC) 2018, pp. 1-50.

Bielak-Jomaa E., Lubasz D. (ed.), *RODO. Ogólne rozporządzenie o ochronie danych. Komentarz*, Warsaw 2018, LEX.

Binns R., Van Kleek M., Veale M., Lyngs U., Zhao J., Shadbolt N., *'It's Reducing a Human Being to a Percentage'; Perceptions of Justice in Algorithmic Decisions*, Proceedings of the 2018 CHI Conference on Human Factors in Computing Systems Paper No. 377.

Blanchette J.-F., Johnson D. G., *Data Retention and the Panoptic Society: The Social Benefits of Forgetfulness*, 18 (1) The Information Society (2002), pp. 33-45.

Bozdag E., *Bias in Algorithmic Filtering and Personalization*, 15 (3) Ethics and Information Technology (2013), pp. 209-227.

Brennan-Marquez K., Henderson S.E., *Artificial Intelligence and Role-Reversible Judgment*, 109 (2) Journal of Criminal Law and Criminology (2019), pp. 137-164.

Brkan, M., *Do Algorithms Rule the World? Algorithmic Decision-Making in the Framework of the GDPR and Beyond*, Terminator or the Jetsons? The Economics and Policy Implications of Artificial Intelligence, Technology Policy Institute (Conference held 22 February 2018 in Washington, D.C., USA), written on 1 August 2017, available at SSRN: https://papers.ssrn.com/sol3/papers.cfm?abstract_id = 3124901, accessed 1 October 2019, pp. 1-29, a revised version of this paper has been published in: 27 (2) International Journal of Law and Information Technology (2019), pp. 91-121.

Burrell J., *How the Machine 'Thinks': Understanding Opacity in Machine Learning Algorithms*, 3 (1) Big Data and Society (2016), pp. 1-12.

Bygrave L.A., *Minding the Machine: Article 15 of the EC Data Protection Directive and Automated Profiling*, 17 (1) Computer Law & Security Review (2001), pp. 17-24.

Bygrave L., *Data Protection Law: Approaching Its Rationale, Logic and Limits*, Kluwer Law International 2002.

Casey B., Farhangi A., Vogl R., *Rethinking Explainable Machines: The GDPR's 'Right to Explanation' Debate and the Rise of Algorithmic Audits in Enterprise*, 34 (1) Berkeley Technology Law Journal (2019), pp. 143-188.

Chabert J. L. (ed.), *A History of Algorithms: From the Pebble to the Microchip*, Springer 1999.

Citron D.K., Pasquale F., *The Scored Society: Due Process for Automated Predictions*, 89 (1) Washington Law Review (2014), pp. 1-33.

Cowgill B., Tucker C., *Algorithmic Bias: A Counterfactual Perspective*, Working Paper: NSF Trustworthy Algorithms, December 2017.

Custers B., Calders T., Schermer B., Zarsky T. (eds), *Discrimination and Privacy in the Information Society*, Springer 2013.

Datta A., Sen S., Zick Y., *Algorithmic Transparency via Quantitative Input Influence*, paper presented at the 37th IEEE Symposium on Security and Privacy, 23-25 May 2016, San Jose, the United States of America, published by IEEE Symposium on Security and Privacy, pp. 598-617.

Datta A., Tschantz M.C., *Automated Experiments on Ad Privacy Settings a Tale of Opacity, Choice, and Discrimination*, 1 Proceedings on Privacy Enhancing Technologies (2015), pp. 92-112.

Di Porto F., *In Praise of an Empowerment Disclosure Regulatory Approach to Algorithms*, 49 (5) International Review of Intellectual Property and Competition Law (2018), pp. 507-511.

Dixon P., Gellman R., *The Scoring of America: How Secret Consumer Scores Threaten Your Privacy and Your Future*, World Privacy Forum, 2 April 2014.

Doshi-Velez F., Kortz M., *Accountability of AI under the Law: The Role of Explanation*, Berkman Klein Center Working Group on Explanation and the Law, Berkman Klein Center for Internet & Society Working Paper (2017), pp. 1-15.

Douglas H.E., *Science, Policy, and the Value-Free Ideal*, University of Pittsburgh Press 2009.

Dumortier J. (ed.), *Recent Developments in Data Privacy Law*, Leuven University Press 1992.

Edwards L. (ed.), *Law, Policy and the Internet*, Hart 2018.

Edwards L., Veale M., *Enslaving the Algorithm: From a 'Right to an Explanation' to a 'Right to Better Decisions'?*, 16 (3) IEEE Security & Privacy (2018), pp. 46-54.

Edwards L., Veale M., *Slave to the Algorithm? Why a 'Right to an Explanation' Is Probably Not the Remedy You Are Looking For*, 16 Duke Law & Technology Review (2017), pp. 18-84.

Eskens S., *Profiling the European Citizen in the Internet of Things: How Will the General Data Protection Regulation Apply to This Form of Personal Data Processing, and How Should It?*, written on 29 February 2016, available at SSRN: https://papers.ssrn.com/sol3/papers.cfm?abstract_id = 2752010, accessed 1 October 2019, pp. 1-69.

Ezrachi A., Stucke M.E., *The Rise of Behavioural Discrimination*, 37 (12) European Competition Law Review (2016), pp. 485-492.

Fayyad U., Piatetsky-Shapiro G., Smyth P., *From Data Mining to Knowledge Discovery in Databases*, 17 (3) AI Magazine (1996), pp. 37-54.

Floridi L., *Soft Ethics and the Governance of the Digital*, 31 Philosophy & Technology (2018), pp. 1-8.

Gleicher M., *A Framework for Considering Comprehensibility in Modeling*, 4 (2) Big Data (2016), pp. 75-88.

Goddard K., Roudsari A., Wyatt J.C., *Automation Bias: A Systematic Review of Frequency, Effect Mediators, and Mitigators*, 19 (1) Journal of the American Medical Informatics Association (2012), pp. 121-127.

González Cabañas J., Cuevas Á., Cuevas R., *Facebook Use of Sensitive Data for Advertising in Europe*, submitted on 14 February 2018, available at arXiv: https://arxiv.org/abs/1802.05030v1, accessed 1 October 2019, pp. 1-15.

Goodman B., *Economic Models of (Algorithmic) Discrimination*, 29th Conference on Neural Information Processing Systems, 5-10 December 2016, Barcelona, Spain, pp. 1-10.

Goodman B., Flaxman S., *European Union Regulations on Algorithmic Decision Making and 'a Right to an Explanation'*, presented at 33rd International Conference on Machine Learning, Workshop on Human Interpretability in Machine Learning, New York, United States of America, 19-24 June 2016, published in 38 (3) AI Magazine (2017), pp. 50-57.

Granka L.A., *The Politics of Search: A Decade Retrospective*, 26 (5) The Information Society (2010), pp. 364-374.

Gutwirth, S., Poullet, Y., de Hert, P., de Terwangne, C., Nouwt, S. (eds.), *Reinventing Data Protection*, Springer 2009.

Henderson, T., *Does the GDPR Help or Hinder Fair Algorithmic Decision-Making?*, written on 21 August 2017, LLM dissertation, Innovation, Technology & The Law, University of Edinburgh (2017), available at SSRN: https://papers.ssrn.com /sol3/papers.cfm?abstract_id = 3140887, accessed 1 October 2019, pp. 1-43.

Hildebrandt M., Koops E.J., *The Challenges of Ambient Law and Legal Protection in the Profiling Era*, 73 (3) Modern Law Review (2010), pp. 428-460.

Hill R.K., *What an Algorithm Is*, 29 (1) Philosophy and Technology (2016), pp. 35-59.

Hornung G., *A General Data Protection Regulation for Europe? Light and Shade in the Commission's Draft of 25 January 2012*, 9 (1) SCRIPTed (2012), pp. 64-81.

Janssens L.A.W. (ed.), *The Art of Ethics in the Information Society*, Amsterdam University Press 2016.

Kamarinou D., Millard C., Singh J., *Machine Learning with Personal Data*, Queen Mary School of Law Legal Studies Research Paper 247 (2016), pp. 1-23.

Kaminski M.E., *The Right to Explanation, Explained*, 34 (1) Berkeley Technology Law Journal (2019), pp. 189-218.

King N.J., Forder J., *Data Analytics and Consumer Profiling: Finding Appropriate Privacy Principles for Discovered Data*, 32 (5) Computer Law & Security Review (2016), pp. 696-714.

Kingston J., *Using Artificial Intelligence to Support Compliance with the General Data Protection Regulation*, 25 (4) Artificial Intelligence and Law (2017), pp. 429-443.

Kitchin R., *Thinking Critically about and Researching Algorithms*, 20 (1) Information, Communication & Society (2017), pp. 14-29.

Klimas T., Vaiciukaite J., *The Law of Recitals in European Community Legislation*, 15 (1) ILSA Journal of International & Comparative Law (2008), pp. 61-93.

Koops B.J., *The Trouble with European Data Protection Law*, 4 (4) International Data Privacy Law (2014), pp. 250-261.

Kosinski M., Stilwell D., Graepel T., *Private Traits and Attributes Are Predictable from Digital Records of Human Behavior*, 110 (15) Proceedings of the National Academy of Sciences of the United States of America (2013), pp. 5802-5805.

Kotsiantis S.B., *Supervised Machine Learning: A Review of Classification Techniques*, 31 (3) Informatica (2007), pp. 249-268.

Kroll J.A., et al., *Accountable Algorithms*, 165 (3) University of Pennsylvania Law Review (2017), pp. 633-705.

Kuner C., Svantesson D.J.B., Cate F.H., Lynskey O., Millard C., *Machine Learning with Personal Data: Is Data Protection Law Smart Enough to Meet the Challenge?*, 7 (1) International Data Privacy (2017), pp. 1-2.

Kuner C., *The European Commission's Proposed Data Protection Regulation: A Copernican Revolution in European Data Protection Law*, Bloomberg BNA Privacy and Security Law Report, 6 February 2012, pp. 1-15.

Leibowitz J., Rosch J.T., Ramirez E., Brill J., Ohlhausen M., *Report to Congress under Section 319 of the Fair and Accurate Credit Transactions Act of 2003*, Washington 2012.

Malgieri G., Comandé G., *Why a Right to Legibility of Automated Decision-Making Exists in the General Data Protection Regulation*, 7 (4) International Data Privacy Law (2017), pp. 243-265.

Malgieri G., *Right to Explanation and Other 'Suitable Safeguards' for Automated Decision-Making in the EU Member States Legislations*, written on 17 August 2018, available at SSRN: https://papers.ssrn.com/sol3/papers.cfm?abstract_id = 3233611, accessed 1 October 2019, pp. 1-21, Computer Law & Security Review (2019), Forthcoming.

Malgieri G., *Trade Secrets v Personal Data: A Possible Solution for Balancing Rights*, 6 (2) International Data Privacy Law (2016), pp. 102-116.

Mantelero A., *Personal Data for Decisional Purposes in the Age of Analytics: From an Individual to a Collective Dimension of Data Protection*, 32 (2) Computer Law & Security Review (2016), pp. 238-255.

Matthias A., *The Responsibility Gap: Ascribing Responsibility for the Actions of Learning Automata*, 6 (3) Ethics and Information Technology (2004), pp. 175-183.

Mednis A., *Obowiązek informacyjny na podstawie art. 13 RODO*, 3 Informacja w Administracji Publicznej (2018), pp. 9-14.

Mednis A., *Prawo ochrony danych osobowych wobec profilowania osób fizycznych*, Wrocław 2019.

Mendoza I., Bygrave L.A., *The Right Not to Be Subject to Automated Decisions Based on Profiling*, University of Oslo Faculty of Law Legal Studies Research Paper Series No. 20/2017, pp. 1-22.

Mittelstadt B., Allo P., Taddeo M., Wachter S., Floridi L., *The Ethics of Algorithms: Mapping the Debate*, 3 (2) Big Data & Society (2016), pp. 1-21.

Mittelstadt B., *Auditing for Transparency in Content Personalization*, 10 Systems International Journal of Communication (2016), pp. 4991-5002.

Mittelstadt B., *From Individual to Group Privacy in Big Data Analytics*, 30 (4) Philosophy & Technology (December 2017), pp. 475-494.

Moor J., *The Dartmouth College Artificial Intelligence Conference: The Next Fifty Years*, 27 (4) AI Magazine (2006), pp. 87-91.

Noto La Diega G., *Against the Dehumanisation of Decision-Making: Algorithmic Decisions at the Crossroads of Intellectual Property, Data Protection, and Freedom of Information*, 9 (1) Journal of Intellectual Property, Information Technology and Electronic Commerce Law (2018), pp. 3-34.

Ntokos I., *Reality Mining: Privacy and Data Protection Dilemmas in the World of Perpetual Behavioral Monitoring*, written on 13 August 2018, available at SSRN: https://papers.ssrn.com/sol3/papers.cfm?abstract_id = 3230139, accessed 1 October 2019, pp. 1-60.

Oastler K., *GDPR Series: Automated Decisions – What Controllers Need to Know*, 18 (5) Privacy & Data Protection (2018), pp. 6-7.

Ohm P., *Broken Promises of Privacy: Responding to the Surprising Failure of Anonymization*, 57 UCLA Law Review (2010), pp. 1701-1777.

Pasquale F., *The Black Box Society: The Secret Algorithms That Control Money and Information*, Harvard University Press 2015.

Perel M., Elkin-Koren N., *Black Box Tinkering: Beyond Disclosure in Algorithmic Enforcement*, 69 Florida Law Review (2017), pp. 181-221.

Picht P.G., Freund B., *Competition (Law) in the Era of Algorithms*, 10 (3) Max Planck Institute for Innovation and Competition Research Paper No. 18-10 (2018).

Picht P.G., Loderer G.T., *Framing Algorithms: Competition Law and (Other) Regulatory Tools*, 10 (5) Max Planck Institute for Innovation & Competition Research Paper No. 18-24 (2018), pp. 1-35.

Powell C., *Race and Rights in the Digital Age*, 112 American Journal of International Law Unbound (2018), pp. 339-343.

Purtova N., *The Law of Everything. Broad Concept of Personal Data and Future of EU Data Protection Law*, 10 (1) Law, Innovation and Technology (2018), pp. 40-81.

Rieke A., Robinson D., Yu, H., *Civil Rights, Big Data, and Our Algorithmic Future: A September 2014 Report on Social Justice and Technology by Robinson + Yu*, September 2014, pp. 1-34.

Roig A., *Safeguards for the Right Not to Be Subject to a Decision Based Solely on Automated Processing (Article 22 GDPR)*, 8 (3) European Journal of Law and Technology (2017), pp. 1-17.

Rossi F., *Artificial Intelligence: Potential Benefits and Ethical Considerations*, European Parliament: Policy Department C: Citizens' Rights and Constitutional Affairs, October 2016, Briefing PE 571.380, pp. 1-8.

Sandvig C., Hamilton K., Karahalios K., Langbort C., *Auditing Algorithms: Research Methods for Detecting Discrimination on Internet Platforms*, Paper presented to Data and Discrimination: Converting Critical Concerns into Productive Inquiry, a preconference at the 64th Annual Meeting of the International Communication Association on 22 May 2014 Seattle, United States of America, available at Semantic Scholar: https://www.semanticscholar.org/paper/Auditing-Algorithms-%3A-Research-Methods-for-on-Sandvig-Hamilton/b7227cbd347666 55dea10d0437ab10df3a127396, accessed 1 October 2019, pp. 1-23.

Sandvig C., *Seeing the Sort: The Aesthetic and Industrial Defence of 'the Algorithm'*, 11 (1) Journal of the New Media Caucus (2015), pp. 35-51.

Schermer B., *The Limits of Privacy in Automated Profiling and Data Mining*, 27 Computer Law and Security Review (2011), pp. 45-52.

Schwartz P., Solove D., *Reconciling Personal Information in the United States and European Union*, 102 (4) California Law Review (2014), pp. 877-916.

Schwartz P., Solove D., *The PII Problem: Privacy and a New Concept of Personally Identifiable Information*, 86 New York University Law Review (2011), pp. 1814-1894.

Selbst A.D., Powles J., *Meaningful Information and the Right to Explanation*, 7 (4) International Data Privacy Law (2017), pp. 233-242.

Sweeney L., *Simple Demographics Often Identify People Uniquely*, Carnegie Mellon University, Data Privacy Working Paper 3, Pittsburgh 2000.

Synodinou T.E., Jougleux P., Markou C., Prastitou T. (eds), *EU Internet Law: Regulation and Enforcement*, Springer 2017.

Tene O., Polonetsky J., *Big Data for All: Privacy and User Control in the Age of Analytics*, 11 (5) Northwestern Journal of Technology and Intellectual Property (2013), pp. 239-273.

Tutt A., *An FDA for Algorithms*, 69 (1) Administrative Law Review (2017), pp. 83-123.

Urgessa W.G., *The Protective Capacity of the Criterion of 'Identifiability' under EU Data Protection Law*, 2 (4) European Data Protection Law Review (2016), pp. 521-531.

Veale M., Binns R., *Fairer Machine Learning in the Real World: Mitigating Discrimination Without Collecting Sensitive Data*, 4 (2) Big Data and Society (2017), pp. 1-17.

Veale M., Edwards L., *Clarity, Surprises, and Further Questions in the Article 29 Working Party Draft Guidance on Automated Decision-Making and Profiling*, 34 (2) Computer Law & Security Review (2018), pp. 398-404.

Wachter S., Mittelstadt B., *A Right to Reasonable Inferences: Rethinking Data Protection Law in the Age of Big Data and AI*, 2 Columbia Business Law Review (2019), pp. 494-620.

Wachter S., Mittelstadt B., Floridi L., *Why a Right to Explanation of Automated Decision-Making Does Not Exist in the General Data Protection Regulation*, 7 (2) International Data Privacy Law (2017), pp. 76-99.

Wachter S., Mittelstadt B., Russell C., *Counterfactual Explanations Without Opening the Black Box: Automated Decisions and the GDPR*, 31 (2) Harvard Journal of Law & Technology (2018), pp. 841-887.

Wiedemann K., *Automated Processing of Personal Data for the Evaluation of Personality Traits: Legal and Ethical Issues*, 10 (1) Max Planck Institute for Innovation and Competition Research Paper No. 18-04 (2018).

Williams R., *Rethinking Deference for Algorithmic Decision-Making*, written on 31 August 2018, available at SSRN: https://papers.ssrn.com/sol3/papers.cfm?abstract_id=3242482, accessed 1 October 2019, pp. 1-40.

Zarsky T., *The Trouble with Algorithmic Decisions an Analytic Road Map to Examine Efficiency and Fairness in Automated and Opaque Decision Making*, 41 (1) Science, Technology & Human Values (2016), pp. 118-132.

Žliobaitė I., Custers B., *Using Sensitive Personal Data May Be Necessary for Avoiding Discrimination in Data-Driven Decision Models*, 24 Artificial Intelligence and Law (2016), pp. 183-201.

Zuboff S., *Big Other: Surveillance Capitalism and the Prospects of an Information Civilization*, 30 (1) Journal of Information Technology (2015), pp. 75-89.

Other Sources

40th International Conference of Data Protection and Privacy Commissioners, *Declaration on Ethics and Data Protection in Artificial Intelligence Adopted at 40th International Conference of Data Protection and Privacy Commissioners*, adopted on 23 October 2018 in Brussels.

Angwin J., Parris T.Jr., *Facebook Lets Advertisers Exclude Users by Race*, Propublica, 28 October 2016, available at: https://www.propublica.org/article/facebook-lets-advertisers-exclude-users-by-race, accessed 1 July 2019.

Cambridge Dictionary, 'meaningful', available at: https://dictionary.cambridge.org/dictionary/english/meaningful, accessed 1 June 2019.

Copeland J., *What Is Artificial Intelligence*, May 2000, available at: http://www.alanturing.net/turing_archive/pages/reference%20articles/what%20is%20ai.html, accessed 1 June 2019.

Dastin J., *Amazon Scraps Secret AI Recruiting Tool That Showed Bias Against Women*, Reuters, 10 October 2018, available at: https://www.reuters.com/article/us-amazon-com-jobs-automation-insight/amazon-scraps-secret-ai-recruiting-tool-that-showed-bias-against-women-idUSKCN1MK08G, accessed 1 May 2019.

Diakopoulos N., Friedler S., *How to Hold Algorithms Accountable*, MIT Technology Review, available at: https://www.technologyreview.com/s/602933/how-to-hold-algorithms-accountable/, accessed 1 June 2019.

Encyclopædia Britannica: Definition of Algorithm, 15th edition, 2010.

Encyclopædia Britannica: Definition of Data Mining, 15th edition, 2010.

FEDMA Code of conduct of 6 September 2000, available at: http://www.oecd.org/sti/ieconomy/2091875.pdf, accessed 1 November 2018.

How Might Your Choice of Browser Affect Your Job Prospects?, Economist, 11 April 2013, available at: https://www.economist.com/the-economist-explains/2013/04/10/how-might-your-choice-of-browser-affect-your-job-prospects, accessed 1 May 2019.

IEEE Global Initiative, *Ethically Aligned Design: A Vision for Prioritizing Human Well-being with Autonomous and Intelligent Systems*, 1st Edition, 2019.

Naudts L., *The Right Not to Be Subject to Automated Decision-Making: The Role of Explicit Consent*, 2 August 2016, available at: https://www.law.kuleuven.be/citip/blog/the-right-not-to-be-subject-to-automated-decision-making-the-role-of-explicit-consent/, accessed 1 May 2019.

Privacy International, *Data Is Power: Profiling and Automated Decision-Making in GDPR*, 2017, pp. 1-17.

Schwab K., *The Fourth Industrial Revolution: What It Means, How to Respond*, World Economic Forum, 14 January 2016, available at: https://www.weforum.org/agenda/2016/01/the-fourth-industrial-revolution-what-it-means-and-how-to-respond/, accessed 1 May 2019.

The World's Most Valuable Resource Is No Longer Oil, but Data, Economist, 6 May 2017, available at: https://www.economist.com/leaders/2017/05/06/the-worlds-most-valuable-resource-is-no-longer-oil-but-data, accessed 1 May 2019.

Table of Cases

Case Law and Opinions of Advocates General

Table of Treaties and Other Documents

International Agreements

United Nations General Assembly, Universal Declaration of Human Rights, 10 December 1948, 217 A (III), **5**

Council of Europe, European Convention for the Protection of Human Rights and Fundamental Freedoms, as amended by Protocols Nos 11 and 14, 4 November 1950, ETS 5, **30**

Vienna Convention on Diplomatic Relations of 18 April 1961, United Nations, Treaty Series, vol. 500, pp. 95 et seq., **27**

Vienna Convention on Consular Relations of 24 April 1963, United Nations, Treaty Series, vol. 596, pp. 261 et seq., **27**

Convention on the Grant of European Patents of 5 October 1973, United Nations, Treaty Series vol. 1065, pp. 199 et seq., **88**

Convention for the Protection of Individuals with regard to Automatic Processing of Personal Data of 28 January 1981, European Treaty Series No. 108, **11, 97**

Agreement on Trade-Related Aspects of Intellectual Property Rights of 15 April 1994, Marrakesh Agreement Establishing the World Trade Organization, Annex 1C, 1869 United Nations Treaty Series 299, 33 I.L.M. 1197, **88**

World Intellectual Property Organization Copyright Treaty, adopted in Geneva on 20 December 1996, TRT/WCT/001, **88**

European Union Legislation

Directive 95/46/EC of the European Parliament and of the Council of 24 October 1995 on the protection of individuals with regard to the processing of personal data and on the free movement of such data, Official Journal of the European Union L 281, 23 November 1995, pp. 31-50, **xvii**

Directive 2000/31/EC of the European Parliament and of the Council of 8 June 2000 on certain legal aspects of information society services, in particular electronic commerce, in the Internal Market ('Directive on electronic commerce'), Official Journal of the European Union L 178, 17 July 2000, pp. 1-16, **23**

153

Regulation (EU) 2016/679 of the European Parliament and of the Council of 27 April 2016 on the protection of natural persons with regard to the processing of personal data and on the free movement of such data, and repealing Directive 95/46/EC (General Data Protection Regulation), Official Journal of the European Union L 119, 4 May 2016, pp. 1-88, **xvi**

Directive (EU) 2016/943 of the European Parliament and of the Council of 8 June 2016 on the protection of undisclosed know-how and business information (trade secrets) against their unlawful acquisition, use and disclosure (Text with EEA relevance), Official Journal of the European Union L 157, 15 June 2016, pp. 1-18, **89**

Regulation (EU) 2018/1725 of the European Parliament and of the Council of 23 October 2018 on the protection of natural persons with regard to the processing of personal data by the Union institutions, bodies, offices and agencies and on the free movement of such data, and repealing Regulation (EC) No. 45/2001 and Decision No. 1247/2002/EC, Official Journal of the European Union L 295, 21 November 2018, pp. 39-98, **23**

National Legislation

An Act to amend the Federal Deposit Insurance Act to require insured banks to maintain certain records, to require that certain transactions in United States currency be reported to the Department of the Treasury, and for other purposes enacted 26 October 1970 (The Fair Credit Reporting Act), title VI of Public Law 91-508, 84 Statutes at Large 1114, 15 U.S. Code §§ 1681 et seq., **28**

Data Protection Act 1998 (c 29), **38**

Personal Data Act issued on 29 April 1998 (1998:204), unofficial English translation available at: https://www.wipo.int/edocs/lexdocs/laws/en/se/se097en.pdf, accessed 1 July 2019, **38–39**

Bundesgesetz, mit dem das Datenschutzgesetz 2000 geändert wird (Datenschutz-Anpassungsgesetz 2018), 1761 der Beilagen XXV. GP – Ausschussbericht NR – Gesetzestext, German language version available at: https://www.parlament.gv.at/PAKT/VHG/XXV/I/I_01761/fname_643605.pdf, accessed 1 July 2019, **53**

Data Protection Code, Legislative Decree No. 196 of 30 June 2003, unofficial English translation available at http://www.privacy.it/archivio/privacycode-en.html, accessed 1 July 2019, **39**

T/623. Számú törvényjavaslat az információs önrendelkezési jogról és az információszabadságról szóló 2011. évi CXII. törvénynek az Európai Unió adatvédelmi reformjával összefüggő módosításáról, valamint más kapcsolódó törvények módosításáról, **53**

Gesetz zur Anpassung des Datenschutzrechts an die Verordnung (EU) 2016/679 und zur Umsetzung der Richtlinie (EU) 2016/680 (Datenschutz-Anpassungs- und -Umsetzungsgesetz EU – DSAnpUG-EU), Bundesdatenschutzgesetz vom 30. Juni 2017 (BGBl. I S. 2097), official English translation available at: https://www.gesetze-im-internet.de/englisch_bdsg/englisch_bdsg.html#p0310, accessed 1 July 2019, **53**

Data Protection Act 2018, (c 12) available at: http://www.legislation.gov.uk/ukpga/ 2018/12/pdfs/ukpga_20180012_en.pdf, accessed 1 July 2019, **53**

Data Protection Act 2018 (Number 7 of 2018), available at: http://www. irishstatutebook.ie/eli/2018/act/7/enacted/en/pdf, accessed 1 July 2019, **53**

Ustawa o ochronie danych osobowych z dnia 10 maja 2018 r. (Dz.U. z 2018 r. poz. 1000), **53**

Uitvoeringswet Algemene verordening gegevensbescherming (UAVG), geldend van 25 mei 2018 (Stb 2018, 144), unofficial English translation available at: https:// www.akd.nl/o/Documents/UAVG%20ENG%20DEF.pdf, accessed 1 July 2019, **53**

LOI n° 2018-493 du 20 juin 2018 relative à la protection des données personnelles du 20 juin 2018, JORF n°0141 du 21 juin 2018 texte n° 1, **53**

Ustawa o zmianie niektórych ustaw w związku z zapewnieniem stosowania rozporządzenia Parlamentu Europejskiego i Rady (UE) 2016/679 z dnia 27 kwietnia 2016 r. w sprawie ochrony osób fizycznych w związku z przetwarzaniem danych osobowych i w sprawie swobodnego przepływu takich danych oraz uchylenia dyrektywy 95/46/WE (ogólne rozporządzenie o ochronie danych) z dnia 21 lutego 2019 r. (Dz.U. z 2019 r. poz. 730), **53, 54, 86**

Komunikat Prezesa Urzędu Ochrony Danych Osobowych z dnia 17 czerwca 2019 r. w sprawie wykazu rodzajów operacji przetwarzania danych osobowych wymagających oceny skutków przetwarzania dla ich ochrony, (Monitor Polski 2019 Poz. 666), **112**

Documents of the European Union Institutions, Agencies and Other Bodies

Commission of the European Communities, Amended proposal for a Council Directive on the protection of individuals with regard to the processing of personal data and on the free movement of such data, COM(92) 422 final – SYN 287, 15 October 1992, **46**

Commission Staff Working Paper, Executive Summary of the Impact Assessment accompanying the document Regulation of the European Parliament and of the Council on the protection of individuals with regard to the processing of personal data and on the free movement of such data (General Data Protection Regulation) and Directive of the European Parliament and of the Council on the protection of individuals with regard to the processing of personal data by competent authorities for the purposes of prevention, investigation, detection or prosecution of criminal offences or the execution of criminal penalties, and the free movement of such data, Brussels, 25.1.2012, SEC (2012) 73 final, pp. 1-9, **2**

Commission Staff Working Paper, Impact Assessment accompanying the document Regulation of the European Parliament and of the Council on the protection of individuals with regard to the processing of personal data and on the free movement of such data (General Data Protection Regulation) and Directive of the European Parliament and of the Council on the protection of individuals with regard to the processing of personal data by competent authorities for the purposes of prevention, investigation, detection or prosecution of criminal offences or the execution of criminal penalties, and the free movement of such data, Brussels, 25.1.2012, SEC (2012) 72 final, pp. 1-241, **1**

Communication from the Commission to the European Parliament, the European Council, the Council, the European Economic and Social Committee and the Committee of the Regions on Artificial Intelligence for Europe, Brussels, 25 April 2018, COM(2018) 237 final, **17**

Communication from the Commission to the European Parliament, the Council, the European Economic and Social Committee and the Committee of the Regions, *Safeguarding Privacy in a Connected World: A European Data Protection Framework for the 21st Century*, Brussels, 25 January 2012, COM (2012) 9 final, pp. 1-12, **2**

Communication from the Commission to the European Parliament, the European Council, the Council, the European Economic and Social Committee and the Committee of the Regions, *Coordinated Plan on Artificial Intelligence*, Brussels, 7 December 2018, COM(2018) 795 final, **17, 18**

EU study on the impact of marketing through social media, online games and mobile applications on children's behavior, March 2016, available at: https://ec.europa. eu/info/publications/study-impact-marketing-through-social-media-online-ga mes-and-mobile-applications-childrens-behaviour_en, accessed 1 November 2018, **59**

European Economic and Social Committee, Opinion on '*Artificial intelligence: anticipating its impact on work to ensure a fair transition*', 6 December 2018 (2018/C 440/01), **17, 18**

European Parliament Committee on Civil Liberties, Justice and Home Affairs, Report on the Proposal for a Regulation of the European Parliament and of the Council on the Protection of Individuals with Regard to the Processing of Personal Data and on the Free Movement of Such Data (General Data Protection Regulation) of 21 November 2013, A7-0402/2013, **45, 76**

European Parliament resolution of 14 March 2017 on fundamental rights implications of big data: privacy, data protection, non-discrimination, security and law-enforcement, 2016/2225(INI)), P8_TA(2017)0076, **13**

Opinion of the European Economic and Social Committee adopted on 23 May 2012 on the Proposal for a Regulation of the European Parliament and of the Council on the protection of individuals with regard to the processing of personal data and on the free movement of such data (General Data Protection Regulation), CES1303/2012, **55**

Position (EU) of the Council at first reading with a view to the adoption of a Regulation of the European Parliament and of the Council on the protection of natural persons with regard to the processing of personal data and on the free movement of such data, and repealing Directive 95/46/EC (General Data Protection Regulation), adopted by the Council on 8 April 2016, Official Journal of the European Union C 159/1, 3 May 2016, pp. 1-82, **7**

Position of the European Parliament adopted at first reading on 12 March 2014 with a view to the adoption of Regulation (EU) No .../2014 of the European Parliament and of the Council on the protection of individuals with regard to the processing of personal data and on the free movement of such data (General Data Protection Regulation) (Text with EEA relevance), P7_TC1-COD(2012)0011, **7, 10, 45, 55, 76**

Proposal for a Regulation the European Parliament and of the Council on the protection of individuals with regard to the processing of personal data and on the free movement of such data (General Data Protection Regulation) of 25 January 2012, COM(2012) 11 final, **2, 55, 76**

The Europeans Commission's High-Level Expert Group on Artificial Intelligence, *A definition of AI: Main capabilities and scientific disciplines*, Brussels, 18 December 2018, **17**

United Nations General Assembly, Human Rights Council, Resolution: *The right to privacy in the digital age*, adopted on 22 March 2017, A/HRC/34/L.7/Rev.1., **31**

Index

EUROPEAN MONOGRAPH SERIES

1. Lammy Betten (ed.), *The Future of European Social Policy*, 1991 (ISBN 90-654-4585-4).
2. Annemarie Loman, Kamiel Mortelmans, Harry H.G. Post & Stewart Watson, *Culture and Common Law: Before and After Maastricht*, 1992 (ISBN 90-654-4638-9).
3. John A.E. Vervaele, *Fraud against the Community: The Need for European Fraud Legislation*, 1994 (ISBN 90-654-4634-6).
4. Philip Raworth, *The Legislative Process in the European Community*, 1993 (ISBN 90-654-4690-7).
5. Jules Stuyck, *Financial and Monetary Integration in the European Economic Community*, 1993 (ISBN 90-654-4718-0).
6. Jules Stuyck & A.J. Vossestein (eds), *State Entrepreneurship, National Monopolies and European Community Law*, 1993 (ISBN 90-654-4773-3).
7. Jules Stuyck & A. Looijestijn-Clearie (eds), *The European Economic Area EC-EFTA*, 1994 (ISBN 90-654-4815-2).
8. Rosita B. Bouterse, *Competition and Integration: What Goals Count?*, 1995 (ISBN 90-654-4816-0).
9. René Barents, *The Agricultural Law of the EC: An Inquiry into the Administrative Law*, 1994 (ISBN 90-654-4867-5).
10. Nicholas Emiliou, *Principles of Proportionality in European Law: A Comparative Study*, 1996 (ISBN 90-411-0866-1).
11. Eivind Smith, *National Parliaments as Cornerstones of European Integration*, 1996 (ISBN 90-411-0898-X).
12. Jan H. Jans, *European Environmental Law*, 1996 (ISBN 90-411-0877-7).
13. Síofra O'Leary, *The Evolving Concept of Community Citizenship: From the Free Movement of Persons to Union Citizenship*, 1997 (ISBN 90-411-0878-5).
14. Laurence W. Gormley (ed.), *Current and Future Perspectives on EC Competition Law*, 1983 (ISBN 90-411-0691-X).
15. Simone White, *Protection of the Financial Interests of the European Communities: The Fight against Fraud and Corruption*, 1998 (ISBN 90-411-9647-1).
16. Morten P. Broberg, *Broberg on the European Commission's Jurisdiction to Scrutinise Mergers*, 4th Edition, 2013 (ISBN 978-90-411-3339-7).
17. Doris Hildebrand, *The Role of Economic Analysis in the EC Competition Rules: The European School*, 2nd Edition, 2002 (ISBN 90-411-1706-7).
18. Christof R.A. Swaak, *European Community Law and the Automobile Industry*, 1999 (ISBN 90-411-1140-9).

19. Dorthe Dahlgaard Dingel, *Public Procurement: A Harmonization of the National Judicial Review of the Application of European Community Law*, 1999 (ISBN 90-411-1161-1).
20. John A.E. Vervaele (ed.), *Compliance and Enforcement of European Community Law*, 1999 (ISBN 90-411-1151-4).
21. Martin Trybus, *European Defence Procurement Law: International and National Procurement Systems as Models for a Liberalized Defence Procurement Market in Europe*, 1999 (ISBN 90-411-1167-0).
22. Helen Staples, *The Legal Status of Third Country Nationals Resident in the European Union*, 1999 (ISBN 90-411-1277-4).
23. Damien Geradin (ed.), *The Liberalization of State Monopolies in the European Union and Beyond*, 1999 (ISBN 90-411-1264-2).
24. Katja Heede, *European Ombudsman: Redress and Control at Union Level*, 2000 (ISBN 90-411-1413-0).
25. Ulf Bernitz & Joakim Nergelius (eds), *General Principles of European Community Law*, 2000 (ISBN 90-411-1402-5).
26. Michaela Drahos, *Convergence of Competition Laws and Policies in the European Community*, 2002 (ISBN 90-411-1562-5).
27. Damien Geradin (ed.), *The Liberalization of Electricity and Natural Gas in the European Union*, 2001 (ISBN 90-411-1560-9).
28. Gisella Gori, *Towards an EU Right to Education*, 2001 (ISBN 90-411-1670-2).
29. Brendan P.G. Smith, *Constitution Building in the European Union*, 2001 (ISBN 90-411-1695-8).
30. Friedl Weiss & Frank Wooldridge, *Free Movement of Persons within the European Community*, 2nd Edition, 2007 (ISBN 978-90-411-2545-3).
31. Ingrid Boccardi, *Europe and Refugees: Towards an EU Asylum Policy*, 2002 (ISBN 90-411-1709-1).
32. John A.E. Vervaele & André Klip (eds), *European Cooperation Between Tax, Customs and Judicial Authorities*, 2001 (ISBN 90-411-1747-4).
33. Wouter P.J. Wils, *The Optimal Enforcement of EC Antitrust Law: Essays in Law and Economics*, 2002 (ISBN 90-411-1757-1).
34. Damien Geradin (ed.), *The Liberalization of Postal Services in the European Union*, 2002 (ISBN 90-411-1780-6).
35. Nick Bernard, *Multilevel Governance in the European Union*, 2002 (ISBN 90-411-1812-8).
36. Jill Wakefield, *Judicial Protection through the Use of Article 288(2) EC*, 2002 (ISBN 90-411-1823-3).
37. Sebastiaan Princen, *EU Regulation and Transatlantic Trade*, 2002 (ISBN 90-411-1871-3).
38. Amaryllis Verhoeven, *The European Union in Search of a Democratic and Constitutional Theory*, 2002 (ISBN 90-411-1872-1).
39. Paul L.C. Torremans, *Cross Border Insolvencies in EU, English and Belgian Law*, 2002 (ISBN 90-411-1888-8).

40. Malcolm Anderson & Joanna Apap (eds), *Police and Justice Cooperation and the New European Borders,* 2002 (ISBN 90-411-1893-4).
41. Christin M. Forstinger, *Takeover Law in EU and USA: A Comparative Analysis,* 2002 (ISBN 90-411-1919-1).
42. Antonio Bavasso, *Communications in EU Antitrust Law: Market Power and Public Interest,* 2003 (ISBN 90-411-1974-4).
43. Fiona G. Wishlade, *Regional State Aid and Competition Policy in the European Union,* 2003 (ISBN 90-411-1975-2).
44. Gareth Davies, *Nationality Discrimination in the European Internal Market,* 2003 (ISBN 90-411-1998-1).
45. René Barents, *The Autonomy of Community Law,* 2003 (ISBN 90-411-2251-6).
46. Gerhard Dannecker & Oswald Jansen (eds), *Competition Law Sanctioning in the European Union,* 2004 (ISBN 90-411-2100-5).
47. Nauta Dutilh (ed.), *Dealing with Dominance: The Experience of National Competition Authorities,* 2004 (ISBN 90-411-2211-7).
48. Stefaan van den Bogaert, *Practical Regulation of the Mobility of Sportsmen in the EU Post Bosman,* 2005 (ISBN 90-411-2327-X).
49. Katalin Judit Cseres, *Competition Law and Consumer Protection,* 2005 (ISBN 90-411-2380-6).
50. Philipp Kiiver, *The National Parliaments in the European Union: A Critical View on EU Constitution Building,* 2006 (ISBN 978-90-411-2452-4).
51. Alexander Turk, *The Concept of Legislation in European Community Law,* 2006 (ISBN 978-90-411-2472-2).
52. Dimitrios Sinaniotis, *The Interim Protection of Individuals before the European and National Courts,* 2006 (ISBN 978-90-411-2498-2).
53. M. Holoubek & D. Damjanovic, M. Traimer (eds), *Regulating Content: The European Regulatory Framework for the Media and Related Creative Sectors,* 2006 (ISBN 978-90-411-2597-2).
54. Anneli Albi & Jacques Ziller (eds), *The European Constitution and National Constitutions: Ratification and Beyond,* 2006 (ISBN 978-90-411-2524-8).
55. Gustavo E. Luengo, *Regulation of Subsidies and State Aids in WTO and EC Law: Conflicts in International Trade Law,* 2007 (ISBN 978-90-411-2547-7).
56. Eniko Horvath, *Mandating Identity: Citizenship, Kinship Laws and Plural Nationality in the European Union,* 2007 (ISBN 978-90-411-2662-7).
57. Rass Holdgaard, *External Relations Law of the European Community: Legal Reasoning and Legal Discourses,* 2007 (ISBN 978-90-411-2604-7).
58. Jill Wakefield, *The Right to Good Administration,* 2007 (ISBN 978-90-411-2697-9).
59. Dimitry Kochenov, *EU Enlargement and the Failure of Conditionality: Pre- accession Conditionality in the Fields of Democracy and the Rule of Law,* 2008 (ISBN 978-90-411-2696-2).
60. Despina Mavromati, *The Law of Payment Services in the EU: The EC Directive on Payment Services in the Internal Market,* 2008 (ISBN 978-90-411-2700-6).

61. Anne Meuwese, *Impact Assessment in EU Lawmaking*, 2008 (ISBN 978-90-411-2720-4).

62. Ulf Bernitz, Joakim Nergelius & Cecilia Cardner (eds), *General Principles of EC Law in a Process of Development*, 2008 (ISBN 978-90-411-2705-1).

63. Johan van de Gronden (ed.), *The EU and WTO Law on Services: Limits to the Realisation of General Interest Policies within the Services Markets?*, 2008 (ISBN 978-90-411-2809-6).

64. Alina Tryfonidou, *Reverse Discrimination in EC Law*, 2009 (ISBN 978-90-411-2751-8).

65. Mikael Berglund, *Cross-Border Enforcement of Claims in the EU: History Present Time and Future*, 2014 (ISBN 978-90-411-4564-2).

66. Theodore Konstadinides, *Division of Powers in European Union Law: The Delimitation of Internal Competence between the EU and the Member States*, 2009 (ISBN 978-90-411-2615-3).

67. Mattias Derlén, *Multilingual Interpretation of European Union Law*, 2009 (ISBN 978-90-411-2853-9).

68. René Barents, *Directory of EU Case Law on the Preliminary Ruling Procedure*, 2009 (ISBN 978-90-411-3150-8).

69. Yan Luo, *Anti-dumping in the WTO, the EU and China: The Rise of Legalization in the Trade Regime and Its Consequences*, 2010 (ISBN 978-90-411-3207-9).

70. Patrick Birkinshaw & Mike Varney (eds), *The European Union Legal Order after Lisbon*, 2010 (ISBN 978-90-411-3152-2).

71. Thomas Gr. Papadopoulos, *EU Law and Harmonization of Takeovers in the Internal Market*, 2010 (ISBN 978-90-411-3340-3).

72. Bas van Bockel, *The* Ne Bis In Idem *Principle in EU Law*, 2010 (ISBN 978-90-411-3156-0).

73. Veljko Milutinović, *The 'Right to Damages' under EU Competition Law: From* Courage v. Crehan *to the White Paper and Beyond*, 2010 (ISBN 978-90-411-3235-2).

74. Amandine Garde, *EU Law and Obesity Prevention*, 2010 (ISBN 978-90-411-2706-8).

75. Leonard Besselink, Frans Pennings & Sacha Prechal (eds), *The Eclipse of the Legality Principle in the European Union*, 2011 (ISBN 978-90-411-3262-8).

76. Sacha Garben, *EU Higher Education Law: The Bologna Process and Harmonization by Stealth*, 2011 (ISBN 978-90-411-3365-6).

77. Dimitry Kochenov (ed.), *EU Law of the Overseas: Outermost Regions, Associated Overseas Countries and Territories, Territories Sui Generis*, 2011 (ISBN 978-90-411-3445-5).

78. Pablo Ibáñez Colomo, *European Communications Law and Technological Convergence: Deregulation, Re-regulation and Regulatory Convergence in Television and Telecommunications*, 2012 (ISBN 978-90-411-3829-3).

79. Elise Muir, *EU Regulation of Access to Labour Markets: A Case Study of EU Constraints on Member State Competences*, 2012 (ISBN 978-90-411-3823-1).

80. Tim Corthaut, *EU Ordre Public*, 2012 (ISBN 978-90-411-3232-1).

81. Oana Ştefan, *Soft Law in Court: Competition Law, State Aid and the Court of Justice of the European Union*, 2013 (ISBN 978-90-411-3997-9).
82. Francesco Rossi dal Pozzo, *Citizenship Rights and Freedom of Movement in the European Union*, 2013 (ISBN 978-90-411-4660-1).
83. Jens Hartig Danielsen, *EU Agricultural Law*, 2013 (ISBN 978-90-411-3280-2).
84. Ulf Bernitz, Xavier Groussot & Felix Schulyok (eds), *General Principles of EU Law and European Private Law*, 2013 (ISBN 978-90-411-4683-0).
85. Michelle Everson, Cosimo Monda & Ellen Vos (eds), *European Agencies in between Institutions and Member States*, 2014 (ISBN 978-90-411-2843-0).
86. Stefan Leible & Matthias Lehmann (eds), *European Contract Law and German Law*, 2014 (ISBN 978-90-411-2588-0).
87. Piero Leanza & Ondrej Pridal, *The Right to a Fair Trial: Article 6 of the European Convention on Human Rights*, 2014 (ISBN 978-90-411-4855-1).
88. Patrick J. Birkinshaw, *European Public Law: The Achievement and the Challenge*, 2014 (ISBN 978-90-411-4744-8).
89. George Cumming, *Expert Evidence Deficiencies in the Judgments of the Courts of the European Union and the European Court of Human Rights*, 2014 (ISBN 978-90-411-4123-1).
90. Vesna Rijavec, Tomaž Keresteš & Tjaša Ivanc (eds), *Simplification of Debt Collection in the EU*, 2014 (ISBN 978-90-411-4854-4).
91. Nina Półtorak, *European Union Rights in National Courts*, 2015 (ISBN 978-90-411-5863-5).
92. Kyriaki-Korina Raptopoulou, *EU Law and Healthcare Services: Normative Approaches to Public Health Systems*, 2015 (ISBN 978-90-411-5013-4).
93. Torsten Frank Koschinka & Piero Leanza, *Preliminary Injunctions: Germany, England/Wales, Italy and France*, 2015 (ISBN 978-90-411-5833-8).
94. Vesna Rijavec, Tomaž Keresteš & Tjaša Ivanc (eds), *Dimensions of Evidence in European Civil Procedure*, 2016 (ISBN 978-90-411-6662-3).
95. Stefan Leible (ed.), *General Principles of European Private International Law*, 2016 (ISBN 978-90-411-5955-7).
96. Patrick J. Birkinshaw & Andrea Biondi (eds), *Britain Alone!: The Implications and Consequences of United Kingdom Exit from the EU*, 2016 (ISBN 978-90-411-5832-1).
97. René Barents, *Remedies and Procedures before the EU Courts*, 2016 (ISBN 978-90-411-6614-2).
98. Luca Prete, *Infringement Proceedings in EU Law*, 2017 (ISBN 978-90-411-6900-6).
99. Robert van den Hoven van Genderen, *Privacy Limitation Clauses: Trojan Horses under the Disguise of Democracy*, 2017 (ISBN 978-90-411-8599-0).
100. Mariusz Krzysztofek, *Post-Reform Personal Data Protection in the European Union: General Data Protection Regulation (EU) 2016/679*, 2017 (ISBN 978-90-411-6237-3).
101. Gianni Lo Schiavo, *The Role of Financial Stability in EU Law and Policy*, 2017 (ISBN 978-90-411-8230-2).

102. Emmanuel Guinchard & Marie-Pierre Granger (eds), *The New EU Judiciary: An Analysis of Current Judicial Reforms*, 2017 (ISBN 978-90-411-6834-4).

103. Kirsten Henckel, *Cross-Border Transfers of Undertakings: A European Perspective*, 2017 (ISBN 978-90-411-9227-1).

104. Vesna Rijavec, Wendy Kennett, Tomaž Keresteš & Tjaša Ivanc, *Remedies Concerning Enforcement of Foreign Judgements: Brussels I Recast*, 2018 (ISBN 978-90-411-9416-9).

105. Albert Sanchez-Graells & Constant De Koninck, *Shaping EU Public Procurement Law: A Critical Analysis of the CJEU Case Law 2015–2017*, 2018 (ISBN 978-94-035-0160-4).

106. Andrea Biondi, Patrick J. Birkinshaw & Maria Kendrick, *Brexit: The Legal Implications*, 2019 (ISBN 978-90-411-9540-1).

107. Mariusz Krzysztofek, *GDPR: General Data Protection Regulation (EU) 2016/679: Post-Reform Personal Data Protection in the European Union*, 2019 (ISBN 978-94-035-0594-7).

108. Giovanni Bassani, *The Legal Framework Applicable to the Single Supervisory Mechanism: Tapestry or Patchwork?*, 2019 (ISBN 978-94-035-0872-6).

109. Piotr Staszczyk, *A Legal Analysis of NGOs and European Civil Society*, 2019 (ISBN 978-94-035-1251-8).

110. Patrizio Messina, *Finance for SMEs: European Regulation and Capital Markets Union – Focus on Securitization and Alternative Finance Tools*, 2019 (ISBN 978-94-035-0161-1).

111. Jacques H.J. Bourgeois (ed.), *EU Framework for Foreign Direct Investment Control*, 2020 (ISBN 978-94-035-1883-1).

112. Ulf Bernitz, Xavier Groussot, Jaan Paju & Sybe de Vries (eds), *General Principles of EU Law and the EU Digital Order*, 2020 (ISBN 978-94-035-1165-8).

113. Aleksandra Drożdż, *Protection of Natural Persons with Regard to Automated Individual Decision-Making in the GDPR*, 2020 (ISBN 978-94-035-2045-2).